Social Care Markets

Two week loan

Please return on or before the last
date stamped below.
Charges are made for late return.

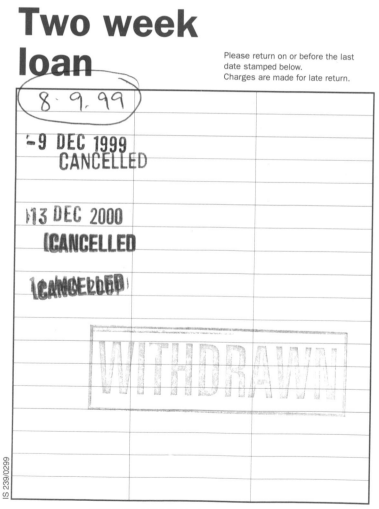

8. 9. 99

-9 DEC 1999
CANCELLED

13 DEC 2000
CANCELLED

CANCELLED

WITHDRAWN

IS 239/0299

INFORMATION SERVICES PO BOX 430, CARDIFF CF1 3XT

Public Policy and Management

Series Editor:
Professor R.A.W. Rhodes, Department of Politics, University of Newcastle.

The effectiveness of public policies is a matter of public concern and the efficiency with which policies are put into practice is a continuing problem for governments of all political persuasions. This series contributes to these debates by publishing informed, in-depth and contemporary analyses of public administration, public policy and public management.

The intention is to go beyond the usual textbook approach to the analysis of public policy and management and to encourage authors to move debate about their issue forward. In this sense, each book both describes current thinking and research, and explores future policy directions. Accessibility is a key feature and, as a result, the series will appeal to academics and their students as well as to the informed practitioner.

Current Titles Include:

Social Care Markets

Progress and Prospects

Gerald Wistow, Martin Knapp, Brian Hardy, Julien Forder, Jeremy Kendall and Rob Manning

Open University Press
Buckingham · Philadelphia

Open University Press
Celtic Court
22 Ballmoor
Buckingham
MK18 lXW

and
1900 Frost Road, Suite 101
Bristol, PA 19007, USA

First Published 1996

A catalogue record of this book is available from the British Library

ISBN 0 335 19546 6 (pb) 0 335 19547 4 (hb)

Library of Congress Cataloging-in-Publication Data
Social care markets : progress and prospects / Gerald Wistow . . . [et al.],
    p. cm.
  Includes bibliographical references and index.
  ISBN 0-335-19547-4 (hb). — ISBN 0-335-19546-6 (pb)
  1. Social service – Great Britain – Marketing. 2. Public relations
– Social service – Great Britain.   I. Wistow, Gerald, 1946–
HV245.S614   1996
361′3.0068′8–dc20   95-49780
                                                                      CIP

Typeset by Dorwyn Ltd, Rowlands Castle, Hants
Printed in Great Britain by St Edmundsbury Press Ltd, Bury St Edmunds, Suffolk

Contents

Preface

The overarching aim of the research programme jointly undertaken by the Nuffield Institute for Health and the Personal Social Services Research Unit (PSSRU) is to describe, monitor and evaluate the developing mixed economy of social care in England. The research programme comprises three interrelated activities:

- Description and evaluation of the organization and structure of local authority commissioning functions, with particular regard to the perceptions and beliefs of local authorities, their policy positions, and their arrangements for purchasing.
- Description and evaluation of the organization and structure of supply, including analysis of the incentives and motivating forces as they affect providers, and the implications of a mixed economy for providers in the various sectors.
- Description and evaluation of the development and regulation of social care, including forms of relationship between purchasers and providers, and the respective balance of power or influence between them in different market settings.

This book builds on a mapping of the development of the broad mixed economy undertaken between 1990 and 1992, which provided a detailed account of the intentions and actions of a representative sample of twenty-five English local authority social services departments in relation to the early implementation of the community care legislation in general, and their promotion of a mixed economy in particular. The findings of this earlier phase of the research were described in *Social Care in a Mixed Economy* (Wistow *et al*. 1994), which should be seen as a companion volume to this book. By returning to those same authorities for this second examination of the mixed economy, the findings from the 1990–92 work provided us with a broad baseline for the study of more recent changes in policy and practice, as described in this book.

Methodology

The chapters in the book are organized into two sections: the first is mainly descriptive (Chapters 2 to 6) and the second is primarily evaluative (Chapters 7 to 9). Our intention in the former is to identify: the perceptions and beliefs of purchasers about social care markets; the behaviour and actions of purchasers, mainly in terms of purchasing and commissioning arrangements and also their collection of information about providers; and the motivations and behaviour of providers.

Our aim in investigating perceptions and beliefs is to provide an account of the *assumptive worlds* of both purchasers and providers. The approach is analytic in being constructed within a particular frame of reference, but the focus is description rather than causal explanation (Chapters 3 and 4). Gaining an understanding of the assumptive worlds in which key stake-holders operate is a prerequisite for the construction of the *causal* predictions of behaviour reported in the second part of the book.

The second, complementary, task of Chapters 2 to 6 is to describe *behavioural consequences*. In particular, we look at the information systems that local authorities are operating, the types of information they are collecting (including the characteristics of providers), and the ways in which these data are processed (Chapter 4). We also look at the purchasing and commissioning arrangements that local authorities are putting in place, such as provider selection mechanisms, devolved purchasing and contract types (Chapter 5). Constructing this picture is crucial if we are to explore the relationships between motivations and perceptions, and between events, actions and consequences.

In Chapter 6 we map the motivations and behaviour of a particular group of providers: those in the independent sectors running residential homes for elderly people. We can then examine how well local authority purchasers' understandings match such provider motivations and therefore how well placed they are to manage and shape local markets.

In Chapters 7 to 9 we analyse and evaluate the organization of social care with reference both to a set of public policy goals (particularly choice, independence, cost-effectiveness and innovation) and to a set of more fundamental socio-political and economic goals. We employ a two-pronged approach to evaluate the organization of social care relative to these performance criteria. First, we look at the attainment of public policy goals directly, by eliciting the views of some key policy stake-holders (Directors and Assistant Directors of Social Services, Chairs of social services committees, and a small number of independent sector providers). In doing so, we are adopting an *internal* perspective, reporting experiences of the reforms largely according to the assumptive worlds of these stake-holders (Chapter 7).

Our second approach takes an *external* perspective in applying a theoretical framework, the core presuppositions of which are not *fundamentally* context-specific. We employ an amalgam of 'new institutional' economics and mainstream microeconomic theory, tailored, for our purposes, to observations of the organization and structure of social care and the motivations and perceptions of key stake-holders. The approach can then be used to assess authorities' commissioning arrangements: that is, to form hypotheses about how well these arrangements will work relative to the performance criteria. The intention is to use this framework to derive a set of advantages and disadvantages of operating with particular purchasing arrangements.

In Chapter 9 we begin to bring these various strands together. We build upon the descriptive material from the first part of the book and the latter evaluative approach in order to gauge local authorities' commissioning arrangements and market management in the medium term. The propositions derived throughout the book are then used to develop a set of implications for local authorities, particularly concerned with what constitutes appropriate governance and what key tasks local authorities should be considering. Our future intention is to collect data on commissioning arrangements in order to test systematically the predictions that emerge. Although this is mainly beyond the scope of the current book, we none the less have some data from our study of providers to illuminate specific hypotheses.

The research which provided the platform for this book was funded by the Department of Health, and also informed by the findings of research and other activities commissioned from the Nuffield Institute and the PSSRU by other bodies. The views expressed in this publication are those of the authors and not necessarily those of the Department of Health. Officers and members in the twenty-five local authorities in our sample were generous with their time and advice, and a great many providers in the private and voluntary sectors willingly took part in some aspects of our research. We are very grateful to them all for their assistance. We also thank Sally Sugden and Maureen Weir for secretarial excellence; Jane Dennett for subediting, typesetting and encouragement; and the members of our Advisory and Reference Groups for their advice.

Part I

Markets in social care

1

Developing social care markets: background and context

Introduction

The creation of social care markets lay at the heart of the community care changes, which were set out in the 1990 NHS and Community Care Act and came into effect between April 1991 and April 1993. Under these changes local authority social services departments were required to assume new roles and responsibilities for market development and market management, which, it was widely recognized, would demand a revolution in systems, attitudes and behaviours at all levels in social services departments (see, for example, Audit Commission 1992b).

Local authorities were, however, ambivalent in their attitudes towards these changes, with enthusiasm for the central principles of needs-led and user-centred services tempered by the suspicion that the government's principal motivation was capping the growth of social security spending and promoting the interests of private sector providers. Having campaigned for the lead role in community care, local authorities could scarcely reject it, especially when other responsibilities and budgets were being curtailed. Yet they feared being handed the 'poisoned chalice' of increased responsibilities and inadequate resources. Moreover, the transfer of functions from social security to social services had clear drawbacks for them. As principally purchasers of services from the independent sector, local authorities were now required to encourage and create other organizations to take over their historic core responsibilities for providing services to the most vulnerable members of their local communities. This 'price' was compounded by the local authority perception that many of these organizations were motivated by self-interest rather than public service. Prior to implementation there were, therefore, major questions not only about local authorities' commitment to their new role, but also about their competence to fulfil their new statutory duties, even though it was accepted that the changes could not be realized overnight but only through a long-term programme of change.

As we showed in *Social Care in a Mixed Economy* (Wistow *et al.* 1994), less than two years before the implementation of the reforms departments lacked either the expertise or commitment to operate in a market environment. This book records how they responded to those challenges between 1991 and 1994. It demonstrates the emergence of more positive attitudes towards their new tasks, but suggests that their understandings remained flawed and their capabilities limited. It concludes by arguing for a conceptualization of the purchaser role as the management of inter-organizational relationships rather than the adoption of crudely competitive behaviours.

The initial phase of the research reported here had found little understanding of markets in local social services departments or enthusiasm for the injection of market forces into the delivery of social care (Knapp *et al.* 1994; Wistow *et al.* 1994). The study, conducted in a representative sample of twenty-five English authorities during 1991, had identified widespread reservations about the adoption of commercial principles which were seen to be alien to the values of social care and social work. Furthermore, the characteristics of social care consumers and their needs were seen to be such that their exposure to market forces would be inappropriate and ineffective: vulnerable users are unable to act as informed consumers; outcomes are difficult to specify and measure; and the fluid nature of individual needs and relationships demand changing packages of care, not baskets of standardized products.

The main aim of that initial phase of research had been to identify the intentions and actions of social services departments in England in relation to the implementation of the community care legislation in general, and the promotion of a mixed economy in particular. Its principal findings may be summarized in the following terms. First, there was widespread support among the sample authorities for the reforms' social policy objectives of promoting a shift to needs-led, individualized and home-based services. Yet such support was matched by almost equally widespread reservations about using markets to achieve such a shift. Second, those reservations were due to a number of factors including:

- a lack of support for an enabling role defined as one of market development rather than personal or community development;
- the perceived scarcity, unsuitability, unwillingness or inability of independent sector providers to play a more extensive role in a mixed economy; and
- a view transcending local political boundaries that 'social care is different' from other goods and services in ways which made market mechanisms inappropriate.

Third, the development of independent sector provision was proceeding cautiously and selectively. Authorities generally preferred to work with voluntary rather than private providers because of their known track record, shared values, mutual trust and the lower transactions costs which flowed from those characteristics of established voluntary/statutory relationships.

Fourth, the development of purchasing capacities in social services departments was embryonic: only a minority of authorities had begun to map need and supply systematically, and only three of the twenty-five had drawn up service specifications or contracts. The decision to phase the reforms' implementation over a two-year period meant that the new purchasing arrangements would not come into effect until 1993. As a result, such activities were not seen to be immediate priorities when we conducted our fieldwork in 1991. Moreover, with a general election due before this final implementation stage was reached, some authorities questioned whether the reforms would ever be introduced in their entirety. Others positively hoped they would not and, overall, there was a tendency to 'hasten slowly'. Even so, the final conclusion from the 1991 study was that cultural change was beginning to be evident in the management of social services departments. Such change was particularly demonstrated by the growing acceptance that local authorities should actively promote a mixed economy in which public services operated alongside a greater diversity of supply and suppliers in the independent sectors.

This book presents the findings from a follow-up study conducted within the same localities in the immediate aftermath of the reforms' implementation in April 1993. It provides evidence of changing attitudes towards social care markets on the part of social services Directors and Chairs, including a growing tendency to see such markets as mechanisms with potential for achieving social goals. However, such perceptions existed alongside a continuing under-development of the purchasing role, a finding which raises questions about the capacity of local authorities to secure those social goals in practice. Before beginning to present such evidence, however, it is necessary to outline both the nature of the reforms and the initiatives taken by central government to assist local authorities' preparations for fulfilling their new roles and responsibilities.

Social care markets: means and ends

Social care markets can be interpreted as both the means and ends of government policy. From the perspective of the White Paper *Caring for People* (Secretaries of State 1989), they were advocated as the means for strengthening the capacity of local authorities to secure the reforms' underlying aims of 'promoting choice and independence' for individuals and their carers (Secretaries of State 1989: para. 1.8). The perceived failure of traditional administrative hierarchies to deliver services sufficiently responsive to individual needs and preferences was seen to demand new organizational approaches. More particularly, the Audit Commission, whose earlier

6   Social care markets

(1986) report had effectively prompted the Government to develop these new policy initiatives, saw the White Paper as setting in motion 'a process of change . . . which will turn organisations upside-down' (Audit Commission 1992a: para. 45). It emphasized that the policy changes required 'a shift in influence from those who provide services to those who use them'. The need to redress the balance between service providers, users and carers reflected a – by no means unjustified – perception that the bureaucratic and professional power structures of state welfare had become impersonal, self-seeking and insufficiently accountable to those they were intended to serve (see, for example, Deakin and Wright 1990; Wistow and Barnes 1993). The separation of purchaser and provider responsibilities, together with the development of service specifications and contracts, were to provide a set of interrelated mechanisms for securing greater responsiveness to the needs of individuals. Thus, it was envisaged that the interests of users and carers would no longer take second place if responsibility for service provision was detached from that of commissioning social care. Service specifications and contracts would provide commissioners at both macro (community) and micro (individual) levels with tools to ensure that providers adjusted service patterns and service delivery processes to the needs of users and carers. In addition, and most crucially, the devolution of budgets to care managers would enable them to purchase individual packages of care specifically tailored to the

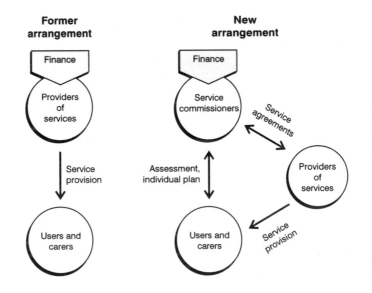

Figure 1.1   The changing funding arrangements
Source: Audit Commission (1992a: 22). Crown copyright is reproduced with the permission of the Controller of HMSO.

needs they assessed and thus to make the best use of the resources available.

It followed that the purchaser/provider split would necessarily have a fundamental impact on the processes by which resources were allocated to services through the substitution of contractual for hierarchical relationships. Traditional bureaucratic hierarchies allocate resources directly to service providers through a budgetary process, which routinely rolls forward each year with little if any challenge to baseline activities and their continuing relevance to need. By contrast, the introduction of contracts or service-level agreements was designed to prevent this semi-automatic allocation of resources to service providers by placing them in the hands of commissioners purchasing on behalf of users and carers. Figure 1.1 illustrates this difference between a commissioning process based on contracts or service-level agreements and line relationships based on guaranteed funding and little incentive to increase responsiveness to need. In principle, the new arrangements introduced the possibility of competition between providers, with care managers and users being able to choose services which more closely matched the needs and preferences of the latter. The White Paper specifically envisaged that competition would provide a tool for promoting 'choice, cost-effectiveness and innovation' (Secretaries of State 1989: para. 3.4.3). Thus, the opening up of public services to external and internal competition was expected to stimulate the development of a wider range of better-quality services. Competition was also expected to reduce inefficiencies and, thereby, meet users' interests by expanding the purchasing power of the public purse and providing 'more for less'.

Taken together, then, the new organizational and funding arrangements were advocated on the grounds that market forces and decentralized purchasing provide more effective instruments for securing long-established social goals summarized in the White Paper as the promotion of 'choice and independence'. Whether or not they meet that objective successfully is, of course, an empirical question which this programme of research is beginning to address. While definitive judgements cannot be made on the basis of data collected at the beginning of a long-term process of change, our research does reveal the extent to which the competence and compliance of implementing agencies are significant determinants of policy outcomes.

The above discussion is predicated on the assumption that social care markets were introduced to provide more effective means for securing the social policy goals which were described as lying at the heart of the community care White Paper. At the same time, however, the reforms may be seen as part of a wider policy framework whose objective is to replace traditional forms of government through public sector bureaucracies by what Self has termed 'government by the market' (1993: 56). From this perspective, social care markets are not merely better means for achieving long-established welfare goals; rather, they are ends in themselves which exist within a hierarchy of policy objectives whose ultimate purpose is to change the nature of the state no less than that of state welfare. Thus, the introduction of social care markets is to be seen as a reflection in a particular policy field of

> a powerful new ideology which has become politically dominant over the
> last two decades. This new ideology has overthrown or undercut the
> previous dominant ideology often described as the Keynesian welfare state.
>
> (Self 1993: 56)

The post-war welfare state rested upon a consensus about the role and
capacity of government to intervene in the market. Moreover, it stressed the
essential interdependence of such interventions in the spheres of both
economic and social policy: full employment was an essential pillar of the
welfare state and Keynesian economics provided the tools to manage markets
in the pursuit of prosperity and social welfare. The apparent inability of the
market to deliver such objectives during the period between the two world
wars both spurred the growth of state intervention and also reinforced a notion
of government as a beneficial influence acting in the general interest. By
contrast, private decisions taken by individuals in a free market were broadly
agreed to produce 'inferior welfare outcomes than appear possible under public
or non-market decision-making' (Dunleavy and O'Leary 1987: 77). Thus,
Beveridge's proposals on social insurance (1942) and full employment (1944)
provided the basis for a major expansion in the role of government to
compensate for the failure of unregulated markets. Their interlocking
components combined demand management with the protection and creation
of employment opportunities, together with new and expanded social programmes.

However, as Deakin (1994) demonstrates, the underlying consensus about
the efficacy and desirability of 'big' government had a relatively short life,
although it did not finally crumble until the sterling crisis of 1976. The collapse
of international confidence in the British economy that summer led to an
International Monetary Fund loan on terms which required a reduction in
public borrowing and the proportion of the gross domestic product allocated
to public expenditure. The introduction of these measures was a historical
turning point which, as Deakin argues, 'more than any one single act finally
knocked the props away from under the post-war certainties' (Deakin: 62).
From then on, full employment ceased to be an objective of public policy,
economic goals took precedence over social goals and public expenditure was
viewed in a new light. Having been regarded

> throughout most of the postwar period as a benign instrument for
> securing the goals of social policy and the final guarantor against the
> return of economic depressions (public expenditure) had changed sides:
> from being an essential part of the solution, it had now become part of
> the problem.
>
> (Deakin: 63)

The new orthodoxy – which became a fundamental part of the Thatcherite
canon – simply reversed the post-Keynesian consensus by holding that markets
were generally beneficent and government intervention was the source, rather
than the necessary consequence, of market failure (Self 1993). The route to

economic prosperity lay in reining back a public sector which had so grown in size that it 'crowded out' productive investment (Bacon and Eltis 1976) and could be funded only through inflationary borrowing which, in turn, led to increased unemployment.

The influence of these elements of monetarist economics was reinforced by the contribution of public choice theorists who applied the tools of economic analysis to the study of the political process and the behaviour of public sector bureaucracies (for example, Buchanan 1978, 1986). Their case was that government not only had an in-built tendency towards economically damaging expansion, but also that it favoured provider rather than consumer interests. It is an approach which has both demand- and supply-side dimensions. The former builds on Downs' (1967) characterization of democracy as an electoral market place in which political leaders compete for votes. Thus, public choice theory argues that pressure groups are able to exercise excessive influence over the politicians who should hold them to account. The latter are motivated by short-term electoral interests which make them more likely to placate, rather than to challenge, organized producer interests in order to win or retain power. They are able to accede to such demands in the knowledge that the costs of so doing are likely to be less evident than either the benefits of meeting such demands (such as more teachers, doctors or other public services) or the political costs of not meeting them. By contrast, taxpayers as a group are less well organized, and the electoral process offers them a crude and infrequent vehicle for expressing their preferences, especially compared with their role as consumers in the market place. The consequence is that government expands inexorably while the costs of its bargaining with individual producer groups are either deferred through deficit financing or dispersed in the global pool of public expenditure. In Friedman's terms, 'the benefits are concentrated; the costs are diffused; and you have a bias in the market place which leads to ever greater expansion in the scope of government' (1976, quoted in Gamble 1988: 52). As a result, both individual liberty and economic welfare are threatened by the growth of the state and its inflationary borrowings.

A second dimension of public choice theory deals with the supply side of government. It asserts that demand-side pressures from producer interests are reinforced by the tendency of government bureaucracies to pursue their own interests rather than those of the public. As Self argues, public choice theorists

> are unable to accept the traditional view that bureaucrats are guided, at least to some extent by a sense of public service . . . Instead they postulate that bureaucrats are primarily motivated by their private interests over pay, status and personal convenience or ambition.
>
> (Self 1993: 32)

According to Niskanen (1971, 1978) government bureaucrats are monopolistic suppliers of services to whom the 'normal' rules of monopoly apply.

Accordingly, they are able to exploit their position to secure excessive budgets which they spend on some combination of oversupply or inefficiency. Consequently, and as would apply in the private sector, exposure to competitive forces would enable costs to be cut without reducing the quantity and quality of services to end users.

Both the supply-side and demand-side arguments of public choice theorists lead to a position which is pro-market and anti-state. In policy terms, it implies creating space for market forces by reducing the role of government in both economic management and direct service provision. This 'new right' or neo-liberal thinking was a growing influence on the programmes of successive Conservative governments since Mrs Thatcher's first election victory in 1979. In broad terms, those governments sought to secure a new balance between state intervention and market forces by pursuing two complementary strategies which may be described as 'taking government into the market' and 'bringing the market into government'. The former comprised full-scale privatization in the sense of the sale or transfer of government functions to the private sector. The sale of the former nationalized (and sometimes subsidized) industries provides the most substantial example of this approach, although the sale of council houses, transfer of responsibility for certain sickness benefits to employers, and fiscal incentives for employees to take up private pensions are all examples of privatization in the social policy field. However, the latter has been more generally characterized by a second strategy of introducing competitive forces into the supply of services while retaining public sector funding. The progressive extension of compulsory competitive tendering for local government services and the creation of quasi markets based on the separation of purchaser and provider functions in health and social care provide examples of this strategy. Moreover, as the distinctive elements of the health and social care markets indicate, competition may be introduced within and between government bureaucracies, as is primarily the case of the former, or between government and independent sector producers, as is primarily the case of the latter.

As will be evident from the above analysis, the community care reforms are best seen as the product of a complex, and in some respects interlocking, mix of social, economic and political goals. Each of them shares the objective of rebalancing the needs and interests of the consumer/user against those of the producer/professional. Each also sees some advantage in diversifying supply in the interests of cost-effectiveness, responsiveness to need and flexibility in delivery. As a result, the health and social care reforms produce the paradox of public sector professionals endorsing them as the embodiment of best-practice thinking about user-centred services, and the new right pursuing them as a means of undermining those same professional interests. Notwithstanding this apparent consensus, however, markets and social care are normally considered to be driven by opposing forces: the former by self-interest and profit maximization; the latter by an altruistic concern to represent the interests of others and maximize welfare outcomes on their behalf. Indeed, it was this perceived conflict between self- and other-regarding motivations, reinforced by the perception that social care is different, that underpinned the resistance to the reforms encountered in the earlier phase of this study. The findings presented here provide evidence about the extent to which opposition to the 'commercialization of care' affects the support of implementors for the objectives of central government.

Implementing the reforms

It was accepted from the outset that the translation of the policies outlined in *Caring for People* would require a complex and long-term process of implementation. The policies were seen to represent not only a 'cultural revolution' in terms of traditional behaviours, ways of working and organizational systems; in many respects, they also amounted to a leap in the dark (Wistow 1995a; see also Henwood and Wistow 1994). Thus the Audit Commission (1992b) spoke of the need for 'fundamental changes to organisational cultures' and described the necessary changes in the operation of social services departments over the next decade as amounting to 'a revolution'. The nature of this revolution in management and service delivery processes has been indicated above in discussing the need to shift the balance of influence between users and providers in favour of the former. In terms of the specific functions and tasks involved, it has been usefully summarized as follows:

> Authorities must therefore go through significant readjustments to reorientate their approach to implement the new policies. They must identify needs more systematically; policy formulation must become more clearly defined and overt, and must be shared between authorities; operational arrangements for commissioning care must be aligned with delegation of authority where appropriate, with budgets to match; and a host of other adjustments must be made to assessment procedures, service agreements, information systems, quality control and to the management of individual services.
>
> (Audit Commission 1992a: para. 51)

Establishing any one of these processes and systems was a formidable implementation task in itself when compared with existing ways of working. Taken together, they provided challenges of the highest order to staff at all levels in management and service delivery, not least because they were being introduced alongside so many other changes in the health and social services: the almost continuous revolution in NHS structure and management arrangements; the administrative and political uncertainty flowing from the Local Government Review; and the requirements of major legislative change in the fields of child care and criminal justice. Moreover, the community care reforms were based on limited previous experience:

Much of the new approach is theory – as yet untried and untested on any large scale. Much of it is based on research projects usually run by people with high abilities and high motivation, often with extra funding.
(Audit Commission 1992a: para. 52)

Even such an assessment might be considered overgenerous. In practice, the reforms combined ideology and rhetoric with minimal evidence. Most of their key elements were based on untested assumptions and nowhere was this more so than in the case of the benefits which markets were claimed to provide in the field of social care. For example, no evidence was produced to demonstrate whether or not sources of market failure were inherent in characteristics of social care or its consumers. Similarly, the evidence for the gains to be derived from the assessment and care management systems was based on a small number of initiatives. Although it would be untrue to suggest that the policy had no empirical foundation, the balance between ideology and assumption, on the one hand, and evidence, on the other, lay towards the former. This relative absence of evidence-based policy-making has not been uncommon in the field of social care for adults. An independent review of research and development in the personal social services, commissioned by the Department of Health, contrasted the 'significant impact' of research on child care policy with the situation in respect of adult user groups. In the latter context, it reported 'a perception that policy had too often been politically-led with, in recent years, an emphasis on cost containment' (Smith 1994: paras 26, 29). The influence of care management research on the *Caring for People* objectives was recognized as a necessary qualification to this general perception. However, one of the purposes of this book and the programme of Department of Health funded research of which it forms a part is precisely to review critically the assumptions on which the policy was based and secure empirical evidence about their robustness.

The largely untested nature of the changes did contribute to a recognition in the Department of Health that their introduction would be politically risky – a factor compounded by the basic lack of trust in local authorities, their managerial capacity and political commitment to take on complex market-based reforms. Partly as a reflection of such considerations, the Department began to signal, from the outset, that evolutionary rather than overnight change was the essence of the social care reforms. Thus, the full title of the 1989 White Paper was *Caring for People: Community Care for the Next Decade and Beyond*. An early letter to Directors of Social Services from the then Chief Inspector of the Social Services Inspectorate (SSI) began a process of separating those elements of the reforms which required more immediate attention from those which would be addressed in the longer term (Department of Health 1990c). This distinction became the starting point for a monitoring and development programme which aimed to ensure that all authorities met the minimum requirements of the 1990 Act by the time of its final implementation in April 1993 (Henwood and Wistow 1995).

The evidence base for this implementation programme was provided by findings from monitoring visits to all health and social services authorities carried out in September 1991 by officers of Regional Health Authorities and the Social Services Inspectorate. This monitoring round concluded that, while authorities were making 'largely satisfactory progress . . . many detailed and difficult issues of implementation will need to be tackled positively over the next few months' (Department of Health 1992a: 1). Accordingly, a joint letter was sent to all health and local authorities in March 1992 by the Deputy Chief Executive of the NHS (Andrew Foster) and the Chief Inspector of the SSI (Herbert Laming) in which they set out the Department's 'expectations of the work which needs to be done over the next twelve months so that a smooth transition to the new arrangements can be achieved' (*ibid.*: 1). The approach adopted was to specify two minimum implementation requirements for April 1993: arrangements for assessing care needs; and arrangements for securing the provision of care in response to such assessments. It also emphasized the importance of focusing on the estimated 100,000 people who would previously have been supported by the social security system but would now approach local authorities for an assessment of their needs.

The so-called Foster/Laming letter further identified 'eight key tasks on which authorities would need to concentrate to meet those requirements' (see Box 1.1). Other elements of the reforms were identified as requiring continuing work and development over the longer term. These included: the development of care management; further clarification of the purchaser and provider roles within SSDs; a wider role for the independent sector; development of innovative purchasing arrangements; joint assessment of population needs; joint community care plans as purchasing strategies; joint information requirements; and a needs-based approach to service provision and the proper involvement of users and carers both in planning services and in making arrangements for individuals (Department of Health 1992a).

To assist authorities fulfil the eight key tasks, the Department sponsored a national development programme designed to generate practical guidance and disseminate good practice. This approach was refined and reinforced by a second 'Foster/Laming letter' in September (Department of Health 1992b) based on further monitoring results. In addition, a 'Community Care Support Force' was established at the same time to assist authorities identified through the monitoring visits as giving 'significant cause for concern'. The Support Force was also responsible for identifying good practice, disseminating it and publishing practical guidance on a range of issues, including market management.

The final elements in the implementation framework came some weeks later with an announcement of the amount of resources to be transferred from the social security budget to local government, together with the conditions under which the transfer would be paid. The Griffiths Report (1988) had proposed that the transfer be effected through a specific grant subject to social services departments satisfying a number of conditions. These included the submission of an annual community care plan demonstrating evidence of their

---

Box 1.1   Eight key tasks, 1992

1   Agreeing the basis for required assessment systems for individuals.

2   Clarifying and agreeing arrangements for continuing care for new clients in residential and nursing homes including arrangements for respite care.

3   Ensuring the robustness and mutual acceptability of discharge arrangements.

4   Clarifying the roles of GPs and primary health care teams.

5   Ensuring that adequate purchasing and charging arrangements are in place in respect of individuals who will be receiving residential or nursing home care.

6   Ensuring that financial and other management systems can meet the new demands likely after 1 April 1993.

7   Ensuring that staff are suitably trained, wherever appropriate on a joint basis.

8   Informing the public of the arrangements made by the authority for assessment and the provision of care.

Source: Department of Health (1992a).

---

collaboration with health and housing services, their willingness to work with the independent sectors, and their development of effective management processes and information systems (Wistow 1990). However, the government had rejected this recommendation in its response to Griffiths (Clarke 1989). The White Paper proposed that the social security transfer should be included within the general revenue support grant: an approach which necessarily gave local authorities wide discretion over its allocation, including the extent to which it should be spent on social services and their new community care responsibilities at all. It was, therefore, to some considerable surprise that the Secretary of State announced a form of earmarked grant in her speech to the annual social services conference in October 1992: funds would be transferred to social services departments in four annual instalments which would be ringfenced for the year in which they were transferred (Bottomley 1992). Thereafter, the transferred sums would be included in the overall revenue support grant and thus, in principle, be available to local authorities to use for other purposes. Over the first three years, this grant would build up to a total of £1,568 million, which was equivalent to 32 per cent of the 1992/93 estimated budget for social services current expenditure.

This limited form of ringfencing (and what was considered to be a relatively generous total) did much to disarm critics in local government who had lobbied for a specific grant since the publication of the White Paper. Their position had been supported by the House of Commons Social Services Committee (1990) and many of the interested parties who gave evidence to the Committee. The Government had consistently rejected such an approach ever since Griffiths (1988) had proposed it, arguing in its response to the Social Services Committee that

> The government does not accept the argument that it is necessary to 'protect' community care funding through ring fencing . . . [it] has found no reason to change its conviction that the widely shared objectives of the White Paper can be achieved without the constraining measures of a large specific grant and that the disadvantages of such a grant firmly outweigh any possible advantages.
>
> (Department of Health 1990b: 3–4)

The government's change of heart was hedged around with a number of conditions limiting local authorities' discretion to spend the grant. These conditions reflected the centre's concern about whether local authorities could be trusted to spend the money effectively and in ways which safeguarded the interests of the NHS and independent sector providers (Wistow 1995b). Thus, authorities were told that they risked being excluded from receiving the grant if they did not sign agreements with the health service on hospital discharge and the purchase of nursing home places before 31 December 1992. In addition, they were required to spend 85 per cent of the transferred resources on services provided by the independent sector. By this means they were prevented from greatly expanding their own services. A further directive gave individual users the right to enter the home of their choice, within financial limits (Department of Health 1992c). Finally, social services departments were directed to consult with the independent sector providers in the preparation of community care plans (Department of Health 1993b).

Thus, the Department of Health produced a skilful blend of incentives and sanctions to ensure that local authorities created and worked within a social care market rather than invested substantially in direct provision. None the less, these conditions and, indeed, the entire national monitoring and development programme were indicators of the degree of nervousness at the centre about the possibility of a highly visible implementation failure. They reflected a lack of confidence at the highest levels of government in reforms which extended the responsibilities and resources of local authorities. Indeed, the policy was never fully secure until close to the final implementation date and was called in for review by Downing Street as late as the summer of 1992 (Brown 1992: 7). The early monitoring findings about the lack of readiness for implementation in the NHS as well as in local government fed those underlying concerns. Thus, the Departmental implementation support programme, together with the statutory directives and financial conditions, were designed against a backcloth of fears that 'another poll tax' débâcle was a real possibility.

In practice, however, the new arrangements duly came into effect. All authorities signed discharge agreements as required and thus qualified for receipt of the grant. A fourth round of monitoring was conducted in January 1993, and the Langlands/Laming letter of March 1993 noted that 'rapid moves forward' had been made since the previous monitoring exercise in September 1992. Importantly, it also concluded that there 'appears to have been some evening-up of performance. All authorities should have the basic elements in place by April' (Department of Health 1993c). The scene was set, therefore, to achieve the 'smooth transition' to the new arrangements which the Government had set as its target in March 1992.

Against this background of preparations at national level, this book records the experiences of twenty-five local authorities in the initial months following implementation of the reforms.

2

Enabling and market configuration: steering and rowing

Introduction

One of the main findings of our fieldwork in 1991 was that there was a range of understandings of the term 'enabling' among the sample local authorities. These were interpreted by us – rather than being described by those concerned – as comprising three models: enabling as personal development, community development, and market development. Only the first two interpretations had strong historical roots in the personal social services: the third model of enabling as market development – given emphasis in the *Caring for People* White Paper – has a different pedigree and was widely regarded in 1991 as incompatible with the values and nature of social care.

The roots of this interpretation of enabling as market development lie in the wider attempt by successive Conservative governments during the 1980s and 1990s to alter the basis upon which not only local authorities but also the public sector as a whole operates. Such an approach, described by one Conservative MP as 'civic Conservatism', applies to 'those parts of society which cannot simply be left to the free operation of the market', the institutions of which nevertheless will benefit by incorporating 'some of the best features of markets – choice and competition' (Willetts 1993). This is a policy shift which in the case of local authorities is well encapsulated in Nicholas Ridley's earlier description (1988) of their proper, and future, role as 'enabling not providing'. In other words, a move away from their traditional function of service provision to planning and managing the delivery of services principally, but not wholly, by others.

It is important to recognize that more generally this reflects a policy shift which is not confined to the personal social services but which has been effected across the public sector in this country and abroad. One of the best-known characterizations of this general, and international, shift – from 'traditional administration' to 'new public management' – is by Osborne and Gaebler (1992). Although insistent that government and business are fundamentally different, their view is that, even if government cannot be run as a business, it can be more business-like. They describe the nature of emergent entrepreneurial governments in terms of ten guiding principles, among which are the following:

- that government should be catalytic, its prime task being that of steering rather than rowing;
- that government should be market-oriented, encouraging change through the market rather than bureaucratic mechanisms;
- that government should be competitive, injecting competition into service delivery and catalysing all other sectors; and
- that government should empower citizens by pushing control into the community.

Although based on American experience of central and local government, much of Osborne and Gaebler's diagnosis and prescriptions chime with developments which have had their parallel – contemporaneously – in Britain (see Butler 1994). In the particular context of social care, it is also clear that many of these principles are consonant with the thrust of *Caring for People* and subsequent policy guidance: notably the *a priori* preference for markets, the focus on catalysing, and the emphasis on steering not rowing as government's prime task.

Under such principles – whether in the language of Osborne and Gaebler or in the language of *Caring for People* – the job of governments is to forgo doing everything themselves in favour of managing, monitoring and regulating others. It is, however, a much more proactive role than implied by a straightforward withdrawal from one of the prime traditional functions of local government in this country: that of service delivery. The argument is not that governments should necessarily 'do less' (much less 'do nothing') but that in redefining their role they should indeed do less of some things – notably service provision via traditional bureaucracies – but also that they should do more of others. In the case of local government they should in particular do more to engage (or catalyse) the fullest range of stake-holders and use their unique power and influence as facilitators: as enablers. This role can be described as one of strategic commissioning in the broadest sense: that is, it could be seen as setting, or helping to define, the architectural brief and thereafter *overseeing* – but not *undertaking* – the design, construction and running of the building. In this way, it combines both senses of the term steering, distinguished by Dunsire and Rhodes as process and effect (Rhodes 1995): it is both setting the direction and supervising the moves in that direction.

In the context of the *Caring for People* changes it is, of course, of the essence that local authorities both steer and row. Although they are indeed required to promote alternative service provision, they are expected to develop and manage a mixed economy of care in which an essential part of the mix is the public sector. One of the main issues we were exploring in 1993, as outlined in this chapter, was the range of stances among authorities in terms of the extent to which they intended to reduce their direct provision – their rowing – and concentrate upon, and even increase their capacity for, steering.

We discussed in Chapter 1 the broad context within which recent Conservative governments have challenged the historic equation of public services not only with public funding but also with direct public provision (Wistow *et al.* 1994). Beginning with the contracting out of ancillary services such as cleaning and catering, this challenge has been extended in recent years to such core local authority services as education and housing; with, in both services, the gradual diminution or erosion of the traditional local authority role of hierarchical service management and provision. Likewise in the health service, and more widely with the 'next steps' initiative across the civil service (Ibbs 1988), one of the fundamental changes has been the organizational separation of the planning and purchase of services from their actual provision. The prime objective of this shift, as we discussed in Chapter 1, has been to expose such organizations to the discipline of competitive market forces and thereby increase their efficiency and responsiveness to consumers (see Flynn 1990; Harrison *et al.* 1990; Metcalfe and Richards 1990; Willetts 1993). It is, however, important to note that the 'next steps' initiative was not a hiving off or privatization of government functions: it was 'simply about reorganising executive functions within government' (Butler 1994).

One interpretation of the *Caring for People* approach to enabling might, in the extreme case, reduce local authorities to one council meeting a year in order to let contracts. This is the Nicholas Ridley version of an enabling council. This narrow or minimalist version of local authorities as enabling councils contrasts sharply with a different, broader, view of enabling which has been developed within the field of local government. Here Clarke and Stewart (1988, 1990) and Brooke (1989) have propounded a view of enabling as potentially entailing not a reduction to some residual responsibilities but an increase of responsibility whereby local authorities act as instruments of a broader community governance (see also Stewart and Walsh 1992). We found in 1991 that this latter view of enabling was much more consonant with understandings of the term within the personal social services field where enabling traditionally has been construed as personal or community development. Our evidence was that many of the reservations which local authorities had about the government's community care proposals stemmed from a perceived clash between such traditional understandings of enabling and the form in which it was expressed by Griffiths – and subsequently by *Caring for People* – as market development. These reservations were in part based upon a fear that stimulating a mixed economy would not only involve a diminution in public sector provision but also, almost inevitably, a growth in private sector provision. Traditionally within the personal social services, enabling has meant fostering and supporting large and diffuse networks of voluntary organizations. Such agencies could claim community roots in so far as they were generally established and putatively run to meet perceived local needs. Founders of these local bodies had traditionally included respected national organizations, unaffiliated community groups, or those with obvious expertise and experience including carers or the clients themselves. In tapping such resources, local authorities were dealing with organizations with apparently shared values in one crucial respect – their perceived orientation towards altruistic or public goals, as opposed to private gain. Local authorities' reservations in 1991 thus comprised a combination of civic pride – a view that local authorities have long produced many excellent services and facilities – and fears either that too few alternative suppliers existed, or that many incumbent and potential providers were unfit, either because they were profit-motivated or because they were managerially ill-equipped.

We began our fieldwork in 1993 by asking about then current understandings of enabling and whether these had changed in the previous two years. (We need to remember here that fewer than half – 44 per cent – of the Directors interviewed in 1993 had been in post in 1991.) We also sought to locate this understanding within a broader local context: that is, whether the individual local authorities corporately regarded themselves as being, or as becoming, enabling councils.

We were also exploring what advantages or disadvantages people expected to accrue from the development of social care markets. One of the most notable findings of the 1991 mapping was the widespread view that, however appropriate for other goods or services (local authority and other), markets in the field of social care were inappropriate because social care is inherently 'different'. Was this still a prevalent view two years later?

It was important to gauge such attitudes towards enabling because they govern both the pace and direction of local change. They help to explain authorities' preferences for particular types of providers and their willingness or unwillingness to fragment or forgo their own 'market share' in particular areas of provision. They also help to explain why social care is perceived to be different and why certain types of market and market mechanisms are therefore seen to be more appropriate than others.

Changing perceptions among sample authorities

As we have argued previously, the three models of enabling are neither mutually exclusive nor necessarily mutually reinforcing (Wistow et al. 1994: 134). Indeed, community and market development can be viewed, at least in part, as alternative means to achieving the ends specified in the personal development interpretation of enabling. In positing the existence of three models we were interpreting and attempting to distinguish between the widely different views of enabling expressed by interviewees in 1990/91: views which helped explain the widely differing ways in which authorities were approaching their implementation task. In asking interviewees in 1993 about their understandings of the term enabling we were not seeking to validate the three models, but to explore how understandings of what enabling involves and entails had altered.

In 1991 we described enabling as market development in terms of an emphasis on market creation, separation of purchasing and provision, and the introduction of a contract culture. Implicitly, the defining characteristic of this model of enabling is the active promotion by local authorities of alternative service provision and, simultaneously, the ending of their own sole or near-monopoly provision.

In theory, the two ends of the supply spectrum are sole local authority provision and non-local authority provision. In practice, no local authority has ever been a sole provider, but many have been near-monopoly providers, especially for services such as domiciliary and day care. The general shift being urged – and now being seen – is along the spectrum, therefore, from near-monopoly provision to non-provision, where the latter comprises local authorities merely steering, acting solely as the commissioners within, and regulators of, social care markets. In 1993 we found only two of the twenty-five sample authorities where the complete cessation of in-house provision was regarded as a possibility, with the authority becoming solely a commissioning and regulating body; and, even here, these were possibilities envisaged only in the long term. In one of these cases the Director said that the authority 'would like to contract out everything if they could'. However, the likelihood – at least in the short to medium term – was that, in social services if not in other parts of local government, there would be both in-house and external provision. Partly this was because of concern 'about not fragmenting the welfare market too much'. Also, however, in the Director's view 'the injunction to become enabling authorities was specifically designed to give greater user choice not just between the type of service, but also between the types of service provider'.

This rejection of the extreme minimalist position echoes the findings of earlier research carried out across local government services as a whole. In their sample of 201 local authorities throughout Great Britain (39 per cent of the total), Ennals and O'Brien (1990) found very few authorities taking what they and others (see Clarke and Stewart 1988; and Brooke 1989) have described as the 'narrow' view of enabling. Thus, there were some authorities which saw it

> as a desirable objective to slim themselves down to a small core organization which carries out only those functions which strictly have to be performed by the authority itself.
>
> (Ennals and O'Brien 1990: 13)

By contrast, 73 per cent of the authorities in Ennals and O'Brien's sample were not proposing to put out to compulsory competitive tendering any services that they were not required to: 'The majority of authorities, including Conservative controlled authorities positively want their direct service organizations (DSOs) to succeed in winning contracts' (Ennals and O'Brien 1990: 16). Similarly, in the majority of authorities in our sample, what was being considered, both in principle and in practice, was a shift along the spectrum away from near-monopoly provision (where this currently existed) towards, but short of, non-provision: in other words, a broad acceptance of the concept of enabling as market development in which local authorities see their role as 'facilitators' working alongside and with other providers, as 'honest brokers' of a range of provision, as being not the main rowers but one among many.

Supplementary or substitute provision

There are two principal means by which local authorities can pursue this sort of market development and effect a shift in market configuration. First, they can retain their own direct provision and encourage other, additional, suppliers to supplement it; and second, they can simultaneously decrease their direct provision and encourage alternative suppliers (existing or new) to replace it. That is, they can change both market size and market share. Only one sample authority argued that it should and would be pursuing the former option. Here the Director said that the objective was:

> to increase the number of players in social care and increase the capacity of existing non-statutory providers . . . it was not to enable other people to manage the services that are currently run.

Indeed, across the authority as a whole the aim was 'to keep all direct services direct'. In only one other authority were similar views expressed, but these were already changing: in a Labour-controlled metropolitan district the Director said that while the members:

> see their job as providing the best possible service to citizens in X . . . [and] see that service as being very much a direct service managed by the local authority . . . and not the enabling authority in terms of enabling other agents to provide a service on our behalf . . . [The latter was] developing very quickly as a viable alternative.

Of the remaining authorities aiming in effect to alter their market shares – irrespective of political control – two issues were being considered: first, what should be the size and shape of the remaining direct provision; and second, by which mix of alternative providers should such public provision be replaced – existing organizations, newly created 'not-for-profit' organizations formed by the externalization of local authority services, or other, newly encouraged provision?

Even if resigned or grudging, this widespread acceptance by local authorities of a diminished role as rowers – or providers of social care – and an increased role as steerers – as promoters and regulators of other forms of supply – can be contrasted with what we found in 1991. Then we reported finding near-universal support for the service principles espoused in *Caring for People*, but widespread reservations about or hostility to the White Paper's organizational principles: the enabling role and development of a mixed economy of care (Wistow *et al.* 1994). The growing acceptance of these two organizational principles is undoubtedly based in part on a growing realization that there is no inherent incompatibility between the three models of enabling. In particular, it was due to a recognition that the term market development presupposes neither a single market form, nor a certain distribution of market shares among provider types; nor does it preclude authorities from developing markets in which some providers are preferred to others. In other words, authorities have the ability, if they wish, actively to promote markets dominated by providers whom they trust and with whom they feel some affinity in terms of values and service principles.

For many authorities, voluntary and not-for-profit providers are those with whom they have had long-standing relationships: relationships often built up by the local authority, as indicated previously, acting as enablers of community development. In four authorities interviewees referred specifically to the fostering or enabling of community development as their preferred route for developing a mixed social care market. Indeed, one Director argued that enabling 'has always been about community development, looking at what the community needs'.

It ought to be said that, although widely accepted as inevitable, there was less than universal enthusiasm for the reduction in direct local authority provision. There was often said to be what one interviewee described as 'an air of realism around that is touching everybody . . . CCT [compulsory competitive tendering] has had an impact'. But there was also 'sadness' and 'resignation' about local authorities' reduced role, including the Conservative-controlled authority in which the Director said that the council would prefer to provide the services itself 'because it believes it can provide better value for money than the private sector'. In an echo of Nicholas Ridley's description of a future enabling local authority, the social services Chair in the same authority envisaged:

> In a few years' time [the authority would need only] a chief executive, a computer, a finance director and the rest of us can go and jump in the nearest lake . . . that's what we're here to do really, to cut our own throats.

In the sample as a whole, interviewees in only two authorities voiced unambiguous enthusiasm for the reduction in direct local authority provision. By contrast interviewees in ten authorities – while acknowledging its inevitability – expressed strong reservations about this aspect of enabling. In one of these authorities, the Chair described the encouragement of alternative providers as the 'positive' meaning of enabling, but described 'running down and providing less of the local authority service' as its 'negative' side – or as 'disabling'. In another authority the two members who were interviewed said respectively that:

> I'm suspicious of enabling as a political concept because it's all about getting rid of local authorities and reducing member influence, and it's all about setting contracts once a year.

> We have no choice but to do it through partnerships because we won't have the money to do it ourselves, not by direct provision.

Size and type of market share

A number of reasons were given by local authorities for retaining some in-house provision, however diminished their actual market share. First, echoing the findings two years previously, they needed a *contingency in case of failures* among other providers. Second, allied to this, authorities referred to the need to *avoid destabilizing local markets*, especially in the short term when there is a shortage of alternative providers either in some services (for example, domiciliary or day care) or in some localities, particularly rural areas. In relation to this argument, two interviewees (both in county councils) said that enabling meant different things in different markets within the same locality. 'An enabling authority', it was said, 'behaves in a different way depending on the market place': in other words, it is dependent upon market maturity. Thus, in this particular county when the local authority was, and still is, the dominant provider in the domiciliary care market, its task was said to be 'to enable a foothold to be gained by independent providers'. However, where the authority was a minority provider – as it has been for a long time in the residential care market – it will seek to remain a small, specialist niche provider. The reason for retaining such a 'foothold in the market place' as a provider was to retain sufficient knowledge of practice not only to be able to specify and identify where service developments might take place but also to regulate the market. As one Director said, one way to regulate the market 'is having a proportion . . . ourselves'.

The next reason adduced for retaining direct local authority provision – once again echoing a finding from 1991 – was to enable the authority to act as a measure for quality standards and *an exemplar of good practice*. As we have already noted, there was, among local authority members especially, considerable pride in much public sector provision, and also a belief that the best local authority services and facilities match or exceed the quality of those in other sectors. Allied to this civic pride is the scale of the financial investments involved – notably in the building or refurbishment of residential homes – and also members' personal and political investment.

The other main reason given for retaining local authority provision was *the promotion of sectoral choice*. By definition, a 'mixed economy of care' was interpreted as requiring a presence in the market place of variety in terms of ownership and sector, embracing public as well as non-public provision: without such a mix, user and carer choice, it was argued, is reduced. As one Director stated:

> [On the one hand,] if you run a sort of monopolistic approach to care, then you're not giving appropriate choice, [but, on the other hand] market development includes the development of the local authority's own services.

Complementing these various rationales for the retention of direct provision, there was evidence of a growing acceptance between 1991 and 1993 of the need for authorities to define and concentrate on their core social services functions or 'businesses': that is, not just a slimming-down of service provision for its own sake but also a planned retraction to certain defined core services. As one Director remarked, the task is:

> sticking with what we do best and doing it ourselves [and] not being afraid to contract with other people who can do things better. We aren't experts in food, so why are we running a meals-on-wheels service? On the other hand, we are experts at child protection investigations and there are no other alternatives.

Underlying many of these comments about the diminution in public sector provision there remained the view that, in some important senses, social care is different. As we discuss in the following section, there is a conviction among many interviewees that, for example, choosing a residential care home is fundamentally different from choosing, say, a bar of chocolate; and that contracts for personal social services are not only precisely that – personal and individual – but are made with or on behalf of the most vulnerable of people.

It is these underlying beliefs which inform not only local authorities' decisions about appropriate public and non-public market shares but also which are the most appropriate (that is, their preferred) non-statutory providers. Across the sample as a whole, fourteen authorities expressed a preference for voluntary and 'not-for-profit' over private providers: in the remaining authorities no clear preference was expressed. However, in three of the above fourteen authorities, it was emphasized that such a preference did not imply antagonism towards the private sector. According to the Chair in one hung county council, there was a preference for the voluntary sector because:

> We share many of the same perceptions . . . voluntary organizations also have this feeling that this isn't really right; but it's what we're being forced to do . . . there is a real partnership in that way with them because we share common ideals.

Nevertheless, the authority was also working with the private sector in the residential care field: there is 'a real commitment towards doing that in a genuine way . . . not in any antagonistic way at all'. Among the other eleven authorities there were some which explained their preference in terms of doubts, in principle, about the suitability of profit-motivated providers in the field of social care; although in only one authority did interviewees (members in this case) speak of 'moral repugnance' among council colleagues at making a profit out of vulnerable and disadvantaged people. One of these members added that 'people have a job realizing that you can be equally caring in the private sector'. More typical were the interviewees in two authorities who spoke of being 'more comfortable' working with the voluntary sector.

In Chapter 4 we look in more detail at the options considered and decisions taken by authorities in promoting alternative patterns of supply either by encouraging private or voluntary providers or by externalizing existing local authority provision. However, in the next section of this chapter we address authorities' views about whether 'social care is different' and what advantages or disadvantages accrue from the development of social care markets. Together with attitudes towards enabling, this is what broadly dictates authorities' preferred routes for market development.

Perceived appropriateness of markets in social care

In 1991, Chairs and Directors commonly questioned whether the market had a place in the production and delivery of social care. Typically their view was that social care differed from purely private as well as other local authority services in ways which made it inappropriate to extend market mechanisms to this sphere of social policy. The belief that 'social care is different' appeared to be wedded to the view that it was inappropriate to expose social care to market mechanisms. In our 1993 fieldwork, we deliberately untangled these two issues, an approach which proved to be valuable in illuminating understandings and motivations. Our findings are presented in Table 2.1. Among Directors, opinion was almost evenly divided: nine considered that it was different and ten did not. However, opinion was less divided about the advantages and disadvantages of markets for the delivery of social care: sixteen Directors perceived overall advantages compared with only three who saw overall disadvantages, albeit sometimes with a hint of resignation.

Six responses could not be clearly categorized either way. The views of

Table 2.1 'Social care is different': views of directors of social services, 1993

	Yes (N)	No (N)	Not available[a] (N)
Social care is different	9	10	6
Overall the market has comparative advantages	16	3	6
Social care is different and overall the market has comparative advantages	5	1	3

[a] Either these issues were not explicitly covered in the interview, an explicit response was not made, or it was impossible readily to categorize responses.

the Directors who agreed that 'social care is different' were particularly revealing: of the nine in this category, only one saw overall disadvantages to social care markets; in three cases no clear view was expressed; and the remaining five perceived overall advantages. Thus, the majority of those who considered that 'social care is different' also thought that, on balance, the market had more advantages than disadvantages.

For the vast majority of interviewees, the market was fast becoming an accepted fact of life. For example, when asked if there were any disadvantages to using the market, one Director replied 'No, I don't think so. You've got to work with it'. This response was the more significant since it came from an authority where the members had previously been well-known for their reluctance to develop a mixed economy. Yet, in spite of this legacy of antipathy they were now said to be working positively with the private sector, a relationship which the Director said they 'had embraced magnificently'.

By contrast, one Labour Chair suggested that enabling 'meant privatization by the back door'; and the Director in a different Labour authority expressed fears about 'the market place' being used 'to lower the level of public entitlement, citizens' entitlement to having a need met'. The same interviewee also argued that the local authority 'having to put the money in to enable a profit [to be made] . . . is the biggest ideological bar to the idea of a market place'. This view was, however, unique among the Directors interviewed and rare among Chairs. Much more typical was the Director who suggested in 1993 that answers in 1991 to the question whether social care is different had been 'based on the kind of anti-commercial model of understanding rather than a more mature understanding of values and quality systems'. Other Directors also maintained that understanding and attitudes had changed over the two years. One simply stated that 'If I said social care was different last time, I've changed my mind'. According to a fellow Director:

> I think we've moved on. A lot of the personal prejudices, resistance to change, had to be put in some sort of perspective. Some of the absolutes that people set are really quite daft. I think that the market economy, as defined by the government, is here, if not to stay, is here for a very long time; and I think social carers are great adaptors.

Thus, the small number of market enthusiasts we identified in 1991 were in 1993 accompanied by a larger number of 'market pragmatists' who were questioning taken-for-granted assumptions which had underpinned their previous antipathy. Neither of these groups, however, was entirely uncritical about the developing social care market. Most identified potential disadvantages or argued that careful management would be necessary to overcome inherent weaknesses. In addition, as we have already noted, views about whether 'social care is different' were almost equally divided among Directors, and those in each category identified features which distinguished social care from other services. None the less, relatively few Directors or Chairs had well-developed views about the distinctive features of social care markets or their potential strengths and weaknesses. At this point in what was widely acknowledged to be a steep learning curve, knee-jerk anti-commercialism was apparently being replaced by a willingness to engage with the new community care arrangements. However, that willingness was based upon pragmatism rather than a full and considered understanding of their implications.

Is social care different?

Differences between social care and other goods and services – even within the public sector – were identified by authorities along five main dimensions. First, interviewees in a number of authorities underlined the *vulnerability of users* as a distinguishing feature of social care markets. For example, three London boroughs referred to the well-publicized murder of a user in Hammersmith and Fulham by an 'employee' of a private domiciliary care agency. One commented that 'it is a pretty crude kind of example, but it does make you realize the potential hazards and potential risks'. Elsewhere, a Director reported the argument which he had often put to his members, that:

> Making contracts for window cleaning is one thing because if the contractor fails to clean 10 per cent of the windows you're alright; but if a domiciliary or residential care provider doesn't feed 10 per cent of your clients, you're really in trouble.

Concerns about the vulnerability of users and the accountability of public agencies for them led those interviewed to underline the importance of effective registration and inspection on the one hand (especially in the case of domiciliary services), and contract specifications on the other. The Director who had used the window cleaning analogy concluded that 'therefore, it has to be a very different kind of contract' in the case of social care. However, others argued that the 'different' nature of social care as a product made contracting inherently complex. Reflecting on the Hammersmith and Fulham case, one Director said 'I don't have too much worry about profit-making companies and personal care, although I do suspect there has to be an awful lot of work on specification, monitoring and quality'. Others were concerned, however, that social care did not readily lend itself to conventional specification processes, several stressing that individual needs could not be met in a uniform way: social care is not a standard product 'like tins of beans flooding out – each person with a stroke is going to have to have a specially designed [package]'.

A second distinction was the *capacity to act as consumers*: very few interviewees related the characteristics of users – or their carers – specifically to their ability to function as well-informed consumers. The following view was exceptional for its elaboration of this issue:

> There's a belief that the end users and their carers can act economically sensibly within the market place, but it's a decision that you only make

once or twice or three times . . . in your life. So it's different from going into a sweet shop and deciding whether to have a Mars bar or a Twix. Buying sweets is very common. That's part of the market you are operating in every day. Social care is something that's very, very special . . . it's not something you find out about very quickly. You don't know about the market and, secondly, when you go to visit somewhere, what you see are the physical things – is there any smell about, what's the decoration like, how big is the room, what is the view like, how far geographically from where I live, how long will it take me to drive there?

Third, there was the *complexity of outcomes*. It was suggested that social care outcomes were difficult to specify, and one Director, emphasizing the inappropriateness of standard corporate contracting processes in this field, said: 'You can't go for the sorts of tenders which are about how high you want the grass and how often you want it cut'. Social care is seen to be different because it involves organizing a multiplicity of providers and elements of care in order to meet individual need and also because it is difficult to specify desired outcomes like 'dignity, quality of life, involvement in the local community, health and safety'.

Fourth, mention was made of what we might call the *continuity imperative*. It is the very personal nature of such care that requires continuity on the part of the provider and also the right personal characteristics. Thus, as one interviewee remarked:

It may not matter who . . . picks up your rubbish bag in the street [but] it does matter who wipes your bum . . . And that ought to be the same person day in and day out because it's a very personal service and you have to trust that person.

The final dimension of difference was *political sensitivity*. A number of interviewees referred to the particular vulnerability of users as being not only a special characteristic of social care but also a source of vulnerability too for publicly accountable agencies. In the latter context, a Director emphasized the 'fundamental difference between somebody placing themselves and the local authority placing them' in terms of the latter being required to account for any difficulties which emerged subsequent to the placement. The Director in one Labour-controlled authority highlighted the difference between individuals placing themselves in residential care and local authorities using the same money to place them as being one of political accountability: 'our bosses', he said, 'have to account to the electorate every four years'. A similar point was made in a Conservative-controlled authority, where it was suggested that 'you won't need many deaths of elderly people at the hands of their carers before there'll be a tremendous pulling away from all of this'.

This comment is the more significant for having been made in an authority which was clearly a market enthusiast and by an individual who could also be described in such terms. It further serves to underline the more general point that views about whether 'social care is different' should not necessarily be equated with negative attitudes towards the market (although a minority of respondents did take this view). Rather, the perceived differences may be regarded as issues which need to be taken into account in developing and regulating the market.

It ought to be said that, alongside such differences, a smaller number of interviewees also identified similarities between social care and other services. These included the belief that experience in the private sector demonstrated that management skills could be transferred between different kinds of markets so long as managers understood the nature of their product and their market. A related view was that social services departments were moving towards a 'Marks & Spencer' approach based on specifying the values suppliers were expected to embrace as the basis for a trusting relationship between purchasers and providers. If such similarities were less frequently mentioned than the differences, it should be recalled that we categorized the majority of Directors as perceiving overall advantages in using the market to deliver social care.

Perceived advantages of social care markets

A large number of actual or potential advantages of using the market were identified by local authority interviewees. They can be discussed under four heads: stimulus to change; opportunities for cost reduction; purchasing power and quality; and diversity and choice.

Stimulus for reappraisal and change

Competition was seen to be the principal force for change. The more enthusiastic supporters of competitive market forces described them as breathing new energy and vitality into management processes. This view was typified by the Director who described the advantages of the market in terms of:

> the opportunities for innovation, the release of energy and drive in people, new approaches, new thinking, new ways of tackling problems, improved management practices.

Similarly, another Director was emphatic that 'undoubtedly, and controversial as it might be, competition doesn't half sharpen your thinking'. Other respondents spoke of departments being shaken out of a long-established complacency. At least three consequences were said to flow from this sharpening-up of departments and their liberation from the forces of inertia. First, departments were beginning to adopt a more customer-focused approach: the market approach, it was said, 'takes away the complacency and reminds you whom you're in business for'. Second, it was forcing departments to look more critically at costs. In the view of one Director: 'I wouldn't have credited the speed, if you'd asked me this nine months ago, how fast we've moved into overtly talking about unit costs'. Third, as indicated earlier in this chapter, social services departments are increasingly defining their core businesses and becoming clearer about the circumstances in which, and the extent to which, they should provide services directly: 'It helps to focus your mind on what bit of the market you want to provide. If you are a monopoly supplier, you are not going to have to think about priorities.'

We would not wish to claim that all or even the majority of authorities were acting in response to these forces for change: some, indeed, were responding to these forces for change without actually identifying them as *market* forces. However, the potential for such change was widely recognized, and across all kinds of authorities. It is significant, for example, that the above three quotations used to illustrate the consequences of what respondents perceived to be the liberating forces of competition were from, respectively, an authority with a long-established Conservative majority, a hung council (formerly Conservative) and a traditional Labour authority.

Opportunities for cost reduction

A substantial number of authorities associated the market with opportunities to reduce unit costs in both the public and independent sectors. Several linked this issue to pressure on public expenditure and their responsibility to use limited resources as effectively as possible (see Chapter 3). The market was said to be 'healthy because it extends the public purse further than it would otherwise go'. A number of authorities had already negotiated, or envisaged being able to negotiate, reductions in the cost of residential care provided by the independent sector. These authorities included one of the three which was generally unsympathetic towards the market. In addition, two Labour-controlled authorities highlighted the advantages of exposing the costs of public services to competitive forces either by floating them off into an arm's-length trust or putting them onto a separate trading account within the authority. In both cases, such developments were expected to lead to a review of employee working practices and employment conditions. It is worth noting, however, that this was at a time when the implications of the TUPE (Transfer of Undertakings and Protection of Employment) regulations and of the European Union's Acquired Rights Directive were unclear.

It should also be noted that authorities used or interpreted the term 'cost improvements' only in relation to their own budgets. Often this means shunting some of the cost to relatives or to providers. A number of interviewees believed that the lifestyles of some private home providers were evidence of what were perceived to be excess profits which, therefore, gave ample scope for cost reductions. It is also important to note that, as indicated below, some local authorities were concerned about protecting their own staff (and maintaining their terms and conditions of service) as well as about what they perceived to be poorer terms and conditions for staff in the private sector.

Purchasing power and quality

The creation of a purchasing role for social services departments was seen as the instrument for securing the cost improvements referred to above. In addition, authorities were beginning to appreciate that this role provided wider opportunities for influencing the shape and quality of services and provider organizations. According to one Director, who was critical of many aspects of the market economy, the purchasing role put departments 'in the driving seat for quality and specifications, regulation and accreditation'. Others were also beginning to appreciate that, in a situation of oversupply, the market in principle enabled them to purchase strategically and thus express their preferences between types of provider and the quality of provision. In this group were at least two Labour-controlled authorities who had expected independent sector providers to be in the driving seat. Somewhat to their surprise, the lower than anticipated demand for residential and nursing home places had shifted that balance towards the local authorities.

Alongside this emerging perception of their capacity to shape the market through the exercise of purchasing power, authorities also emphasized that the purchasing role (the process of steering) required them to develop a clearer and more explicit sense of purpose (the direction of steering). Part of this process derived from the need to specify criteria to guide decisions about what should be purchased externally and what should be produced internally. A traditionally Conservative-controlled (but recently hung) authority described this feature of the new arrangements in the following terms:

> The market economy therefore requires that kind of business clarity for resource input through to service output to outcome, customer outcome. It has generated . . . [or assisted] what used to be called a public service orientation backed by purchasing power to identify . . . the demands of the consumer.

Similar views were advanced in other authorities, particularly with reference to the potential for using their purchasing power to drive up quality. Thus, one Labour-controlled authority referred to the advantages of the market which would flow from clearer specification processes:

> You are going to say, you don't have to put up with sitting in wet urine for half an hour. It's unacceptable to you. It's unacceptable to society, it's unacceptable to the social services department because we're paying for it and if it happens too often we are going to go to that home and say, we're not going to do business with you any more.

Diversity and choice

Most interviewees who expressed views about the anticipated benefits of the social care market referred either to diversity or choice or both. The following typifies these views:

The advantages are that it does enable more diversification. It does genuinely enable choice. It seems to me that, however laudable your objectives, if you run a . . . monopolistic approach to care, then you're not giving people appropriate choice. People do need vastly different things from services. So if we are going to develop proper alternatives, proper flexibility, I think the market helps.

More specific advantages that were mentioned included the ability of the independent sector to provide a local residential service to a dispersed population (although other respondents noted its uneven development geographically) together with its capacity to broaden the base of domiciliary care by offering cleaning and shopping services. A further perceived advantage was in creating a market place for ideas, models of service and ways of responding to need. Lastly, one Director with a generally negative view about the market emphasized the advantage of allocating budgets to disabled people as a means of enabling them to exercise choice directly.

Perceived disadvantages of markets

Although the balance of views expressed broadly stressed the advantages of social care markets, a range of potential or actual disadvantages was also identified: some straightforwardly reflected views about whether social care is different (which are not repeated here); others were the mirror image of the above advantages and included the following concerns.

First, there was some anxiety about provider cartels, or simply monopoly power accruing to one large non-statutory provider. The effect, it was argued, would be to limit the beneficial effects of competition, with prices driven up and quality driven down as profit maximization became the dominant value in the market place. The ultimate consequence of the process would be to reduce rather than enhance choice (see also Chapter 7).

Second, it was alleged that the new management culture provided 'increased opportunities to fiddle' and created competitive attitudes where consensus and collaboration were necessary to deliver seamless care. One Director feared that the results of 'a competitive culture could be absolutely chaotic' as a result of everyone 'taking a different approach and not discussing what they are doing because it's a commercial operation'. In another authority, there were similar concerns about the consequences of a market 'free for all' in which people played to their own agendas rather than working at 'getting a degree of consensus which makes it work and is productive'.

Third, while developing and managing social care markets might be in the interest of entrepreneurial managers, it could prove to be 'the thin end of the wedge' for other staff. Dangers of 'exploitation' already existed in the private sector where conditions and pay were perceived to be less advantageous than in the public sector. Moreover, it was widely feared that the exposure to market forces of public services was likely to lead to a levelling down of terms and conditions of service.

Fourth, it was feared that extending the range of providers carried with it the risk of 'bringing in new organisations that haven't understood perhaps the market they are in and . . . won't be able to provide'. An associated disadvantage was the 'danger of fragmentation' in what was supposed to be a seamless service. The American experience of 'hundreds of contracts' and 'vast bureaucracies' (Gutch 1992) was seen to be an example which should not be repeated.

Alongside these specific concerns was a more general issue about the disadvantages of allowing market forces to operate freely. While the stimulus to change was necessary, the danger of market collapse was no less real. One Director observed:

> You need enough turbulence to create change and a wider range of services but not too much so that the market collapses . . . and I don't know how you do that unfortunately . . . that's a trick that we are going to have to keep practising as we move forward.

Other interviewees raised this issue in terms of the desirable balance between the market and planning. Thus, the Director of a Labour authority suggested that 'if the provision of services is totally dependent on market forces, then strategic planning can be problematic'. Similarly, the Director of a hung (but until recently Conservative) authority emphasized 'we actually want to build a quality service and that requires some strategic planning and some strategic thinking'. The same Director also drew attention to the political constraints on allowing market forces to operate freely:

> I cannot see that you can give individual practitioners in a publicly-accountable organization unlimited purchasing power because there are very real decisions that this council feels it has a right to make, and I believe that the members of the council are elected to make those decisions.

Conclusion

This chapter has provided evidence of a shift in attitudes between 1991 and 1993 towards an acceptance of enabling as market development. Perhaps the most striking finding is that whereas in our 1991 interviews we identified only three authorities as *market enthusiasts*, the fieldwork in 1993 identified only three authorities in which the disadvantages of a social care market were thought to outweigh the potential advantages. Across the sample as a whole, authorities were either enthusiastic about the market or, more commonly, seeking to work pragmatically with it: none was wholly uncritical of the market and collectively they identified many issues which would need to be taken into account if the market was to operate effectively.

It would be misleading, however, to suggest that there was universal understanding of what enabling entailed, let alone a consensus about its meaning. According to Leach et al. (1994) it is a term still open to a wide variety of interpretations. Their view, however, is that while local authorities still have scope to choose what sort of authority to become they no longer have the choice of being a traditional bureaucratic authority. The latter, they contend, is best seen as 'the historical starting point from which radical change has become necessary' (Leach et al. 1994: 2). It is also clear that local authorities will not take an internally uniform view of what an enabling role entails: views will reflect differing professional roots and values. Thus, as suggested in this chapter, social work professionals are likely to take a different view of the appropriateness of developing markets in their field from colleagues in, for example, highways departments: the nature of the 'goods' being delivered is different and part of the difference will have a direct bearing on the extent to which service professionals (and their members) regard it as appropriate to externalize all services (and concentrate purely upon steering) or as appropriate to contract with for-profit providers for such 'goods'.

Leach *et al.* argue that the increased emphasis on the enabling role underlines the importance of inter-organizational relationships: the understanding of local authorities as being focal points in networks of other public, private and voluntary organizations. These are, however, service-specific networks which differ markedly in their composition. One of the principal characteristics of social care networks (unlike, for example, highways networks) has always been the importance of voluntary agencies; and the essence of the relationship between local authorities and such organizations, as compared with their relationship with the private sector, has often been conceived, in theory at least, as one of partnership based on a degree of trust and commonality of values and interests, although voluntary organizations have historically often lamented the perceived imbalance of power in favour of their statutory 'partners'. This we found to be one of the principal reasons for local authority preferences for working with the voluntary sector, rather than the private sector, in 1991. It is this relationship which the development of social care markets is sometimes thought to threaten. Lewis, for example, argues that 'the process of creating the mixed economy has profound implications for relationships between different types of providers and between purchasers and providers' (1993: 191) and questions whether voluntary organizations in future will be 'partners, competitors or also-rans in the provision of care' (Lewis 1993: 191). We would argue that, on the basis of the most recent evidence, considerable advantages to voluntary agencies should also be recognized (Kramer 1994; Richardson 1995), although experiences have been uneven and there have been losers as well as winners (Kendall and Knapp 1995, 1996; Russell *et al.* 1995). Voluntary organizations may gain in terms of clarity of relations, security and income from these developments. The dependence of local authorities on voluntary sector providers for the delivery of key services may put more power into the hands of the latter than they have exercised historically, and the danger of loss of identity may have been exaggerated.

The enabling task for local authorities – which they were beginning to recognize in 1993 – is to foster and build collaborative *and* competitive networks of providers across all sectors, as appears appropriate to the particular market context which they face. This will vary geographically, by client group, and by service type. In defining their core activities, local authorities are unlikely to come to a uniform view across all services about how much they comprise steering and how much rowing. In certain services it may be wholly the former: in social services it is likely to continue to be both steering and rowing. This is not simply because a mixed economy, by definition, requires some public provision but because the very nature – the vulnerability – of the services' end-users requires a public safety net. This interpretation of local authorities' roles was made in the recent High Court judgement in which Wandsworth Council was told that it could not externalize all its direct services but must retain some (albeit an unspecified portion) as directly run local authority residential accommodation. Although subsequently overturned in the Appeal Court, it seems that even those authorities most enthusiastic about interpreting the enabling role as that of steering may wish to retain the capacity for rowing.

Increasingly, the enabling role for social services – whatever the balance between steering and rowing – will require an acknowledgement that fostering networks of preferred providers means acknowledging the vulnerability of providers too. This is an issue to which we turn in later chapters. In the next chapter, we extend the above analysis by reviewing the changing balance of barriers and opportunities surrounding the creation of a mixed economy that were perceived in 1993.

3

Opportunities and barriers revisited

Introduction

The development of a mixed economy of care is not wholly within the control of local authorities. There are many externally-generated barriers to be surmounted and opportunities or incentives to be considered. It was therefore not surprising that members and officers described a range of opportunities and barriers during our interviews, both in 1991 and 1993.

In our first look at the mixed economy in our sample authorities – in early 1991 – the incentives included fiscal pressures, expectations of improved cost-effectiveness, a wider choice for users and purchasers, and the sloping playing field of financial advantages for non-statutory providers. Each of these factors was cited by several local authorities – and often by a large majority – as working to encourage development of the mixed economy in the early months after passage of the NHS and Community Care Bill through Parliament. Among the impediments there were also fiscal pressures (different authorities responding to similar external forces in rather different ways), together with fears about loss of control, a strong local commitment to public sector provision, the perceived underdevelopment or unpreparedness of voluntary and private sector providers, and – in some quarters – the hope or expectation that the general election, imminent in 1992, would sweep away the market reforms before implementation. Ideological positions played a major part in framing the stances of members towards a mixed economy, although there was no simple division into opposing camps along party political lines. There were Labour members in 1991 who welcomed the further mixing of the economy of care, just as there were Conservative councils openly expressing doubts about the advisability or feasibility of this direction of central government policy.

Our discussions with local authorities in 1991 addressed the *broad* mixed economy and community care reform. They did not give a great deal of attention to markets as such. One reason for this was the breadth of our research brief, but also that social care markets were not widely recognized as being important at that time, not least because social services departments were busily preparing for implementation of other elements of the 1990 legislation, introducing new organizational and practice arrangements required by the 1989 Children Act, and establishing new links with the NHS.

As we described in Chapter 2, our return visits to local authorities in 1993 immediately confirmed that social care markets were of considerably greater importance than in 1991. Consideration of barriers and opportunities revealed a similar change of focus. We first look at the opportunities and incentives to develop a mixed economy, and then turn to the barriers or impediments. It should be noted that, in both 1991 and 1993, the barriers and opportunities were largely reported to us without specific prompting. (In the later round we asked about the effect of the 85 per cent special transitional grant (STG) requirement, but did not prompt on other factors.) Because a particular incentive or difficulty was not mentioned by an authority should not therefore be taken to imply that it was irrelevant, merely that it was not uppermost in the mind of the interviewee.

Opportunities and incentives

Resource factors

One of the most marked developments in the mixed economy in the early 1990s – even earlier in some areas – was the transfer of some Part III accommodation from the local authority to independent private or voluntary organizations or quasi-independent trusts. The latter were established using a variety of legal forms, allowing authorities to retain a degree of control while making residents eligible for income support (Wistow et al. 1994: Chapter 6). In 1991, three factors had combined to encourage the majority of our sample authorities to investigate the possibility of 'externalizing' or 'hiving off' residential homes, and a smaller number actually to do it: fiscal pressures, limiting the expansion of local authority provision and curtailing maintenance and improvement programmes; the income support rules, providing a strong incentive for local authorities to transfer some of their homes to independent status; and the intro- duction of arm's-length inspection units, expected to reveal discrepancies in standards between independent and public provision. In 1993 the first of these remained influential in the continued development of local mixed economies; the second had some relevance but the 1990 Act reforms obviously lessened its importance; and no one mentioned inspection units. More importantly, new fiscal pressures were emerging, notably the restrictions on spending the STG.

Demographic and other need-generating changes, including earlier discharges from hospital, combined with general fiscal pressures, imposed tight limits on both revenue and capital expenditure. These were mentioned by sixteen of our twenty-five sample authorities as factors which acted to promote the mixed economy.

> The main incentive must be the rising tide of clients . . . If we are going to meet that need, and public expenditure is going to be reduced, we are forced into finding more innovative and cost-effective ways of providing care.

Lower costs in the private and voluntary sectors, sometimes mentioned in the same breath as better non-statutory quality of care, were also clearly attractive.

> The contrast between the unit costs of the in-house provision and external service provision is stark. Councillors can't ignore that. I can't ignore that.

Financial pressures were perceived as both national – gloom on the public expenditure front, tight standard spending assessments (SSAs) – and local, such as the siphoning of funds to grant-maintained schools. As in 1991, the knock-on effects of these pressures were felt especially in relation to residential care, partly because of the sheer volume of activity in that area and its large contribution to total expenditure, partly because of 'capital starvation' over a period of years in some cases, and partly because some authorities were introducing approved provider standards which were even more demanding than the registration standards which some of their homes were already failing to meet. The financial pressures loomed large in the first year after implementation of the 1990 Act because of the 'steady state' volume requirement imposed by the Department of Health, limiting the local scope for manoeuvre.

Some Labour authorities which appeared to be resisting these financial pressures in 1991 had faced the 'uncomfortable' need to alter the balance of provision in 1993. But the fiscal pressures could be used to some advantage. More than one authority had used the reforms and their highlighting of differences in standards to improve the quality of its own provision, and many others were looking to reduce their own costs so as to compete more effectively with non-statutory provision. Some were making efforts to prepare a range of services for 'exposure to the market': drawing up business plans, calculating accurate unit costs, extending coverage of domiciliary care to weekends and evenings, and so on. There was also the view that compulsory competitive tendering (CCT), through the 'fear of competition' alone, was sharpening the performance of some in-house units, producing efficiency gains and 'shaking them out of their complacency', as one Director described it. However, as we describe in Chapter 5, a number of authorities were already exploiting the excess supply of residential and nursing home places to drive independent sector prices down even further, so we should not be too sanguine about the possibilities of cost equalization; while some other authorities were using their purchasing power, within oversupplied markets, to drive up quality rather than to 'screw the price down'. They saw themselves becoming 'skilled purchasers', able to manipulate quality rather than, or in addition to, price.

The 1990 Act did not remove the sloping playing field, although it did reduce the gradient, creating a second resource encouragement to develop the mixed economy. Before the Department of Health's August 1991 guidance, which removed the 'preserved rights' status enjoyed by residents of Part III homes transferred before that date (see Chapter 2), local authorities were able to shunt some of their revenue costs onto the social security vote by creating arm's-length trusts. Although this possibility no longer exists, the non-payment of the residential allowance in the public sector provides some incentive to continue transfers, though less marked than the earlier effect of income support. In the words of one Director, the residential allowance was 'driving parts of the local authority out of business'. Other officers also recognized that their authorities would have to plan carefully to define their provider roles:

> It would be false of me to say that I know exactly what our niche is going to be, but we are in the process of trying to identify it from identified need as time passes this year, and we have bought ourselves twelve months of block contracting our own services. Hopefully towards the end of that time we will have a clearer idea . . . It will tell us what we need to get rid of, and what we're going to retain.

In many authorities the most important financial pressure to develop the mixed economy was the '85 per cent rule' governing the spending of the social security transfer element of the special transitional grant (STG). Eventually, the funds transferred from the social security system to the personal social services will represent an average expenditure increase at local level of more than 30 per cent, although only a proportion of that amount was transferred in the first year. (The House of Commons Health Committee 1993b: para. 86, reported that twenty-six local authorities had *less* to spend than they had budgeted for in 1992/93 despite their additional STG allocation.) In areas where there was little independent provision and/or which were previously 'net exporters' of people outside the authority, there was a greater struggle to find services on which authorities could spend their transfer moneys, even though they received fewer funds than 'net importers' or authorities with large income support-funded independent sectors. Inner London boroughs faced big problems.

> There isn't the private sector provision in the borough, particularly in residential care. We are inevitably going to be purchasers, but our money is locked up in Dorset, West Sussex and Hampshire. We've found out that 25 per cent of our residents have gone to Hampshire and West Sussex, and 50 per cent were scattered all over the country. So we are predominantly purchasers without a purchasing budget.

In order to make full use of the transferred funds, authorities with comparatively few independent sector places were often contemplating floating off some of their own provision to, say, the voluntary sector. There were perceived to be dangers in rushing such transfers of ownership in terms of distorting the overall balance between residential and non-residential care. However, the Director in a metropolitan authority described the STG as 'peanuts compared to the amount we spend on community care', and a shire county Director similarly saw no problems with the conditions:

> There is a large and vibrant independent sector, and one that has shown some willingness and ability to diversify out of residential care.

Not surprisingly, some Directors interpreted the 85 per cent rule differently. From their perspective, all of the transferred funds were previously spent in the private and voluntary sectors, so that the transfer arrangements arguably gave local authorities a 15 per cent margin for flexibility, notwithstanding the first year requirement to maintain a 'steady state' in relation to the balance between residential and domiciliary services. This did not necessarily mean a gift for the public sector equivalent to the 15 per cent, but it did offer slightly more flexibility than some had previously feared.

About a quarter of our sample authorities had been successful in bidding for additional funds under the Caring for People Who Live at Home initiative. These funds (for three years only) provided a direct stimulus to domiciliary and associated provision within the independent sector, enabling authorities to further the development of the mixed economy of non-residential care. Projects supported by this initiative included: development of domiciliary services to prevent premature admission to residential care; stimulation of respite and domiciliary services for people from black and ethnic minority groups; establishment of training courses in domiciliary care and enterprise skills; and initiatives to facilitate diversification by existing providers.

Ideological influences

In 1991, it was clear that the transfer of local authority residential homes to the independent sector and the formation of quasi-independent trusts were predominantly resource-driven, and the consequent diversification of supply and creation of a more mixed economy at that time was generally incidental. Although, as we have just seen, there were continuing resource incentives to develop the mixed economy, other factors – particularly ideological influences – were beginning to play a larger role.

The gradual refocusing of enabling as market development over the past two years appeared to be both a consequence and a cause of changes in ideological position, certainly in relation to social care *markets*. If we put to one side the May 1993 county elections and their effects on political control and (eventually) local policy – effects which were too early to discern at the time of our fieldwork – we can identify broadly four patterns of 'ideological change'.

First, although there were apparently no damascene conversions to the free market faith, there were a handful of 'fairly significant cultural shifts', as one Director described them. Most authorities were willingly building market strategies, and most officers had clearly moved some distance in coming to terms with some aspects of market shaping, commissioning and price negotiation. But the roots of these changes should not be misinterpreted. The majority of members and officers saw benefits for users and council tax payers flowing from greater clarity in commissioning, from offering users and carers more information before they made their choices, and from tighter contractual links between authorities and independent providers. However, few of them cited *competition* as the primary cause of these potential improvements.

Second, a common pattern was a degree of attitudinal change in favour of developing the mixed economy, often due to fiscal pressures. These attitudinal changes were pragmatic responses to a rapidly changing environment: 'adaptation, rather than revolution'. For example, in two London boroughs, one Conservative-controlled for many years and the other with a large and enduring Labour majority, the officers described how members' views had changed:

> The members here were originally quite chary about what enabling might mean, but when we pointed out to them the large sums of money they could save and that they would still be able to maintain a large amount of control, they became very happy with it.

> I think the authority's attitude to a mixed economy has moved on. It is more open than it was. I think there's an air of realism around that is touching everybody. Elected members are very aware that the role is going to change. We're going to become much more a commissioning strategic authority. Some recognize that, want to take hold and go with it, but on the basis of doing the right thing by the electorate: being in control of pacing it and shaping it; as opposed to head in the sand, reactive and the next election will be won.

Both authorities were 'pragmatic gradualists', part of the largest group in our sample, and including authorities whose staff were showing 'enthusiasm . . . to try and meet the challenges, regardless of what philosophical personal views they have'.

The third ideological pattern can be referred to as 'unreconstructed civic pride'. The principal feature of this third pattern was the view that the most appropriate way to demonstrate a continued commitment to a public service ethos was to continue to be a large-scale direct provider. As we argue in later chapters, local authorities interpret and demonstrate 'civic pride' in various ways: continued large-scale provision is just one of them. An example of fairly trenchant civic pride came from the Director who told us that members refused to allow officers to enter into any dialogue with private sector domiciliary care agencies or their association. An unwillingness to contemplate the closure of local authority facilities was another manifestation of this ideological position. As one Director explained:

> There is a commitment in [this authority] to provide local services for local people, and employ local people to do that, and to see the local state clearly having an upfront leadership role.

In a county where the council had been Conservative-controlled before the 1993 elections but which then became hung, officers had put forward a strategic plan which suggested that contracting should be considered as the first option for service development, with direct provision only if contracting was impossible or undesirable. The social services committee rejected this suggestion. The same authority had earlier considered and rejected a plan to float off some residential facilities. Indeed, in common with a number of authorities which found themselves as minority providers of residential care within their boundaries, they had taken the decision to keep 'a significant but not substantial part of residential care in direct management'. As in 1991, there was no simple correlation between political control and pride in public sector provision. It was, however, linked to another widespread view across authorities that part of this ideological change was an acceptance that social services departments must increasingly identify and focus upon a set of core activities.

Finally, a small number of sample authorities showed no ideological shift between 1991 and 1993. These were the authorities which we labelled 'market enthusiasts' in 1991, and included two which might eventually turn themselves into purely commissioning agencies. Their commitment to the development of a mixed economy showed no sign of waning.

Enhanced choice

Caring for People and subsequent policy guidance and ministerial statements laid great emphasis on the need for the community care system to broaden the range of service options available to users. Enhanced choice was and remains a central objective. The Government's Direction on Choice (National Assistance Act 1948 (Choice of Accommodation) Directions, 1992), issued in December 1992, was the clearest statement of this aim. At least one interviewee feared other directives – perhaps CCT for community care – if local government did not develop a vibrant mixed economy.

Some of our interviewees cited the promotion of choice as the primary incentive to develop the mixed economy, although it is also an important reason for retaining some public sector provision, especially if the independent sectors prove reluctant to offer services for more dependent people or certain other groups. The Director in one of the authorities which was characterized by 'unreconstructed civic pride' commented:

> If you are going to have needs assessments and an input from users and

carers, . . . provided you can overcome the prejudice about private providers which our members are saddled with, I think there is a potential to widen choice.

Another Director facing opposition from members to plans for developing markets made a similar point:

People need vastly different things from services, so if we are going to develop proper alternatives, proper flexibility, I think the market helps. It also enables providers, people who have got particular ideas, particular approaches – particular obsessions if you like – to do something about them . . . I think you can get over some of the ideological differences we've had. There is something in it for everyone.

Other Directors expressing optimism that 'market forces' would stimulate new services mentioned the benefits of a clearer commissioning task and provider pluralism in better targeting the needs of black and ethnic minority communities. Each of these interviewees recognized that the rerouteing of social security funds via local authorities and the introduction of needs assessments would initially limit user choice. But their longer-term expectation was that users and carers should be better informed and the range of available options wider. Their optimism would presumably have been based in part on the experiences of those few authorities, some in our sample, which had already 'market-tested' these aspects of the community care reforms.

Barriers and disincentives

Supplier-related obstacles

Arranged against these various encouragements were perceived barriers and disincentives to the promotion of a mixed economy. A common view among local authority members and officers in 1991 was that private and voluntary sector providers were insufficient in number and too deficient in quality and management technique to be able or willing to shoulder a heavier supply burden. This can be associated with so-called structural imperfections and associated market difficulties (see Chapters 5 and 8). By 1993, most interviewees still believed that there were too few independent providers of domiciliary, day and respite care, and many still expressed concerns about both the present capabilities of voluntary and private agencies, and their willingness to diversify. Nevertheless, the outlook from the public sector was nowhere near as desolate as in 1991. Partly this was a result of more extensive supply mapping by authorities, even though their maps of non-residential provision remained incomplete (see Chapter 4). There was also greater optimism because there were more and better links between purchasers and private and voluntary sector providers (and potential providers).

Closely linked to these supplier-related obstacles were a small number of 'socio-economic' impediments. One set of potential difficulties posited by interviewees in 1991 concerned the independent sectors' access to skilled staff, land and property at affordable prices, particularly in London. Despite high unemployment in the south-east, two London Directors reported continuing problems for the independent sectors: they could not easily be competitive in the labour market by offering high wages to attract good staff while simultaneously being competitive in the market for services by charging low prices. This was not reported to be a problem elsewhere, although Directors in two metropolitan authorities described their members' anxieties about 'exploitation' of the workforce by low-paying private sector employers.

To local authorities, the main or at least the initial cost advantages of externalization accrue from lower wages and inferior fringe benefits, but the TUPE regulations and the European Union's Acquired Rights Directive were seen as important obstacles in a sizeable minority of areas. Without the opportunity for wage cuts or other changes to the conditions of employment unfavourable to employees, private sector contractors contemplating taking over public services may not have seen attractive profit margins. TUPE also prompted a number of local authorities to put their service transfer plans 'on hold'.

Attitudinal/ideological obstacles

Earlier in this chapter we described the changing attitudinal patterns, with most authorities approaching the mixed economy in 1993 with fewer reservations than in 1991, and many identifying more advantages for users and carers (and for themselves as purchasers). Nevertheless, important ideological or attitudinal obstacles to change lingered. This was not resistance to *any* change in the direction of a mixed economy – something which we found in a few authorities two years earlier – but a lack of enthusiasm for certain aspects of change.

The most frequently mentioned of these obstacles was reluctance among members to consider some alternative forms of provision, or to fight against 'influential community interests' when, say, proposing the closure of a facility. Most of the issues surrounding the closure, sale or transfer of local authority facilities were the same in 1993 as in 1991 (Wistow *et al.* 1994: Chapter 6), though set in rather different policy and political contexts. What was more evident in the later period was the commencement of 'niche marketing' by some authorities, often focusing their own provider resources on specialist needs.

Generally speaking, the reluctance to countenance major changes to the pattern of local authority provision was not a manifestation of blind protectionism. It was – as we described earlier – usually born of informed civic pride ('which', one interviewee asserted, 'the Government ignores at its peril') and the associated commitment to the quality of direct service provision. Such factors were coupled with management and staff anxieties about change, and sometimes reinforced by mutual ignorance and mistrust between local authorities and the independent sectors. Of course, there were exceptions. In one Labour authority, the Director told us:

> There are still some 'sacred cows' that members will drown with, clutching them to their chests; contract services is an example. You won't change them on that.

Nevertheless, the authority had closed some homes, ploughing the savings into other in-house services. The Director saw his task in the following year to be giving members a clear message:

> We need to be adjusting our service provision in this direction in order to meet demands and what care managers are saying about needs. If we go on willy-nilly just providing what we're providing now, we're dead, because ultimately the customer will go somewhere else.

In another Labour authority, the officers 'haven't been allowed to use the word closure yet', although there is 'recognition that homes will have to close'. In contrast, in one county which had seen a large swing away from the incumbent Conservative council in the 1993 local elections, the first meeting of the Labour group overwhelmingly voted down a proposal that there should be an end to the closure of local authority old people's homes.

There was an air of caution in one or two Conservative authorities following the 1993 county elections and some parliamentary by-elections ruling out further major changes to the balance of provision:

> Suddenly, the borough elections next May [London, 1994] could – with current swings – give us a Labour council. The Conservatives aren't privatizing any home help services between now and then . . . There are 3000 home help clients each of whom has at least three voting relatives, which could swing the vote . . . All the talk about enabling authorities and so on is all very well, but what it boils down to is that Mrs So-and-so's home help will change, and that is bad news politically.

The officers in another authority were warned by members before the May 1993 elections not to 'come up with any suggestions for closures before we've got the elections out of the way . . . Shut up, get on and don't rock the boat for us.' Another Director described the frustration among officers who were unable to 'unlock the money' or 'to get people a different model of service that might be more appropriate' because of the political attitude in the authority.

As we have seen, many authorities continued to query the abilities or willingness of some private and voluntary agencies to provide more or new community care services. In addition, there remained in some areas in 1993 a marked degree of antagonism between local authorities and the private sector, deepened by the former's new responsibilities for assessing needs before funding placements in homes run by the latter. Mutual mistrust grew in the weeks which followed implementation of the new residential care funding arrangements in April 1993 when some private home owners accused social services departments of blocking hospital discharges, refusing to make independent home placements, or favouring in-house providers.

Many reasons can be suggested for this antagonism, including the distance between sectors in the planning process, leading to ignorance of each other's motives and attitudes; local authority anxieties about unregistered organizations delivering domiciliary care; the belief that users and carers preferred public sector provision; and, of course, ideological and practical doubts about the perceived effects of providers' pursuit of profit. In a metropolitan borough, for example, members were not enthusiastic about contracting to spend more taxpayers' money to bolster what they saw as the conspicuously high standards of living of some private home owners. The successes (or perceived excesses) of the few were a stumbling block in another authority:

> Immediately you talk about contracting, certain members and the general public and the press think of the most shabby, charlatan type of private entrepreneur who is only in it for the money . . . As a management team we have been vilified for trying to turn [social care] over to a 'disreputable PLC'.

In one Labour authority, members had agreed to begin purchasing private sector services but were then 'furious' to be faced with legal action over contract conditions. Elsewhere, a Director had been 'staggered' by

> the gross ignorance in the private sector about the changing nature of this business [social care] . . . Many of the small home owners just did not understand what 'assessment for need' meant. They presumed that we were just going to go on doing the same thing, putting people into homes when they knocked on the door and said 'Have you got a bed?'

Mutual mistrust of this depth tended not to characterize relations between local authorities and voluntary organizations, although there were difficulties. Generally, relations were eased by voluntary sector representation on the formal joint planning machinery; overlapping governance structures; long traditions of grant aid; complementary provision; the absence of a profit motive; and the fact that, in some areas, some voluntary sector services were, until recently, part of the local authority. In these circumstances, local authority members could be reassured that they were not necessarily losing control over social services by encouraging a mixed economy of voluntary sector providers. Indeed, one officer asserted that he could control former public sector services now in a 'not-for-profit' agency more easily than he could when they were part of the authority. The importance of control is not lost on a set of public agencies which are being monitored more than ever before and which are increasingly likely to face 'malpractice' litigation.

Local authorities, as major employers, were necessarily wary of proposals to move social care provision to the private or voluntary sectors. Most did not wish to abrogate what they perceived as public responsibilities to their staff, although they recognized the trade-off between being a good and generous employer and providing more or better services to the population.

> The slogan for the Labour party in the 1980s was preserving jobs. For the 1990s it has got to be about preserving services. We are no longer in the job creation business.

Some officers described opposition to the further development of the mixed economy from middle managers and other staff: an 'innate conservatism that people have in carrying on the same way despite your best endeavour'. This was not necessarily an ideological conservatism, although that often played a part, but a need for professional change. In one area, the Director saw it simply as the need for training to raise awareness, and for 'self-motivating, reinforcing change' as staff got feedback from users and carers that the new arrangements were producing better care. Another saw external causes for staff opposition:

> I don't think that the rank and file of staff are fully in touch with some of the threats and opportunities that the market can offer. I think many of them see it as a threat, and I don't blame them, because they see jobs under threat and a Government agenda which talks about a kind of residual role for local government rather than a leading role.

Other obstacles

Some other factors were hampering the development of a mixed economy. Some were not so much tangible obstacles to the mixed economy as a 'constraining or debilitating context' which sapped morale and lessened the enthusiasm for change. They included doubts about whether the community care reforms would be effected and whether local authorities would have lead responsibility, uncertainty about the future and structure of local government, fear of compulsory competitive tendering, and concern about the social security entitlements of residents in 'hived-off' services. Each of these doubts and fears was more prevalent in 1991 than in 1993. The major uncertainty surrounded the local government review. Planning blight was mentioned, although most Directors seemed to take a more phlegmatic line:

> We have always taken the view here that, whatever system we have in terms of governance, we would want to try and ensure that community values are reflected through a democratic process.

There was another uncertainty, not about policy *direction* but about policy implications. None of our sample authorities could confidently predict how far the newly transferred funds would stretch during the first year. Many expressed the strong desire to avoid following the example of those health authorities whose funds had run out before the end of the financial year, although none could afford to be carrying a large surplus by March. As later events showed, these fears were – for many authorities – to be realized.

In 1991 many authorities expected that difficulties or delays in getting financial control and information systems in place would hamper their development of a mixed economy. Some of the authorities expressing more optimism about their IT systems at that time may have altered their views, particularly those experiencing teething problems (system crashes, insufficient capacity, and so on). By 1993, most of our sample seemed to be in the middle of the transition from manual and computer-based accounting and monitoring arrangements. Few authorities had yet developed IT systems which gave them the confidence to delegate full purchasing powers to care managers. Many local authorities had welcomed infrastructure moneys which enabled them to develop IT, whereas in 1991 a number of interviewees complained about the insufficient funds made available to them in comparison with the amounts awarded to health and education.

An important obstacle in 1991 was concern among both members and officers that some of the perceived mistakes of the NHS reforms should not be repeated in social care, but it was difficult to disentangle the genuine misgivings about NHS reform from the widespread dismay which attended the change in composition of health authority membership. The disjunction between NHS and local government agendas and timetables was another short-term difficulty. In 1993, the issues were different. They included: the 'fragmentation of the health service'; mergers and boundary changes; the 'maverick' trusts; uncertainties first about the eligibility and then about the desirability of the NHS as an independent provider; major uncertainties about the roles of GP fund-holders; and rapid changes in patterns of provision (especially in London). Despite these and other difficulties, many authorities had developed good joint mechanisms with health authorities, and joint commissioning was underway in a number of our sample areas.

Conclusion

The opportunities for and barriers to the development of the mixed economy described in this chapter clearly have a bearing on both the shape and functioning of social care markets, and on local authorities' abilities to shape those markets, even if they were not always couched in those terms. There were marked changes between 1991 and 1993 – fewer barriers and the perception of more opportunities – and a dominant impression of what we have called 'market pragmatism'. The chapters which follow will tease out these changes, setting them in their broader context, and identifying their implications for the shape and management of markets.

4

Mapping the market

Introduction

The accurate and comprehensive mapping of need, demand and supply is self-evidently a prerequisite for informed strategic choice by local authorities (and other purchasers) involved in developing a needs-led mixed economy of care. It is only through an improved awareness of both the needs and demands of users and carers, and greater knowledge of the characteristics of the range of existing and potential provision, that the putative benefits of a mixed economy can be secured.

In 1991 we found that the baseline of information from which social services departments were attempting to move forward was extremely fragmented. At that time, the preliminary work was developmental in character (as anticipated in the phased implementation strategy), with more attention expected to be given to this particular task in the following year, in order to meet the Department of Health's April 1992 submission deadline for the first set of community care plans. Although two-thirds of authorities expressed a positive attitude towards the mapping of need, only a third of these (six authorities) were actively doing so (Wistow et al. 1994: 73, Table 5.1). None of the authorities reported having a *comprehensive* view of patterns of extant *service provision*. With only the Department's policy guidance to indicate the broad thrust of the necessary work – Paragraph 2.28 had emphasized the need for 'hard data . . . [on] the broad spread and costs of services as currently delivered for each client group' – and no specific guidance at that time on *how* to undertake such mapping, most authorities were directing their efforts towards the urgent implementation tasks required to be in place by the beginning of April 1993.

No authority in 1991 claimed to have mapped local patterns of supply comprehensively. Knowledge of registered provision (that is, all but the smallest residential care homes) was obviously good, as was that of facilities either subject to planning applications or in receipt of financial or other tangible local authority support. Otherwise, in the fields of independent sector domiciliary and day care, there was little knowledge and – in the case of small-scale, informal, neighbourhood and self-help schemes – even less. These findings were echoed in analysis of the 1992/93 community care plans (Wistow et al. 1993): only a minority of authorities had gone beyond producing limited *service* inventories and attempted to produce the sort of joint *resource* inventories (with details of numbers, staffing, costs) recommended in the policy guidance (Department of Health 1990a: para. 2.11).

In attempting to *map and assess need*, a number of authorities had invested in new management information systems, and were using client group registers, current service user referrals, waiting lists, and annual public health reports, as well as being proactively engaged in consultation meetings with users and carers. Seven of the twenty-four sample local authorities indicated that they were actively planning joint information-gathering strategies with health authorities and Family Health Services Authorities (FHSAs). However, a further eight social services departments had not finalized a strategy for the identification of need, and few, if any, appeared to have explored the interface between the micro or tactical level of individual clients' needs assessments and the broader evaluations of the needs of their populations at the macro or strategic level (Knapp and Wistow 1993: 21). Authorities were still at the first rudimentary stage of pulling together extant utilization data and existing national population data.

The overall picture, therefore, had been one of variability both between and within authorities in the extent to which indicators of need (or even demands or patterns of utilization) were being or could be built up. Nevertheless, attempts were being made to collate existing data in a more *systematic* fashion than had been done before, and some authorities were starting to combine data on local demographic trends with national prevalence rate estimates to construct their first indicative 'top-down' estimates of local need. It is worth bearing in mind that the Department of Health's view, even in 1993, was that 'the whole process of assessing overall population needs . . . is a very difficult undertaking on which authorities are only just beginning to embark' (House of Commons Health Committee 1993a: Q281).

With this caveat in mind, we sought in our 1993 study to ascertain again not only how well authorities were mapping the social care markets in which they were operating (and beginning to manage), but how well they understood some of the basic elements and characteristics of those markets. We sought first to obtain information on *how* authorities had attempted, on the one hand, to identify users' and carers' needs and demands and, on the other hand, to map patterns and types of supply. In each case – as regards needs/demands and supply — we were interested in aggregate and individual levels. Thus we sought to ascertain not only how population-level needs assessment was being undertaken, but also what mechanisms had been established to link the resultant findings to those emerging from assessments of individuals' needs. We also sought to ascertain whether supply mapping included not just details of aggregate provision but also the characteristics of individual providers of residential, day or domiciliary care: for example, capacity, occupancy, staffing, client characteristics, prices and costs. We were interested not in the nature and extent of identified needs and supply as such, but in the range of means used: this being an indicator of the comprehensiveness of the mapping exercise itself. In fieldwork interviews we asked questions about such quantitative market mapping only of Directors of social services and independent sector providers. We then asked both local authority members and Directors questions about their broader market understanding: in other words, how well they understood and had attempted to ascertain not just these quantitative data on patterns of supply, but also the business plans, intentions and motivations of providers in their local market.

Unsurprisingly we found that the focus of most authorities' work in the run-up to April 1993 had been to accomplish the eight key tasks set by the Foster/Laming letter (Department of Health 1992a). Their concentration was upon the basic quantitative mapping of residential and nursing home provision, with attempts to identify not only resident numbers but also residents' places of origin, funding sources and routes of admission. These were and are essential data for authorities' management of the social security transfer element of the special transitional grant.

Most local authorities reported having good information on these numbers by April. All twenty-five said that they knew the numbers of people in residential and nursing homes in their area and twenty (80 per cent) were aware of the funding source of all residents. Information on residents' places of origin was less complete (available in fifteen authorities), as was that on the admission rate for income support recipients: that is, residents who had entered homes either following hospital discharge or from the community. Here information was said to be available in fifteen of the twenty-one (72 per cent) authorities from which there was a response. It ought to be said, however, that such information was in some cases obtained from surveys undertaken six, nine or twelve months before the beginning of April 1993 and seldom with a 100 per cent response rate. For example, one authority's survey of homes was conducted in March 1992 and had an 83 per cent response rate from residential homes and a 64 per cent response rate from nursing homes.

Mapping need

Data sources

Evidence on the incompleteness of authorities' information on needs was forthcoming from other research: an analysis of the second-round (1993/94) community care plans and associated case studies in five of twenty-five sample localities (see Wistow *et al.* 1993; Hardy *et al.* 1994). In this study – using a different sample from the one used in the mixed economy study – we found some evidence of improvement in both the quality and quantity of raw planning data, in terms of mapping the levels and patterns of needs and supply. However, this was from a relatively low base in the first-round (1992/93) plans and an extremely low base hitherto.

The analysis of the 1993/94 community care plans revealed that eleven (44 per cent) of the twenty-five sample authorities had based their assessments of need solely on basic demographic (Office of Population Censuses and Surveys (OPCS)) data: four authorities (16 per cent) had used the same basic demographic data and additional sources for certain individual client groups; only eight authorities (32 per cent) had supplemented basic census data with a range of additional sources across all client groups. It is important to enter the caveat made in the reports of both general analyses of plans that they were based on the plans themselves: if particular means for population-level needs assessment were used but not referred to in the plans themselves, they are unrecorded.

By contrast, in the research on which we report in this chapter we identified the means used for such needs assessment both from published documents and from telephone interviews with social services department planning personnel. All of the sample authorities had used census data, but ten (40 per cent) had not used data from the General Household Survey and seven (29 per cent) had not utilized epidemiological studies of prevalence (Table 4.1). Among other national sources used for needs mapping, the most common were the Department of Health Key Indicators and the OPCS Disability Surveys. Two authorities referred specifically to using the Jarman and Townsend deprivation indices; one referred to using the DoE's Z-score indicators of social need. In general there appeared to be little use of published national research.

Local data sources used for needs mapping are also indicated in Table 4.1, although some of these figures need to be treated with caution. For example, local authorities will be recorded as having used general locality-based research (83 per cent of the twenty-three from which information was available) however small-scale and client group-specific. Thus, in one extreme case, an authority reported hiring a consultant for four days to examine the likely effect on patterns of local demand of the changes to the Independent Living Fund. Moreover, as well as often being very narrowly focused, these data from such reported research were not always up to date. Similarly, the fact that other agencies' surveys were used, typically those of DHAs and FHSAs (reportedly by 77 per cent of the twenty-two sample authorities from which information was available), should not be interpreted as meaning that these comprised comprehensive population-level assessments of need across all client groups: frequently they consisted of references to individual reports by public health directors. However apparently encouraging in terms of the range of national and local data sources used to identify population-level needs, the

Table 4.1 Needs mapping; data sources used by local authorities (May 1993)

	Sample size[a]	Number of authorities	(%)
National sources			
1 Census of population	25	25	100
2 General Household Survey	25	15	60
3 Epidemiological studies of prevalence	24	17	71
Local sources			
1 Client group registers	22	18	82
2 Customer relations plus complaints systems	20	6	30
3 Other agencies' surveys	22	17	77
4 General locality-based research	23	19	83
5 Consultations with/survey of:			
private providers	23	23	100
voluntary providers	23	16	70
users	23	16	70
carers	23	13	57
ethnic minorities	21	9	43

[a] Authorities from whom useable response was obtained.

reality – as interviewees readily testified – was that needs mapping was still at a relatively embryonic stage and was widely regarded as complex, time-consuming and costly by most authorities. In addition, it is important to remember that the guidance on population-level needs assessment commissioned from Price Waterhouse by the Department of Health was published in January 1992, too late to affect that year's community care planning round.

This view of general progress was echoed by the Audit Commission in evidence to the House of Commons Health Committee in January 1993. Local authorities were said to be 'mainly establishing the necessary framework for assessing need', but accuracy was something that would only follow 'in due course': at that stage it was 'a concept that is rather too sophisticated' (House of Commons Health Committee 1993a).

Data gaps and their causes

Unsurprisingly, therefore, when asked about the completeness of their information on users' and carers' needs and demands, most Directors reported that there were still serious gaps and deficiencies. Indeed, one Director claimed that neither the amount nor quality of information was adequate for planning purposes. The following phrases typify the feelings of other Directors, who referred to information on needs: 'very patchy . . . a big gap'; 'patchy'; 'certainly incomplete'; 'not brilliant'; 'extremely incomplete on a population analysis basis'. Others said that they were: 'not confident'; 'not confident at all'; and that the information was 'not as complete as I'd like it to be'. One Director said that on a scale of one to five 'if we're pushing towards three, we're lucky'. Another said that information was 'not terribly complete' and that he and departmental colleagues felt 'very vulnerable about what we actually know about real needs'.

Nine Directors cited deficiencies with local authority information systems and technology as being the main cause of gaps in information on need: according to one Director 'we are still not very far beyond the pen and quill stage when it comes to IT'. Invariably the explanation for this deficiency was historic underfunding: too little investment in management information systems. This, indeed, repeats a finding in 1991. Allied to this historic underinvestment in information technology was a similar underinvestment in planning resources, specifically referred to by three authorities. The Director in one of the latter authorities remarked upon the difficulty, with one full-time planning officer, of acquiring the sort of information on need (and supply) implicit in our questions: 'everywhere across the department there is a very great shortfall and in the present financial context there's not the mood to spend money on additional planners'.

This view was far outweighed, however, by the number of fellow Directors who reported that their authorities had begun – however belatedly – to make significant investments in information technology, where the driving force had been the recognition of the need not only to record individual assessments but also to track expenditure accurately (see Chapter 5). One Director remarked that after receiving the infrastructure element of the STG there was 'no excuse for not getting your information systems in pretty quickly'. Despite this investment she was 'not confident at all [because] the information on which we base our decisions is still not good enough'.

Only seven (28 per cent) of the sample authorities said that they had a joint, or shared, information base with other agencies for assessing existing population-level needs, although this was identified as a development priority in many of the remaining authorities. No interviewee attributed the causes of information deficiencies to the unwillingness of other agencies (DHAs and FHSAs especially) to share information or to work towards joint analysis of population-level need. Most authorities were sharing information with health authorities (and, in many cases, with GPs) and seeking to devise compatible systems. The main problem was not unwillingness but incompatibility of data bases, information systems and technology. Once again, the findings from our sample authorities were echoed nationally by the Audit Commission in evidence to the Health Select Committee. Joint work with health authorities and FHSAs on needs assessment was described (in January 1993) as 'still comparatively rare, although many authorities have begun to discuss strategies to do so' (House of Commons Health Committee 1993a). In subsequent oral evidence to the Committee, one NHS perspective was that 'need assessment is at a very crude stage at the moment'; while another was that population-needs assessment 'is not going to happen overnight' (House of Commons Health Committee 1993a).

Obtaining compatibility between separate systems or devising common systems is both expensive and time-consuming. However, in one authority an alternative was being pursued in the area of housing needs. Here, faced with the problem of a multiplicity of housing agencies operating within a single local authority (statutory authorities and not-for-profit housing associations), a housing needs analyst had been jointly appointed. This person, in effect, had a passport to each of the agencies' data systems and a remit both to identify not only the nature and extent of local specialist housing needs but also system inconsistencies, overlaps and deficiencies.

If a general lack of confidence was the dominant theme, four other main points were made about information available on needs and demands. First, information primarily reflected resource usage, not assessed need. Second, the focus was upon current needs; forecasting of future needs had been attempted by only four authorities and was generally regarded as one of the next main tasks for departments. As one Director said, it is 'early days . . . we're just beginning to do that'. Moreover, such forecasting was understood only in respect of some client groups: for example, children with physical disabilities, where predictions of likely needs in adulthood were relatively straightforward. One other Director referred to the prediction of future need as 'one of the most important questions . . .We're asking that question now [but] we have to go up several notches in terms of our planning expertise in the next three or four years'.

The third main point was that many authorities had much 'soft' data even if they had relatively little 'hard' data. The former – obtained from general consultation exercises with service providers, users and carers – were reported as being a source of information on needs by 70 per cent and 57 per cent of sample authorities respectively. These surveys were invariably associated with the community care planning process. Analysis of the second-round (1993/94) community care plans had also found evidence of users and user groups and carers and carer groups having been consulted about, and involved in the preparation of, the second-round plans more extensively than during the first-round (1992/93) plans (Hardy *et al.* 1994). One Director remarked that although from such 'soft' information the authority 'might not be able to quantify some of the needs . . . we're very clear as to what the range of needs are'. It is important to note, however, that notwithstanding a general increase in involvement, there remained some scepticism among independent sector providers about its value or impact. One voluntary sector interviewee described 'communication with user groups' as being 'quite patchy' and said that information was 'fairly patchy for most care groups'.

The fourth main point to emerge is that information on aggregate need was generally expected to improve significantly after April 1993, as the outcomes of individual need assessments were fed into planning systems, even though it was acknowledged that this still comprised a record of presented and not latent need. One Director, who admitted to being 'not confident at all at this stage' (at the end of May 1993) said 'I'll be more confident in six months and even more confident in twelve months because we are obviously keeping close tabs on it'. Similarly, a fellow Director argued that, with aggregate data emerging from the care management information system and with improved joint 'top-down' analysis of population needs, 'two years from now [end of May 1993] my views would change quite dramatically: we're just at the starting gate at the moment'.

Across the sample as a whole, fifteen authorities (60 per cent) reported having such mechanisms in place for linking assessments of need at individual and population levels. However, three points about this figure need to be emphasized. First, of the ten authorities reported as having no mechanisms in place, many were interviewed in May 1993 when, it was said, such mechanisms were either being developed or were nearing completion. Second, even among authorities which had such mechanisms in place at the beginning of April 1993, there was general caution about whether the systems – installed primarily to record 'bottom-up' individual needs assessment – would work or would yield information which was then fed into, and used in conjunction with, planning data generated from 'top-down' population-level needs assessment. According to one Director, 'we have the ability to do it, we have not yet done much work on actually how we're going to do it . . . [it is] the next big area of work we've got to look at very closely'.

Identifying and recording unmet need

One other Director said that in his authority: 'all the processes are in place; whether they actually come up with the goods, we will have to wait and see'. In this Director's view, however, the issue of such data aggregation 'is plagued by the sort of ridiculous arguments going on about unmet need, which gets worse not better'.

In examining answers to the question about how authorities were recording unmet need, it is important to distinguish between issues of principle and issues of practice. At the level of principle, the general view from twenty sample authorities which responded was that unmet needs should and would be recorded. However, in stating such a principle there was, typically, a conflation of two concerns: obtaining basic information for the purposes of service planning and purchasing; and openness to service users and carers. In terms of the latter, it was said to be contrary to the ethos of the community care changes not to record and make those assessed aware of what it was agreed that they needed but which, for whatever reason, the authority was unable (or unwilling) to provide. One Director, for example, said that 'our whole essence is that we must be an honest organization: if we can't supply it we must tell people why we can't supply it; there are no compromises on that at all'. Another Director said that his authority had 'taken the decision in principle to record unmet need and stated it very very clearly with total political backing [across all parties]'.

However, the dual concerns for openness and for basic planning data should be treated separately. Withholding from clients information on assessed needs which cannot or will not be met does not in itself compromise an authority's ability to record and aggregate for planning purposes this unmet need: they are in effect two different decisions. The decision to pursue a policy of openness – to disclose to users and carers information on unmet need – and the decision to record and aggregate such unmet need are quite separate. Of the twenty-five sample authorities, only two (8 per cent) said that they were proposing to make such information available to those assessed. In both cases this decision – which, as one Director admitted, may mean 'we get our fingers burnt' – was based on the belief that users and carers, if trusted and treated sensibly, would accept the fact that resource limitations inevitably mean that there will be gaps between what it is agreed is necessary and what is in fact available. One other Director remarked that rationing in welfare was nothing new, either to authorities or to service recipients; what mattered – in what ought anyway to be a process of negotiation between both parties – was to agree what was needed, specify what was available and decide what the authority was able and willing to provide. To this Director the crunch in terms of possible legal challenges came only at this point: 'Once we say we can offer it, we have to provide it.'

Only four authorities (16 per cent) said that they did not propose to make available to clients information on unmet needs. In each case a record of service deficiency would be made elsewhere – rather than on the individual care plan – and aggregated for planning purposes. In all, thirteen (65 per cent) of the twenty authorities for which information was available proposed to record unmet needs for planning purposes. Two of these, however, pointed out the definitional problems involved. One Director asked: 'how do you define unmet need; it is as long as a piece of string'. Thus, not only is need capable of being differently assessed by different professionals (and by users and carers themselves) but, from a range of identified needs, there have to be distinctions in terms of both level and immediacy. The other Director said that in this respect the authority was having difficulty with 'partial unmet need': for example, where someone had received a placement (in effect their immediate and paramount need) but not a 'same-race' placement (their assessed and agreed need). Of the remaining authorities, firm decisions on recording unmet need were either awaiting legal advice or the formulation of policy following the May 1993 county council elections.

Summary

In most authorities, needs mapping in 1993 was still at an early stage of development and was widely regarded as complex, time-consuming and costly. Typically, the mapping of needs was restricted to identifying current service utilization and rarely extended to mapping latent or future needs. Many authorities were still grappling with information systems and technology deficiencies and, despite evidence of increasing joint needs assessment with health authorities, the inherent difficulties of such mapping and forecasting were compounded by incompatibility between the respective systems. However, much better 'bottom-up' information was expected after the first year of individual needs assessments, with such data being fed into planning processes together with 'top-down' population-level assessments.

Mapping supply

Aggregate levels and patterns of supply

In May 1993, according to the overwhelming majority of local authorities, information on aggregate levels of service provision was complete in respect of residential and nursing home places. Only two authorities lacked a full picture of numbers of places in residential facilities across all sectors and client groups, while information on nursing home provision was also incomplete for these same two authorities, together with two others. In each case, the gaps arose for only one or two client groups, although one authority was unable to distinguish between voluntary and private provision within the independent sector totals.

Table 4.2 illustrates that the situation with regard to non-residential services was, however, considerably more patchy and fragmented: there was very little evidence of authorities having significantly filled the gaps which were identified in 1990/91, although they were being narrowed as a result of information being generated by, or exchanged during, the contracting process.

The incompleteness of this information in 1990/91 had to some extent been due to the absence of any statutory requirement for non-residential facilities to be registered – as, indeed, is still the case. Thus, information on independent sector domiciliary and day care providers equivalent to that on authorities' residential and nursing home 'maps' was not available. However, at the time of fieldwork in 1993, one London borough and two metropolitan districts had established, or were in the process of establishing, non-compulsory 'quasi registers' either independently or jointly with neighbouring authorities. In one case this was linked to an accreditation procedure, while another authority reported that things were not yet 'systematic'. Interestingly, one of the private sector providers (who had previously been employed in a 'brand-name' national charity for elderly people), when asked about the local authority's impression of private sector providers, mentioned without prompting that she was in favour of legislation in this area to replace the current 'temporary' listing arrangements. This could 'ensure that the quality of service is there . . . I think until the government gets some legislation, regulations together, we could have people that will be providing good care and we could have people that would be providing bad care'.

One local authority officer, referring to independent home care services, talked of

Table 4.2 Local authorities' knowledge of independent sector
non-residential provision (May 1993)

Client groups	Private (%)	Voluntary (%)	NHS (%)
Respite care places			
All	21	25	25
Some	37	46	37.5
None	42	29	37.5
Day care places			
All	42	52	n/a
Some	37	36	n/a
None	21	12	n/a
Home care places			
All	13	16	17
Some	22	33	21
None	65	51	62
Meals-on-wheels			
All	13	17	n/a
Some	21	41	n/a
None	66	42	n/a

n/a = not applicable.

myths and fancies about what they may offer. We think that myths and
fancies would be about their offering a domestic service without the
appropriate ingredient of care thrown in. But we don't *know* what their
supervisory arrangements are; in fact, we don't know their employment
arrangements either.

As in 1990/91, information that had been assembled outside the
residential and nursing home sectors still appeared in 1993 to be acquired
largely incidentally to other activities undertaken by authorities, rather than
reflecting a proactive approach to providers for the sake of mapping these
services *per se*. A notable exception was one London borough which lacked
its own private and nursing residential provision for elderly people, and had

> gone out and mapped where old people have gone over the past two
> years . . . We have also talked with local domiciliary home care providers
> and looked at population statistics and tried to make some sort of settled
> guess at what we've used.

Those authorities which were aware of provision of non-residential services
for all or some sectors and client groups (sometimes for elderly people only)
had assembled their maps from various sources: routine records (including

registration) (90 per cent); the contracting process (65 per cent); surveys of/ discussions with intermediaries (50 per cent); and surveys of/discussions with individual providers (100 per cent). These sources were usually also used to supplement their mappings of residential and nursing home care, for which registration and survey-based data already painted a relatively full picture. Awareness of private sector non-residential provision was often high and easily described because there were few or no existing providers.

One authority had acquired information on respite care while conducting a survey of residential and nursing home facilities, and another had similarly collected data on the day care activities provided by the 85 per cent of homes that had responded to its residential and nursing home survey.

Some 65 per cent of authorities had obtained data across the range of service provision through their own or health authorities' contracting processes. In the case of some local voluntary day care providers, information had also been assembled in the course of processing grant aid or service-level agreement applications (which had often been in existence for many years). Others had found out about service levels either by formal discussions, or by informal word of mouth, and admitted that their views of the sectors were anything but systematic. Taking these various sources together, there appeared still to be greater awareness of voluntary than of private sector non-residential provision, although there was evidence that the gap was narrowing because of increasing dialogue with *both* independent sectors. In 1990/91, discussions with the private sector had been rare (see Wistow *et al.* 1994; KPMG 1992).

Information on individual providers

Turning now from information on aggregate patterns of supply to information on the characteristics of individual providers, Table 4.3 shows that over two-thirds of authorities knew about the range of services and users, and had audited accounts, staffing and users' funding sources information on only some providers. These were sometimes the residential and nursing home facilities and, for 90 per cent of authorities, information collected in the course of statutory registration and inspection fed into this knowledge base. A significant proportion of authorities had, as indicated in the previous section, individually or jointly undertaken one or more surveys of their residential and nursing home sectors between 1990 and 1993.

There were varied reactions from within the private and voluntary sectors to requests made by local authorities for the sorts of information listed in Table 4.3, whether asked for via the contracting process, registration and inspection procedures or through surveys. At one extreme, one private sector domiciliary care provider had actually volunteered information because she felt that 'the more information we can give them about ourselves the better'. At the other extreme, the representative of a private residential care home association was keen to ensure that the members of his association only supplied the legal minimum of details to the authority: 'the latest document [from the local

Table 4.3 Information held on individual providers in own local authority area (residential, domiciliary and day care) in May 1993

	All providers (%)	Some providers (%)	No providers (%)
Range of services	26	70	4
Range of users	13	74	13
Levels of utilization	13	70	17
Audited accounts	0	75	25
Unit costs and prices	4	46	50
Staffing levels	8	71	21
Pay rates	0	22	78
Length of time in business	14	63	23
Users' funding sources	5	77	18

authority] I have sent to my solicitor because I feel it is so outrageous the things they are asking . . . and he will mark up what is legally required'.

This same interviewee went on to outline the view of his association that 'the financial aspects of our businesses are confidential, and we have no desire to disclose . . . turnover, profit margins and accounts or any of our basic book-keeping accounts'. A similar sensitivity to the commercial nature of this information was shared by other private sector providers. For example, one maintained that the disclosure of detailed financial information (rather than 'general accounts') had been a 'widespread problem', and said that 'by nature, self-employed people don't like giving information, [for] those of us that have limited companies general information is available at Companies House anyway'. She said that some of her fears had been allayed by assurances that the information would be retained purely within the authority's treasurer's department, to avoid the repetition of what were claimed to be 'lots of cases' of social workers leaving their jobs, setting up a home 'and competing with the private sector using information that they had got as social workers'. Generally, there was much less reticence about providing the types of non-financial information shown in Table 4.3, although providers were often unsure as to the precise details of what they had submitted.

An even more partial picture emerged when authorities were asked about their knowledge of provision outside their geographical area. For example, one shire county Director contrasted the accuracy of his area's map as 'eight out of ten' with a score of 'one out of ten' for extra-county activity. Although 88 per cent of authorities said they had information on some providers outside their boundaries, only one claimed to have full information: the same Inner London borough which had tracked all types of service provision for its elderly residents. This authority had undertaken an 'extensive mapping' of those providers catering for its residents within a fifty-mile radius of its boundary who wished to join its approved list.

However, other authorities were less confident of completeness, although many had collected details of providers with whom they had entered into contracts, or who were seeking accreditation. The former were described variously as 'voluntary', 'specialist' or 'one-off'. Several authorities were only aware of provision in immediately neighbouring areas. One local authority had responses from outside providers to a national advertisement; one was actively sharing information with surrounding local authorities in the course of compiling a provider Directory; and one was involved in discussions with its neighbouring authorities, as well as being represented on one of these authorities' reference groups.

As with the estimation of future needs, attempts to estimate *future* patterns of supply were rare and informal. One Director commented that he 'was not a clairvoyant', and moreover was not in possession of a crystal ball! Another had managed to refine his impression of potential providers by asking his registration units to keep him informed of approaches to them, and had held joint meetings with the health authority and two large 'corporate players' who were considering their future role. However, even the Director of the London borough which considered itself to be 'ahead of the game', and had commissioned a 'best-practice market review' from well-known external consultants – described as a 'market-testing' exercise – was not confident about this activity. Thus, although the review had included

> some preliminary explorations of who the providers in the market were, how interested they'd be in getting into social welfare provision, and really doing quite a lot of informal work in that way, . . . I don't think we know too much about future patterns of supply at the moment. I think it's too early to tell.

Summary

In general, as with their information or needs, authorities' information on aggregate levels and patterns of supply in 1993 was incomplete. Not surprisingly, given authorities' long-standing registration roles, information was more complete on nursing and residential home provision (and on provision for elderly people as a whole) than on non-residential provision. There was little evidence of authorities having significantly filled the information gaps identified in 1991, although contracting processes were improving the situation. One explanation for such a difference in knowledge was the lack of statutory registration requirements for home-based services. Attempts to forecast *future* patterns of supply were rare and informal.

The amount of information held by authorities on the business characteristics of individual suppliers was similarly poor outside of the residential sectors. Indeed, it was rarely systematically sought. This was also true of information on provision in neighbouring local authorities, which was usually acquired only when 'external' providers either applied to be on an authority's approved list or catered for the specialist needs of those individuals who were placed outside their own authorities.

Beyond such quantitative mapping of supply, few authorities had begun to develop a broader market analysis and, in so doing, developed an understanding not only of providers' business plans and strategic intentions but also of their motivations. It is to such a broader market understanding that we now turn.

Market understanding

In asking about local authorities' knowledge of providers' business plans, intentions and motivations, our interest was in gauging the extent of their broader understanding of local markets: that is, beyond the relatively simple and straightforward quantification of aggregate levels of supply and of individual provider characteristics.

Providers' business intentions and plans

From the replies received from the twelve authorities who discussed this aspect of market understanding, it would be plausible to surmise that this focus was due partly to the fact that few authorities had yet sought to ascertain providers' business plans and intentions, and even fewer had obtained them. This does not mean, however, that discussions had not taken place about service developments and shifts, particularly about diversification from residential to day, domiciliary and respite care. As indicated in the following chapter, independent sector providers had increasingly been involved in discussions with, and negotiations about, service specifications and contracts; but rarely had these discussions included consideration of individual business plans. Without having sought the information, four authorities in 1993 claimed to have 'some knowledge', 'some general view' or 'some understanding' of such plans and intentions. One Director said the authority had 'some understanding' from meetings with residential and nursing home proprietors: 'the knowledge is there'. Two other Directors said that it was difficult to generalize because large organizations were often more willing than small ones to discuss such issues:

> Big conglomerates are very happy to show you their financial statements and how they are going to be able to manage for the next year. But some of the smaller concerns (some of them offering quite good-quality care) have very great degrees of suspicion about why you would need to see that.

This problem was acknowledged in another authority where it was said that 'business plans and intentions for the private market place [are] something that they refuse to divulge to us'.

This general reluctance to discuss business plans was confirmed by one of the private sector providers (not in the authority referred to above). The local authority had asked for business plans but the local home owners association had refused because 'it was considered an unwarranted intrusion'. This particular provider's view was that such complaints were 'much more applicable to sole proprietors than to limited companies', while it was conceded that providers would be much more willing to discuss general business possibilities and preferences than specific plans and intentions. A different explanation for such provider reluctance – unconnected with perceived intrusiveness – was offered by one Director. His view was that:

> A lot of the independent sector providers of care homes and nursing homes are a cottage industry where they've never thought strategically about what they wanted to do . . . I don't believe these are at all clear about their strategic objectives and where they want the business plans to go. I don't think most of them have got business plans and haven't got the foggiest idea what their strategic objectives are.

Purchasers' views of providers' motivations

Our interviews in 1993 included questions, not posed in 1991, on local authorities' *perceptions* of the motivations of voluntary and private providers. As with some of the views on the more tangible characteristics described above, these impressions and perceptions were built up through various consultations, reference groups, meetings, conferences, forums and ongoing discussions and dialogue between the various actors. As we have emphasized – and as was shown by the KPMG study (1992) – the activities started from a much lower base in the case of the private sector. And this was reflected in local authorities' responses. The interviewees varied hugely in the confidence which they placed in their own judgement about providers, ranging from 'a very good understanding' to 'the bottom of a learning curve'. One Director commented that his authority was a 'babe in arms' when it came to understanding the private sector.

A number of the Chairs and other members interviewed in 1993 admitted to knowing very little about independent sector providers' motivations, and few felt it necessary or appropriate to go beyond the simplest dichotomy within the independent sector: private providers were most often identified by their profit orientation, and voluntary sector providers by some reference to their 'voluntary' or 'philanthropic' character, or distinctive ethos. (These terms were not elaborated, other than through one reference to fund-raising.) A noticeable exception was the Conservative spokesperson who said he understood the private sector, and who distinguished between large companies with many private homes across the country and very small individual providers: 'It's very different the sort of care that they're offering, or the sort of services they're offering.' Another exception was a councillor who admitted to some sympathy for a number of the private sector organizations:

> I've had some meetings with the private residential sector and I think from their point of view, they feel that they've got a bad press: 'We care as well. Just because we're into profit [doesn't mean] we don't care', and I think we have to be fair and recognize that there are some very committed professional people involved in the private sector.

Four of the Chairs similarly mentioned the presence of professionals in the private sector, explicitly referring to their public sector social and health care backgrounds. Another commented that there were 'some very high-quality services . . . professional social work standards' in both private and voluntary sectors.

In the residential care market in particular, a number of Directors referred to the heterogeneity of the sector, and pointed out that much of the private sector was 'small-scale', a 'cottage industry' or even likened to 'corner shopkeepers', although some also identified 'huge, big companies' and conglomerates operating within their boundaries. One Director referred to his authority as a potential target for 'big bucks business' because of its perceived undersupply of home places. The Director who drew the analogy with corner shopkeepers remarked that 'they're very fragile . . . they've got one small home and they're good-hearted folk'. Another contrasted those which had 'genuine . . . values, concern for individuals' with 'one or two nice little earners but we tend not to use them, never have'. A number of Directors were sympathetic to the private sector homes which were simply struggling to survive, but one Director reacted to the private providers' apparent difficulties with disdain:

> I don't know how it happened, but Authority X got hold of the accounts of the home they wished to contract, and the profit they make is staggering. When we meet with them, one-to-one, you would think you were forcing them into starvation – you know, reduced to driving minis and things: it's just so untrue and, sad to say, . . . the tales of distress that we hear within our reference group are legion.

The same Director quoted a home owner who had confided that, although many people in the sector had 'good hearts', 'we would all be foolish if we weren't in business to maximize the income that we could earn; that's the name of the game'. Another Director agreed that private organizations were there 'to make money at the end of the day'.

Although one authority held the view that the private and voluntary sectors were 'markedly undifferentiated', this was exceptional. Many referred specifically to their links with the voluntary sector, including interlocking committees, historic funding relationships and various modes of joint working as informing them about the sector's *modus operandi*. Thus, many still exhibited a greater awareness and knowledge of the voluntary rather than the private sector, although the gap had narrowed considerably since 1991. Also, as in 1991, references were made to the differential strength of the sector in the residential, day care and meals-on-wheels service, as well as its delivery of ethnically-differentiated services, its employment of people with a 'community service ideal' and 'traditional values', and its continuing advocacy and campaigning role. Only one Director attempted to differentiate between groups within the sector, making a contrast between types of organization which has now also been made by several commentators in the sector (see Kendall and Knapp 1995 for a detailed discussion of voluntary sector typologies and organizational distinctions):

> The voluntary sector, which voluntary sector? If you are talking about your local church-based luncheon club, its the traditional altruistic, often value-driven activity, and a lot of that goes on. But that is untouched by community care, I don't think it has changed radically. If you're talking about big independent sector providers, then you're really talking about the new bureaucracy, because most of the professional voluntary organizations haven't been voluntary in a real sense for a while.

Expressed motivations of providers themselves

We also directly asked a small number of providers themselves about their own motivations. This was intended as a limited complementary perspective allowing us to gauge the accuracy of purchasers' perceptions in 1993. This was undertaken prior to the study of providers of residential care for elderly people carried out in 1994. The findings of that study are reported in Chapter 6. The following account of a small number of providers' views, from the 1993 fieldwork, should be read in conjunction with that chapter.

The motives cited by the providers themselves were partly consistent with the more considered views expressed by the local authorities. Of the private sector providers, two were positive in their attitude towards their local authorities, two had a more ambivalent relationship, while the fifth's language and attitude were often hostile and adversarial. The first two providers, one with a background working for a 'brand-name' national charity, and the other part of a partnership with her husband and son, both stated simply that they liked working with elderly people, and got satisfaction from the job, while the former added that the delivery of high-quality care was particularly important. The latter described her local authority as 'very open, very willing to communicate, very willing to consult and putting a lot of enthusiasm and energy into what is an extraordinary job', while the former noted that the information supplied to her on needs and demands had been 'very helpful and very informative'. Both appeared to feel that their local authorities had become increasingly aware of their motivations, even if the question had not been explicitly broached. One of these interviewees described her current links as 'more controlled' in contrast to historical political antipathy towards the sector.

The two providers with more ambivalent relationships with their local authorities both owned residential homes. They included a husband-and-wife team with nursing and social care backgrounds who were motivated by the desire to be their own bosses, while at the same time wanting to work in an area closely aligned to their professional backgrounds and offering the opportunity of 'financial reward'; and a Director/share-holder who had previously been involved in property markets. The former commented that:

> The authority has a very good understanding of the provision in terms of resources. Whether they have a good understanding of the individuals is open to debate. They have a basic grasp of the fact that the independent sector is there to make money, which of course is true; nobody can deny that. If you don't make money, you don't have a business, simple as that. So I think they have that grasp; they *don't* have a grasp of my own personal motivations, like being my own boss and maintaining standards, all those things.

This particular home owner was in the interesting position of having previously been employed as a nursing home inspector himself. In his view there was a fairly widespread view among inspectors that 'The independent sectors are coining it in. That obviously is not the case, but that's their general belief.'

The fourth home owner made a similar remark, but suggested that the situation might have improved as a result of personal contact 'at the front line', at least since 1991:

> I think there is a suspicion that certain people are in it just for the money, end of story [although over the past two years] people with whom we are in regular contact have a much better appreciation of what we are doing.

Relationships between this provider's association and the local authority had deteriorated because of inadequate consultation during the preparation of service specifications to such an extent that legal action was briefly considered.

One of the members interviewed had referred to the aggression felt by some parts of the private sector, and this was clearly manifested by the representatives of one local residential homes association who felt deeply threatened by what was perceived to be a hostile authority. The authority was attacked for failing to consult, for safeguarding its own jobs and 'empire', and for working 'hand in hand' with the supposedly independent inspection unit. There was even talk of 'infiltration' by the authority in a consultation meeting in order to eavesdrop on conversations between private residential home owners.

The local voluntary sector intermediary body in this same authority described how the social services voluntary sector consisted of a small number of very large service providers, and a much larger number of user-oriented and self-help groups, with whom the local authority was perceived 'not to be communicating enough'. When asked if officers and members of the local authority understood the motivations of providers, he noted the variety of views and a move away from 'municipal socialist' views expressed in 1991 (although these still emerged to a certain extent if very large sums of money were involved):

> That varies from individual to individual. There are certainly people who see voluntary organizations as very much well-meaning amateurs. There are certainly some who hold organizations in very high respect and treat them as partners and recognize people's experience and skills, and make use of that . . . Although it's not as evident as it was three years ago, there are still some members who feel that the voluntary sector is akin to the private sector, but if we have to have some in, we'll have the voluntary sector. That's very little [changed] compared to what it was two years ago.

The other voluntary organization interviewed was delivering carer support for frail elderly people in one half of a metropolitan district. The project, effectively run by a paid former local authority day care employee (the voluntary management committee were 'all doing their own thing and haven't got an awful lot of time for commitment to it') had historically received grant aid from the authority. This provider echoed comments made by one of the private providers that there was a contrast between those at the higher level of the authority who had grasped the needs-led nature of the reforms, and some of the front-line staff, who appeared to be stuck in the traditional mode of matching clients to services. In addition, the increasingly onerous conditions attached to funding were making it look more and more like a service agreement or even a contract, and in the preceding eighteen months of 'absolute sheer hell' the relationship with the authority had changed from one of 'nurture' to effective independence in order to implement the purchaser/provider split. Adding to increasing awareness of the responsibilities of trustees (clarified in the 1992 Charities Act), the new atmosphere of competition with the local authority and even other voluntary groups had caused a crisis in the organization's traditional management committee structure:

> Right up until recently we had management committee members from social services. But that has been a major, major headache for voluntary organizations in [this area] because obviously as we are now going into contracting and purchaser-provider, all local authority officers on that have had to come off [the committee] . . . So we've now got local authority members [that] come along but they can't partake in any discussions – observers. Which I'm not very happy about, why should they observe?

Conclusion

Our general finding from this chapter is that, while authorities had in 1993 begun to explore the identified blank areas on their local map, the areas of ignorance still exceeded the areas of knowledge; in general, maps were still very incomplete. In most of the sample authorities, needs mapping was still at an embryonic stage of development and was widely regarded as complex, time-consuming and costly. Typically, it was restricted to the identi- fication of current service usage and did not extend to mapping latent or future needs. Many authorities were still faced with deficiencies in their information systems and technology; and despite evidence of increasing joint working with health authorities, persistent problems of systems incompatibilities remained. However, much better 'bottom-up' information was expected after the first year of individual needs assessments, with such data being fed into planning processes along with 'top-down' population-level assessments. In general, the sample authorities' information on levels and patterns of supply was similarly incomplete.

To summarize, the information held on individual provider characteristics shown in Table 4.3 reflects:

- much greater awareness of contractors as opposed to non-contracted providers;
- much more knowledge about residential and nursing homes than other types of care;
- more knowledge about the elderly than about other client groups; and
- greater awareness of the voluntary sector in the delivery of non-residential services resulting from grant aid or service-level agreement procedures, and various other historic (pre-1990) personal and collaborative links.

As far as motivations and understandings of them are concerned, there was some evidence of increasing awareness of the diverse motives behind private sector activity – moving from a very low base in 1991 – although this varied both between and within local authorities. However, antipathy towards the profit motive, sometimes supported with anecdotal evidence of conspicuous consumption, was also widespread. As far as voluntary sector motivations were concerned, the level of understanding seemed to be somewhat greater overall. Another difference was that none of the interviewees identified 'cowboys' or opportunists in this sector as had been described in the private sector. Perceived amateurism was the one dimension of 'philanthropic failure' (Salamon 1987) alluded to by both the purchaser and provider sides. Although two interviewees partitioned the sector into its large (and 'bureaucratic') providers and 'others' (either 'value-driven' and 'altruistic' or oriented to user involvement), more sophisticated partitioning of 'provider types' was not forthcoming from either purchasers or providers. The search for a greater understanding of these issues across and within sectors is the topic to which we return in the 1994 provider study described in Chapter 6.

5
Purchasing intentions and arrangements

Introduction

In this chapter, we examine what services authorities were planning to buy in order to meet assessed needs and the arrangements through which purchases were made. We distinguish the aims and means of commissioning: purchasing intentions and purchasing arrangements. The chapter provides a mapping of authorities' purchasing arrangements at the time of our fieldwork and also indicates the directions in which they were either proceeding or wanted to go. We defer evaluation of these various policy stances until Chapter 8, where we seek to gauge how successful these arrangements are likely to be in meeting the objectives discussed in Chapter 1. In the final part of this chapter we look at the arrangements authorities had made to involve various stake-holders.

Purchasing intentions

The purchasing intentions on which we focus here concern those decisions taken at the strategic (or macro) level, rather than at the individual case (or micro) level, although clearly the two are interwoven. These strategic policy decisions concern: what services to buy and for whom.

Purchasing services

A core policy objective of *Caring for People* was to 'promote the development of domiciliary, day and respite services' to offer independent living (para. 1.11).

While acknowledging the development of non-residential services as a key, longer-term objective, authorities were focusing on residential care services over the next year (1993/94), in line with the guidance provided by the Foster/Laming letter (see Chapter 1). Indeed, the proportion of the social security transfer (SST) to be allocated to (independent) residential and nursing home care averaged 87 per cent across the sample. However, in keeping with the needs-led philosophy of *Caring for People*, three authorities had not specified the services to be purchased because the optimal service mix would depend upon the outcome of individual assessments. At the other end of the spectrum, four had decided that 100 per cent of SSTs would be required to preserve the 'steady state' of institutional provision. The remainder of the SST (13 per cent) was allocated to such purposes as the development of independent sector community-based provision, in-house domiciliary care and contingency funds.

These figures reflect projections made before the beginning of the financial year. However, reference was frequently made in interviews with Directors to the mismatch between actual and projected residential placements. The following comment was typical:

> We went for the first four weeks [of April 1993] making barely any admissions at all . . . [and] four months on, our admissions are 50 per cent less than we had anticipated.

A 1993 Association of Directors of Social Services (ADSS) survey confirmed that this low level of referrals to residential and nursing homes was a nationwide phenomenon (*Community Care*, 30 September 1993: 1). Given the implications of this trend for satisfying the '85 per cent rule' governing the use of their DSS transfer allocation, a handful of authorities were beginning to consider revising their purchasing intentions; for example, an authority that had initially earmarked the bulk of the transfer moneys for nursing home placements reported:

> The demand is for respite placements and so we are having to look at whether we need to move money between service categories to accommodate the increased demand in an area where we hadn't expected it.

Others preferred to delay any revision to their purchasing strategy:

> We've decided to wait . . . because we believe in the winter months the admission rates may start to rise.

The planned allocation of SST moneys to domiciliary care services rarely exceeded 15 per cent, but several authorities had also earmarked a small proportion of their 'infrastructure monies' for services. Across our sample as a whole, 87 per cent of the non-SST element of authorities' grant allocations was for infrastructure spending, the remainder often being apportioned to (in-house or external) non-residential provision. A number of authorities had addressed the imbalance between their own residential and non-residential services by investing savings from home closures and home transfers in the latter.

The paucity of independent non-residential provision was widely reported across the sample. According to one Liberal Democrat Chair:

> If you are looking at the domiciliary care services and so on, if you go down through the *Yellow Pages* you'll find there isn't much out there. The market just doesn't exist and people have tried to set things up and they have failed. There have been quite a few that have gone to the wall.

Similar sentiments were expressed by a London Director, who said that 'there simply isn't a ready-made private sector for parts of our service – there aren't many private suppliers in the market other than for residential care'.

The absence of independent sector non-residential provision was a significant factor in the decision to commit a high proportion of DSS transfer funds to residential placements in order to fulfil the 85 per cent spend requirement. An Inner London Director argued that

> It is easy enough to meet the 85 per cent rule from residential care, but the trick is going to be to meet the 85 per cent rule when you start to move away from residential care.

The potential consequence was that preferences for community-based care might not have been realized over the next year, with the majority of purchasers being unable to offer clients anything outside of standard institutional care. The reasons for this were manifold. First, imbalance of provision at the time was being maintained under the 'steady-state' requirement during 1993/94. Second, the independent sector appeared to be unwilling or unable to develop non-institutional services with sufficient speed. Thus, supply-side factors, rather than need and demand, still appeared to be shaping authorities' 1993/94 purchasing strategies to a large degree. This was one reason why the local authority associations had called for an end to the 85 per cent rule (*Community Care*, 21 October 1993: 1).

Purchasing for whom?

Although authorities were concentrating primarily on residential services for elderly people, many officers and Chairs recognized, and indeed advocated, a shift in the balance of provision between the 'traditional' care groups in favour of people with learning disabilities, mental health problems and physical disabilities. A desire to improve access for groups whose needs had been neglected historically – such as black and other ethnic communities – was also expressed. One London Director explained:

> We discovered that the people who were worse off from our local community were the black people, none of whom were in placements which were appropriate to their needs at all. So we have identified some

proprietors who are willing to work with us directly to develop models of care for old people from black communities.

Similarly, the Chair in a metropolitan borough observed that existing meals-on-wheels and home help services were inappropriate for the elderly Sikh community and had thus approached an Indian Workers' Association about 'the possibility of them offering a limited service which we could kick-start with infrastructure funds'.

The issue of maintaining provision for individuals with HIV/AIDS and people who misuse drugs and/or alcohol was rarely mentioned outside of the London boroughs. Within only a minority of authorities did it appear that individuals (who cut across discrete care groups) were being specifically targeted on the basis of their assessed ability to benefit from intervention. Thus:

> We've got a policy where we only offer domiciliary care to people who were in danger of going into residential care . . . The old lady in her own home who wants the mantelpiece dusting every week can go to [a private provider] and pay for herself . . . We can concentrate on the task of keeping people out of residential care by offering more intensive services.

Preventive services were explicitly referred to in only a handful of areas. However, one Director spoke of the danger of tight eligibility criteria re-defining access in favour of 'crisis management' at the expense of preventive work.

Purchasing arrangements

In moving from purchasing aims to means, local authorities were facing a number of issues as they sought to interpret and translate central and local policy into workable systems. Here we will focus on the main issues at the time of our research. We wished to get a picture of:

- How far had authorities separated purchasing from providing and devolved purchasing power?
- Which types of providers were being used as suppliers and what arrangements were in place for authorities to stimulate supply?
- What mechanisms were being used to select potential providers?
- Were authorities using pre-specified prices (for example, call-off arrangements) or were prices left to float (where purchasers buy in spot markets)?
- Finally, what type of contracts were being used?

The purchaser/provider separation

The practical implications of the purchaser/provider separation depend on where the separation begins and ends, and particularly on the extent of

Table 5.1 Devolved purchasing power: distribution of main purchasing budgets across sample authorities

| | Provision type | |
	Internal (%)	External (%)
Where were budgets held?		
Corporate finance only	0	0
SSD finance only	8	4
SSD finance and team manager	12	16
Team manager only	44	44
Team manager and care manager	28	24
Care manager only	8	12
Total (%)	100	100

N = 25

devolution of purchasing power. Key purchasing budgets for the elderly were held at different levels in the sample authorities (Table 5.1). We distinguish between internal (in-house) and external transactions (with independent providers and other local authority providers), although it can be seen that there was little difference in their treatment.

The majority of authorities had not completely devolved all budgets. Purchasing power mostly resided with the team manager who directed a small team of care managers. In a few cases, some purchasing power was given to individual care managers within this arrangement, but usually this was for buying specific services and/or carried a low expenditure ceiling.

Information from nineteen authorities revealed that fourteen had no trading account, four had a shadow trading account, and one had a full trading account. Every authority had a system for recording committed expenditure (fully computerized system in nineteen authorities, a manual system in two, and a combination in the other four).

Twenty-two authorities described the degree of autonomy (complete or limited) given to care managers with regard to provider choice (complete in 19 per cent of authorities) and contract type (complete in 27 per cent of authorities). By autonomy we meant the freedom to allocate budgets without needing the approval of superiors in the organization. However, the wide-ranging nature of the question means that these summary statistics can only be taken as indicative evidence. None the less, they do suggest some decision-making flexibility and responsibility for care managers. On the whole, authorities had been relatively cautious in the implementation of a full purchaser/provider separation and devolved purchasing. One interviewee said:

> It seemed to us that it was more important in the first instance to get the social workers, the care managers and everybody else actually doing the professional things which they are supposed to be doing effectively.

Another Director went further saying that, during a period in which they were getting good information and assessment functions in place, 'the last thing we wanted to do was to chuck the organization up into the air at the same time and go through a massive organizational change'.

Who to buy from: arrangements to develop supply?

Once authorities have decided which services they wish to commission for which groups, they must then decide who to buy from. In practice, these choices are not made independently of one another, but a separate consideration helps to identify the available options and authorities' behaviours and activities. The latter decision itself has two elements: first, authorities must choose whether they wish to buy in-house or use the independent sector; and second, if they are to purchase from the independent sector, do they take an interventionist or non-interventionist stance?

Authorities had taken a variety of positions on the extent to which they intended to alter the overall balance of provision between the statutory and independent sectors. At one end of the spectrum, there was a commitment to maintain existing levels of direct provision, with external purchase only being entertained where there remained gaps in provision. At the other end was the complete divestment of in-house services. Intermediate positions[1] were usually characterized by a programme of some Part III home closures or transfers, with the resultant savings being channelled into either internal non-residential provision, maintenance programmes for the remaining stock of directly-provided homes, or external projects.

Where authorities had taken a decision to employ the independent sector, we sought to determine the policy stance they had taken in regard to arrangements to promote and develop external provision. Our findings are reported in Table 5.2.

The table shows that the most favoured options – those actively en-couraged – included the establishment of new voluntary sector services, the sale of existing in-house services to voluntary organizations, and the creation of not-for-profit trusts. Throughout the sample there was a clear and strong preference for working with the voluntary sector rather than the private sector. Also, enthusiasm for management and staff buy-outs was relatively rare in our sample.

As indicated in Chapter 4, many authorities favoured the voluntary sector over the private sector because of perceived similarities in values, familiarity through historical relationships such as voluntary sector representation on joint planning machinery, and relative ignorance about large parts of the private sector. Ideological opposition to the private sector was voiced in some areas because of their profit-orientated basis and perceived propensity to award relatively low wages. This did not necessarily correlate with political control; many Conservative authorities shared this view. Conversely, a number of Directors – including those from Labour-controlled authorities – took the view that the creation of profit was incidental if the resultant services were affordable, flexible and of a sufficiently high standard.

Table 5.2 Authorities' development of a mixed economy

		Actively discouraged (%)	Neither encouraged nor discouraged (%)	Actively encouraged (%)
(a)	Management or staff buy-out of some LA services	16	79	5
(b)	Floating-off to a 'not-for-profit trust'	24	29	47
Selling-off services to:				
(c)	voluntary organizations	25	25	50
(d)	private organizations	58	21	21
Setting-up new services in:				
(e)	voluntary sector	16	16	68
(f)	private sector	32	26	42

A fraction of the sample either could not (due, in part, to policy uncertainty because of the shire elections which were imminent at the time of our survey) or did not wish to make responses in such broad terms. The lowest response rate on specific items was 64 per cent.

The results in Table 5.2 illustrate that there was a strong preference for creating new providers where current supply was insufficient. New provision in a particular market can be generated either by diversification of providers from other markets or by new start-ups. In terms of their expectations, most authorities thought the largest proportion of new supply would be developed through the former.

A 'commonality of interests' for purchasers and providers was perceived by a number of authorities, particularly in shire counties where institutional provision was oversupplied. The attractions for users, providers and SSDs of encouraging homes in a rural location to develop outreach services were seen as being considerable. The economies of scope gained through diversification also made this option preferable (in some authorities and to some – but by no means all – providers) to establishing 'new starts', especially as the relatively low profit margins on the latter were often said to preclude investment in the necessary human and physical capital. As one local authority Director succinctly remarked: 'We are more likely to get the residential home providers preparing to diversify than we are to get the domiciliary care providers to build up.'

In addition to offering an *alternative* business option, a small number of existing providers saw longer-run benefits. At least two providers who were interviewed – one of whom had already developed home care services – mentioned that it would enable them to establish good trusting relations with individuals who might require residential care at a later stage, and thus provide them with a future market for residential care:

Once you start to build up a relationship they may be more tempted to say 'Ah well, X provided this care for me at home. I know it's time for me to go into a nursing home so I think I'll go into X.' And then at least we've made some contact. So eventually they may actually come into the nursing home.

Thus, diversification may have the dual effect of reinforcing existing provision and creating new activity. However, some authorities were opposed to diversification for precisely this reason. Other authorities, together with a number of private and voluntary sector representatives, were uncomfortable with the notion of combined models of care, particularly for day and respite care, because of the disruption caused to, and the intrusion into the homes of, long-stay residents.

We found that local authorities also preferred diversification rather than the creation of new supply from scratch. We sought to determine whether authorities – having expressed these preferences – actually had arrangements in place to stimulate their preferred supply options. We found that a large proportion of authorities favoured active policies to intervene in the independent sector:

- subsidies/loans provided (27 per cent);
- secondment of staff (27 per cent);
- premises/equipment provided (29 per cent);
- legal, financial, technical advice and training (44 per cent);
- aid to umbrella organizations (62 per cent); and
- organization of bidders' conferences (16 per cent).

Half the sample (48 per cent) had created a dedicated budget (with or without staff) to stimulate supply, again through diversification or agency creation. The alternative is for authorities to elicit supply simply by specifying their (costed) purchasing intentions and leaving the rest to the market mechanism. The latter approach was illustrated by a Director of social services who said of the private sector:

They don't need an enormous amount of encouragement. They are very keen and are contacting me on the possibility of doing deals on land and any surplus property that we happen to know about. They'd be prepared to do developments and to reduce the costs over a period of time.

Authorities had taken steps to inform providers of their purchasing intentions through a variety of mechanisms, including:

- the establishment of working groups with representatives of trade associations and voluntary bodies;
- public meetings and seminars targeted at various groups according to service type and sector;

- written information circulated to homes regarding the authority's proposed arrangements (frequently combined with an invitation to join an approved list and/or sample specifications and contracts); and
- roadshows and frequent addresses to associations.

However, the information imparted through these mechanisms was not, from the perspective of some providers, of sufficient detail. The proprietor of a dual registered home who was considering offering day and respite care felt frustrated.

> They give us no guidelines as to what would be welcomed, whether they would be interested in it . . . as to at what price range they would consider purchasing . . . Those are just general statements in the community care plan . . . Before we would want to put very much time or money into such a project, we would need much more specific encouragement and detailed information.

Another Director opined that his authority's historical commitment to the mixed economy had given the voluntary and private sectors sufficient confidence to enter the market. The view was that unless authorities devised detailed service specifications and offered some commitment to purchase, a new supply of non-residential care would not be forthcoming.

Provider selection mechanisms

Social services departments face a choice between a preferred provider system or open purchasing. The former usually entailed providers meeting eligibility criteria before they were able to join an approved or select list. We observed that this was often formalized as 'core contracts'. In addition it was noted that eligibility criteria varied significantly from authority to authority. In the majority of cases, specifications covered service standards and quality, reimbursement arrangements and the like. In some cases providers had to meet conditions on price (in the form of a price ceiling). As such, provider selection arrangements were linked closely with pricing arrangements.

In our sample, twenty-one authorities (84 per cent) were using some form of select list system in buying residential or non-residential care for the main client groups. Nine of these authorities were compiling a list by open advertisement, two used some other means (for example, including all organizations which at the time were funded by the authority), and eight used a combination of the two.

At the time of our fieldwork most select list systems were used in buying residential care. However, some interviewees recognized a particular potential for using select list systems for the accreditation of non-residential care where legal registration provisions were absent. There was a clear move in this direction for non-residential care.

Fixed or floating prices: DSS or not?

Local authorities have taken two broad approaches to pricing arrangements in regard to residential care. They have employed either:

- *pre-specified* arrangements, where a reimbursement structure is specified in advance so that all contracts let with providers use this pre-specified or fixed pricing structure; or
- *spot* arrangements, where the local authority purchaser and provider negotiate over the contract reimbursement at the point of the transaction.

In order to understand the consequences of these different pricing arrangements, we need to be clear about the different types of contract (see below) and the different types of reimbursement mechanism. The latter cover a range of options, the two ends of which are:

- Simple fixed price reimbursement: contracts are let with a single fixed price and providers are reimbursed for work carried out as specified. Payment is *not* linked to the actual cost of care for specific clients.
- Simple cost-plus reimbursement: contracts are let according to an agreed formula with providers reimbursed on the basis of actual cost.

Between these two endpoints, contracts can have reimbursement structures which combine fixed-price and cost-plus.

The practical implications of the different types of reimbursement, for example, can be seen in relation to domiciliary care. With a simple fixed-price mechanism, a domiciliary care contract would specify a fixed rate per hour for the care of specific individuals. With cost-plus reimbursement the payment rate would vary according to the cost of the service. In this way it can account for the cost-changing characteristics of the job, such as different dependency characteristics of clients, and the quality and coverage of the service. This is particularly useful when the exact impact of these factors is not known before the service begins.

In the purchase of residential care, the majority of the local authorities in our sample used *call-off* arrangements which are a combination of pre-specified and fixed price reimbursement. The fixed price was often closely tied to DSS rates. Eighteen authorities (72 per cent) were using such an arrangement. Of the remaining seven, just under a half had pre-specified reimbursement arrangements but with a tariff of prices set according to different dependency groups within each service type for each client group. Two authorities had floating price arrangements; although they worked with an implicit fixed tariff they reported taking into account other factors as they arose at the time of the transaction (a common one was location of service). Overall, then, only about one in ten of the authorities had truly floating prices for at least some services.

In our sample, no one reported using anything other than single, lump-sum reimbursement. Although some had said they would take into account potential cost-raising factors such as client dependency in fixing this contract price, no authority linked payment retrospectively to actual costs. None the less, one interviewee thought cost-related payment or budget schemes could be used in the future.

We explore the economic rationales for using different pricing arrangements in Chapter 8. However, it is worth emphasizing that one of the principal considerations for local authorities in choosing pricing arrangements was the perceived need to maintain a steady state:

> It does represent a position on 1 April [1993] that was exactly the same as the position on 31 March. It has enabled us to put into system the same volume of purchasing.

Many authorities were starting with fixed rates but intended gradually to build in more flexibility and allow market forces to operate.

Contract choice

Contract type is usually defined according to whether payment is:

- linked to the client (*case-by-case contracts*);
- linked to the facilities made available by the provider (*block contracts*); or
- a combination of the two (*cost-and-volume contracts*).

Block contracts buy units of particular types of service at the agreed price regardless of whether the services are used. The price determined for block contracts is therefore not contingent on client characteristics because payment is for facilities, not services. Thus block contracts are incompatible with pure cost-plus reimbursement. *Case-by-case* (or spot) contracts link payment directly to clients while they are using the service. Payment can either be as an agreed lump sum or cost-plus. In both cases the pricing structure may be determined in advance. Finally, *cost and volume* contracts are a combination of the two. With these contracts an initial block of purchase is agreed, but there is further provision for purchasers to buy additional units.

The sample authorities were employing different contracts for different services and client groups. They were using case-by-case contracts predominantly for residential care for elderly people (with a mixture of call-off and spot arrangements), although a significant minority were either offering block contracts to providers or planning to use them in the future to buy these sorts of services. Two authorities were using cost and volume contracts. Twelve had block contract arrangements for at least some services: in most cases for specialist services about which there may be more uncertainty as to levels of need (such as for people with drug and alcohol dependencies).

In terms of future intentions, a significant number of authorities wanted to move towards block contracts in the next few years, once they had acquired better information on the longer-run pattern of need and demand. In addition, once their monitoring systems have been fine-tuned, purchasers will have less of an information deficit compared to providers. As we discuss in Chapter 8, such information 'asymmetries' can lead to market failure.

Stake-holder involvement

In considering the degree to which social services departments have involved various stake-holders in the formulation of their purchasing plans and intentions, and in the development of their purchasing arrangements, we restrict our attention to the following 'stake-holders':

- providers, both from the statutory and independent sectors;
- other purchasers, such as health authorities, FHSAs and GP fund-holders;
- users; and
- carers.

These non-purchaser stake-holders may be involved at a number of different levels, ranging from the determination of an authority's broad purchasing strategy (concerning the balance of care between service types, sectors and client groups) to the negotiation of service specifications and contracts. We sought to identify the degree to which authorities had involved stake-holders at the various stages of the purchasing process using a framework developed by KPMG (1992: ii). This has three core elements:

- *participation* – provider representation on a planning group;
- *consultation* – seeking comments from providers on a draft plan; and
- *negotiation* – provider involvement in discussing contracting arrangements.

However, many officers, when addressing these issues during the telephone survey, did not differentiate between participation, consultation or negotiation, although the framework had been applied within at least one authority's community care plan. Therefore, Table 5.3 simply reports on the number of authorities in our sample which had involved stake-holders in various ways.

Table 5.3   Stake-holder involvement in purchasing strategy

| | | | *Stake-holder involvement in:* | | | |
| | *Purchasing strategy* | | *Design of service specification* | | *Design of contracts* | |
	(%)	*(N)*	*(%)*	*(N)*	*(%)*	*(N)*
Providers	71	21	96	23	87	23
Other purchasers	83	23	74	19	55	20
Users	33	21	33	21	24	21
Carers	33	21	29	21	24	21

Provider involvement

The KPMG study, undertaken in 1992 and based on the same sample of authorities as used in our work since 1990, reported some disparity between voluntary and private sector agencies in their level of involvement, noting that the latter:

> are unfamiliar to social services and structures for their involvement are only in construction. In consequence the study showed that private providers typically did not participate in developing plans nor did they feel engaged in effective consultation (iii).

In our fieldwork in 1993 we found that within only one authority were communication channels still inadequate. The Director, remarking that the private sector had been involved 'hardly at all', explained that:

> We've been struggling with all the problems in implementing community care and . . . it has been low down on our list of priorities. But had they been better organized, we would have tried harder to bring them on board. It was just such a blooming effort to get a response from them. We've got greater priorities.

Other authorities have now established a number of different mechanisms for informing and negotiating with provider agencies. But the sentiments expressed at the time of our fieldwork are reflected in the comments of the Director of a shire county:

> The KPMG study was commissioned at the wrong time and therefore came up with the wrong conclusions . . . Virginia Bottomley didn't announce the transfer grant until the ADSS conference . . . So there was nothing to talk about before October . . . A lot of KPMG fieldwork was done in the summer and so it doesn't surprise me that they concluded that there was such a mixed picture across the country.

At the time this sentiment was expressed by other Directors among authorities which varied both by type and political control.

Purchasing strategy

Although authorities had taken steps to inform providers of their proposed purchasing strategies through a variety of media, it was not possible to gauge from our study whether the actual formulation of those purchasing intentions was undertaken in collaboration with agencies across the whole of our sample. However, one Labour-controlled Inner London borough had made the decision not to involve providers at this level because it would 'conflict with a needs-led approach'. A similar attitude was suspected by the Director of the local Council for Voluntary Service (CVS) branch with representation on a joint planning team:

> They are immediately suspicious of people who are from a voluntary

> organization as opposed to being just a user or carer, because they . . .
> feel that . . . this particular organization wants power and recognition
> for themselves and wants to manipulate, etc.

Private agencies within the same authority spoke positively of the opportunity
to comment upon the draft community care plan, although the proprietor of
a dual-registered home stated that:

> Though I understand [from] reading the 1992/93 community care plan
> . . . that they do intend encouraging the private sector to expand its
> range of services . . . we haven't quite got to the stage of having a
> dialogue with the local authority about that.

Involvement simply through consultation on community care plans was
regarded as tokenistic by some providers. Within a Labour-controlled
metropolitan borough, where social services had supported the CVS branch
to encourage and facilitate consultation around the community care plan, a
representative of a local, private residential homes' association held this view.
He felt that those comments upon the draft community care plan which had
been made by a minority of homes failed to find their way into the plan,
arguing that: 'yet again our involvement in it has been surface scratching only'.
    While information was not collected on a sample-wide basis, it appeared
that provider involvement in the formulation of purchasing plans and intentions
had been confined to consultation around the community care plan. This was
either through voluntary sector forums or the comments of individual private
sector agencies or their associations. This may reflect the then under-
development of appropriate participatory mechanisms, although, judging from
the degree of involvement of agencies in negotiating the details of purchasing
arrangements (reviewed below), it may well indicate a desire to develop a
needs-led – rather than a provider-led – purchasing strategy.

Specifications and contracts
The merits of involving providers in drafting service specifications were
summarized by the Director of a shire county thus:

> When drawing up a specification it is done with the provider side as
> well as the purchasing side, . . . because providers know an awful lot
> about the service . . . It would be a nonsense to cut them out . . . If you
> get a spec only drawn up by the purchaser, you find it doesn't work.

However, within a number of authorities, despite various attempts to engage
agencies in negotiation around specifications and contracts, there was an
awareness of provider dissatisfaction. Leedham (1993) also found this
perception for authorities in the north-west of England. Referring to the
feelings expressed by the working group formed by a local, private residential
homes' association, the Director of a metropolitan borough stated:

> They felt our contracts were . . . massively overspecific . . . that [the

overall rates] were low . . . We've worked with them solidly for five months . . . and the contract has been modified and we've reached an agreement . . . Now they want to come back and negotiate price with us.

Representatives of this working group confirmed this:

They are moving towards requiring homes to provide purely single rooms . . . [with] en-suite facilities and, as I say, they did try a very onerous contract on us . . . We have now, through a lot of negotiation and substantial legal expenses to us . . . arranged and negotiated what we think is a much more reasonable contract . . . but we still haven't been able to get what we consider to be a reasonable fee to associate with that contract.

In other areas too, residential home owners felt that consultation had produced little impact on the 'detailed wording of the clauses'.

By contrast, representatives from the private sector within another authority (who noted that the historical antipathy towards the private sector had become 'somewhat more controlled' over the last four or five years), expressed praise for the authority's willingness to alter initial draft specifications in accordance with the organization's wishes. It is notable that relations between social services and providers within this latter authority were more harmonious than those reported elsewhere. The relationship was characterized by cooperation and a willingness to exchange information by both sets of players. The authority had set up an information service which, in the words of one private supplier, 'provid[ed] any information [I] wanted', although another provider spoke of an apparent reluctance to supply unit cost information. Whereas providers within other authorities felt that requests for audited accounts and business plans were 'an unwarranted intrusion', agencies within this authority held a different attitude, saying: 'the more information we can give them about ourselves, the better'.

Even within this authority however – in common with the others – there were claims that the social services department was referring individuals to its own Part III accommodation rather than to the independent sector. The 1993 ADSS survey of placements, which showed that referrals to independent residential and nursing homes had averaged 81.3 per cent (*Community Care*, 30 September 1993: 1)[2] since 1 April 1993, appeared to refute this claim, at least as a nationwide phenomenon.

None the less, despite evidence of detailed consultation, many independent sector providers were dissatisfied with either the final outcome or with the fact that they had invested considerable time, effort and money (particularly through legal expenses) in negotiations. The House of Commons Health Committee reported similar findings, noting that:

Where contracts had been seen,[3] providers were anxious that specifications were in some instances overcomplex and even inappropriate . . .

[Moreover] evidence from providers suggests a substantial amount of money could be lost in transaction costs during the contractual process.
(House of Commons Health Committee 1993a: paras 142, 144)

Anxiety reported by agencies during our own study may have reflected concerns about operating within overprovided markets as well as frustration with social services departments, whose own skills in contract specification and negotiation were still being refined. This frustration was also shared by the voluntary sector, even where representatives had praised the historical support of social services.

The suggestion made to the Health Committee by Methodist Homes for the Elderly found support among providers within our sample. It was that 'a series of standard contract clauses, to be used nationally, would be a more sensible and cost-effective approach for both local authorities and service providers' (quoted in House of Commons Health Committee 1993a: para. 144). Certainly this appeared to be an attractive proposition and it was recommended by the Health Committee as a task for the Support Force successor.

Purchaser involvement

Health authorities
Although social services authorities had negotiated '31 December agreements' with health authorities (see Chapter 1), joint arrangements outside of these schemes were reported to be relatively embryonic. Notable exceptions included reprovision (by social services and the health authority from a joint fund) for elderly mentally infirm people following the closure of a long-stay hospital. It was intended that these arrangements would provide a basis for further joint initiatives but these were plagued by 'various legal difficulties'.

The Director of another authority spoke of joint commissioning intentions:

> We will actually look at developing an understanding of a shadow budget which incorporates all the resources of the FHSA, the DHAs and the social service department to see what opportunity costs there were in making certain decisions where we might actually have saved more money.

Such a scheme, which 'could be a model for the rest of the county' was already operational within a particular locality, where a RHA-sponsored joint commissioning board had been established.

Other authorities were just entering into dialogue with health authorities about joint commissioning opportunities, particularly around learning disabilities. Such developments have since gathered pace; the Langlands/ Laming letter of March 1993 specified joint commissioning as a key area for authorities to carry forward during 1993/94 (Department of Health 1993c) and in November 1994 the Department issued draft guidance.

GP fund-holders

In view of the concern expressed by a number of authorities about 'the threat GP fund-holding has to the management of the market', it was surprising that few authorities had attempted to engage fund-holders in the development of purchasing plans and intentions. A similar picture was painted by the BMA's November 1992 survey of GPs, where 78 per cent of respondents had not been consulted individually on their local authority's community care proposals (see House of Commons Health Committee 1993a: para. 122). However, one Director explained that:

> We went to over twenty locations and talked to them about it . . . They were very excited about being part of that process. It just seemed to me that what we need to do is enthuse them about their role in this process.

This authority had co-located social workers within two GP practices, as had the authority quoted above where locality-based joint commissioning had attempted to integrate GP fund-holders.

Users and carers

If the key policy objectives of user choice and independence, carer support and the development of needs-led services[4] are to be achieved, then, as the Health Committee argued: 'Users must be offered the optimum level of involvement at every stage of the process, from planning through commissioning and delivery to monitoring outcomes of the service' (House of Commons Health Committee 1993a: para. 19).

Purchasing strategy

Most authorities had made serious efforts to involve users and carers, and this often took the form of consultation around the community care plan. However, one authority had user and carer representation upon a joint commissioning board, although the effectiveness of that arrangement was severely questioned by a local CVS representative.

The 'real conflict' between users' and carers' wants was clearly recognized by authorities, which prompted user- and carer-specific conferences, sessions and support meetings. Carer groups, networks, support mechanisms and centres had also been established by many authorities, often with assistance from national initiatives associated with the Kings Fund, the Joseph Rowntree Trust and the Princess Royal Trust.

The representative of a carers' support scheme commented that social services had initially failed to grasp the practicalities of consultation. Money for replacement sitters was offered only after prompting, and carers were sometimes intimidated by the professional jargon used at conferences and meetings.

Clearly, authorities need to grapple with a number of issues if their consultation exercises are to be effective in ensuring that the appropriate services are commissioned.

Specifications and contracts

While the need to involve users and carers in drawing up service specifications and contracts was recognized by authorities, this was often an area highlighted for further development. One Director stated that:

> There is a general view that we should be clear about our specifications, that we should do a lot to involve users and carers.

The fact that only a minority of authorities had included user and carer outcomes in their specifications indicates that they have a considerable task ahead of them if they wish to ensure that services are user-responsive. In sum, it seems as though authorities were making some progress on user and carer involvement, but the impact upon actual services was yet to be realized.

Conclusion

This chapter has sought to describe our sample local authorities according to their stated purchasing plans, their purchasing arrangements and their strategies for the involvement of other stake-holders (particularly providers and users). The majority of sample authorities expressed concerns about the initially low level of residential care placements. Moreover, the demand for respite and domiciliary care was reported to be higher than initial projections. This pattern was not necessarily reflected in the allocation of the Social Security Transfer however, which was spent predominantly on residential care. Many commentators saw the key reason for this spending pattern being the paucity of independent sector domiciliary care providers.

Authorities' purchasing arrangements were considered according to a number of indicators: first, the distribution of purchasing power within the social services department. The majority of authorities indicated that they had not completely devolved budgets. Individual care managers had only partial autonomy and, in the main, budgets were held by team managers.

Second, authorities can be distinguished according to their strategies of provider use and development. Our sample authorities had taken a variety of positions on the extent to which they had externalized residential care provision. In a significant but small minority, a complete divestment of provision was considered to be feasible.

The majority of authorities reported their preferred supply development option to be aid in the establishment of *voluntary* sector providers. Half of our sample authorities had established a dedicated budget to stimulate supply. In addition, diversification by residential care providers was regarded as a key method to create independent domiciliary care.

The third indicator of local authority purchasing arrangements is in respect to provider selection. It was found that the majority of local authorities were using some form of accreditation system, usually in the form of an approved provider list. The fourth indicator concerns how local authorities were paying providers. In our sample, only a small minority of local authorities were *not* fixing prices at which they purchased residential care. Finally, almost all authorities were using spot contracts rather than block contract arrangement. Contract choice was our fifth indicator.

This chapter has also described authorities' various approaches to the question of stake-holder involvement. In summary, most authorities said that they had not engaged the independent sector in regard to their purchasing strategy or design of contacts as much as they would like. However, many had made considerable efforts to involve users and carers. This often took the form of consultation around the community care plan. Users and carers did not always share this view.

These features of local authority policy and practice highlighted a wide range of interpretations by our sample authorities of the Government's community care legislation. This was particularly evident in regard to purchasing arrangements. Indeed, some authorities had gone much further than others in embracing the market development model of enabling. We defer analysis of various policy stances until Chapter 8. We turn next to a consideration of the independent sector providing function.

Notes

1 These were quantified in a minority of cases; two authorities were hoping to shift the balance of their gross budget between internal and external services from a ratio of 88 : 12 to 60 : 40 over four years.
2 In 1991, the independent sector supplied 66.23 per cent of all residential home places and 75.46 per cent of all places within both residential and nursing homes (House of Commons Health Committee 1993a: 2).
3 Contrary to submissions received by the Health Committee, there was no evidence in our study of agencies not having seen contracts, although, as recorded by the Committee, draft contracts were, in some instances, reported to be circulated at a very late stage.
4 See *Caring for People* (paras 1.8–1.11) and the National Assistance Act 1948 (Choice of Accommodation) Directions 1992.

6

Provider motivation and behaviour

Introduction

In their market-shaping role, local authorities need to understand providers' motivations. In previous chapters we described local authorities' perceptions of and attitudes towards providers. In 1991 there had been a broadly-based preference for working with organizations in the voluntary rather than the private sector, a preference based not on *systematic* evidence about the relative outcomes and effectiveness of 'voluntary' or 'private' providers but upon greater familiarity with the former, and beliefs about the extent, or otherwise, of shared values and motives. In particular, user welfare, altruism and public duty were identified as core values shared by local authorities and the voluntary sector. By contrast, private sector providers were often assumed to place their own interests in profit maximization ahead of public service or welfare goals. Such assumptions were frequently based merely on hearsay or anecdotal evidence of conspicuous consumption, but the private sector was often mistrusted because it was considered guilty of making 'excessive' profits under the former social security arrangements. Attitudes towards the private sector, therefore, reflected a relatively crude, knee-jerk reaction against what was often seen as inappropriate commercialization of social care.

In this chapter we explore systematically the accuracy of these perceptions and examine actual provider behaviour. Before seeing what light our 1994 provider study can shed on these issues, we pull together evidence from the earlier stage of the project, and examine a number of streams of theoretical work that informed the approach we adopted in the 1994 study. We can look at both the relevant historical developments and these streams of theory for explanations of the ways in which local authorities conceptualize and understand the private and voluntary sectors. We go on to examine how far our provider study data yield an understanding of these issues and also explore a number of issues related to aspects of diversification.

The historical practice of sectoral relations

In recent years, voluntary organizations and local authorities have often tended to operate alongside each other within social networks, in which mutual dependence has been recognized by both parties. These networks have promoted not only mutual learning but confidence in respective cultures, values and ways of working. Added impetus had been given to this process of mutual learning by central government's mandate in the early 1980s that voluntary bodies participate in the formal community care joint planning machinery, although such involvement was not always as extensive as some voluntary groups would have liked (Wistow *et al.* 1994; see also Chapter 5).

Until relatively recently, this proximity contrasted strongly with a lack of joint working with the private sector. The interviews we undertook with Directors and Chairs in 1991 showed that the majority had no contacts with private providers by that stage. Rather, they relied on a combination of assumptions and anecdotal evidence, sometimes ideologically reinforced, to form rather crude understandings of the nature of private sector providers.

However, as Chapter 4 illustrated, by 1993 there was evidence of a deeper understanding as the contracting process yielded new contacts. Dialogue with providers and their intermediaries or associations across both sectors was becoming more regular. Although still discernible, the gap in the scale of involvement between sectors had narrowed markedly between the first (1992/93) and second round (1993/94) of plans (Wistow and Hardy 1994). As far as the formal planning process was concerned, analyses of the first two rounds of community care plans confirmed the existence of differential levels of involvement in this aspect of joint working, but also showed further change (Wistow *et al.* 1993; Hardy *et al.* 1994).

In view of the negative perceptions of the private sector in many local authorities in 1991, it is noteworthy that relationships with the voluntary sector sometimes developed from a not dissimilar baseline of suspicion and hostility. In particular, support for an expanded role in social care by voluntary organizations at the expense of public sector provision was seen to be a betrayal of the Fabian principles on which the post-war welfare state was founded. As late as the mid-1980s, a study of social policy coordination found that some local authorities were still hostile to organizations that they associated with middle-class charity, an attitude reflected in the position that 'if a job needs doing, the Council will do it and do it well' (Challis *et al.* 1988: 221).

The emphasis on the commonality of core values in the public and voluntary sectors is, therefore, itself of relatively recent origin in at least some localities. Arguably, it reflects actual changes in the nature of the voluntary sector as well as the changed perceptions which flow from practical experiences of intersectoral working. Separate trends towards professionalization and community activism have tended to distance it from its earlier images of 'do-gooding' and charity in the traditional sense of *noblesse oblige*. It could also be argued that, faced with the perceived threat of privatization and contracting out, the local authority preference for the voluntary over the private sector was to some extent regarded as a forced choice between the lesser of two 'evils'. This was because voluntary organizations were thought to have the apparent advantage of not obviously espousing the commercial values of the private sector. However, some earlier commentators tended to regard this position as naïve, considering the voluntary sector to be merely a 'stalking horse' for subsequent commercialization. For them, what was needed was undiluted commitment to publicly owned services (Lawrence 1983; Beresford and Croft 1984; see Kendall and Knapp 1996 for a discussion of the early 1980s ideological debate).

Theoretical insights into provider motivation and behaviour

Turning from historical developments to theory, four bodies of literature appear relevant to the study of motivations within the independent sector, viewed against the backdrop of recent developments in social care described in earlier chapters. These four bodies of literature are: economic approaches; the sociology of professions; theories relating to the distinctiveness of voluntary organizations; and sociological analyses of small, private sector businesses. The first three have developed theoretical 'ideal types', which in turn have been criticized both from within and outside their disciplinary bases, while the fourth stream of work has emerged more atheoretically. We briefly consider the key ingredients of each in turn.

Economic approaches

A core assumption of mainstream economic theory is that suppliers are oriented towards the maximization of personal welfare. *Homo economicus* is conceptualized as a *rational* maximizer costlessly mobilizing and acting upon all relevant information, and suffering no constraints of cognitive ability (cf. Simon 1957, 1961; Leibenstein 1980). The pursuit by *homo economicus* of narrow self-interest is typically realized as the generation of maximum profit.

Although this provides a benchmark for the development of testable theory, it is an abstract model. Indeed, if interpreted as a model of actual behaviour this formulation is open to a number of obvious objections recognized and much debated by economists and others (see Hodgson 1988, 1994). Many of these objections have particular relevance in social care markets.

At this stage, we simply note two of the most fundamental difficulties associated with unmodified mainstream economic theorizing. First, the profit-seeking assumption may be challenged on the basis that behaviour can be motivated by other, non-monetary self-interested goals, as well as by altruism and alternative forms of 'other regarding' behaviour. In particular, behaviour may be conditioned or guided by institutionally-determined norms, ideology, moral codes and other socialization processes – including professional training – whose significance tends to be underplayed in economists' search for parsimony.

Second, the concept of maximization under conditions of full information is challenged by the behaviourist school, which argues that, because of limits to cognitive capacities and computational abilities, the perfect rationality assumption of the core model is too heroic (Simon 1961; Cyert and March 1963; Williamson 1975, 1985). The notion of 'bounded rationality' has been developed by behaviourist and transactions cost economists to take these considerations into account. The comparative regulatory economic model we develop in Chapter 8 draws on this approach, also recognizing the implications of structural imperfections for the analysis of social care markets.

We do not take the view that these difficulties should lead us to jettison this model entirely for two fundamental reasons. First, it can be defended on methodological grounds. Deployed as a Weberian ideal type, its role as a logical extreme that patently distorts reality is

> to organize enquiries, giving focus to the questions they can ask and guidance as to where, in the unmanageable complexity of actual cases, to look for relevant causal connections.
>
> (Hughes et al. 1995: 135)

Second, it reflects the assumptions that apparently underpin government policy on social care markets, being a cornerstone of its rhetoric about the benefits of shifting to more 'market-like' styles of delivery. It also features strongly in the understanding and perceptions of those charged with managing social care markets, whether critics or advocates of market-led reform. As such its influences should not be underestimated.

The sociology of professionals

A central feature of the post-Keynesian welfare state has been the increasing number of professionals and semi-professionals employed within the public sector. It is for this reason that the second body of theory – the sociology of professions – is of potential relevance.

Since the provision of residential and nursing home care within the public sector is the province of various professional and semi-professional groups, it is relevant to ask whether the 'caring values' that these purport to typify are also present in the independent sector. As described in the Appendix, significant numbers of our sample had a background in the health and caring professions.

In theory, 'caring values' would orientate the members of these professions towards meeting the needs of elderly people above all other considerations, through the exercise of professional skills and expertise. This model is traditionally promoted by professionals on the grounds that clients' physical and mental vulnerabilities, together with their lack of expert or technical knowledge, constrain them from making choices on their own behalf. The exploitation of clients is prevented by an emphasis on respecting the trust which dependent individuals place upon professionals, and the reinforcement of such values through training and peer group regulation.

However, this approach is also vulnerable to criticism. The essentially functionalist 'perfectly socialized professional' model is a theoretical construct the relevance of which needs to be explored empirically. Alternative theoretical arguments which take a more sceptical view of professional motivations and orientations have also been developed. Conceptualizing professionals as groupings in society pursuing their own self-interest, Tilly and Tilly (1994: 289–90) characterize the professions as 'exceptional labour markets' in which strong monopolies have been purposefully created by a combination of rendering demand for labour inelastic, and enforcing restrictions on supply. Perkin has argued that professionals' claims to 'indispensability' in recent times have been driven by the desire to 'raise their status and through it their income, authority and psychic rewards (deference and respect)' (1989: 6). For Perkin, the rise of the welfare state was itself 'a practical expression of the professional ideal . . . based on trained expertise and selected by [internally judged] merit' (ibid.: 7). Focusing specifically on the health professions, Harrison and Pollit (1994: 2) refer to the strategy of 'occupational control' – securing advantageous employment conditions and other benefits for themselves – as one aspect of the reality of professional goals. These arguments about the motives of professionals as a group can also be expected to apply to the individuals who populate that profession. From these perspectives, professionals at least in part pursue their own advantage, in much the same way as public choice and 'new right' theorists describe other public servants.

Theories relating to the distinctiveness of voluntary organizations

A body of theory has been developed which explicitly alludes to what are seen as distinctive motivations, norms and values in the voluntary sector. In the American and other international literatures, it has been suggested that voluntary organizations are often formed and operate to meet differentiated or particularistic demands, and provide a vehicle for suppliers to pursue religious or ideological goals (see, in particular, James 1987). DiMaggio and Anheier (1990: 145) suggest that voluntary sector entrepreneurs may be value-rational rather than means-rational. That is, they suggest that the actions of those who found and control voluntary organizations may not be instrumental in the sense of choosing means to meet an end, but instead be 'determined by a conscious belief in the value for its own sake of some . . . form of behaviour, independently of its prospects of success' (Weber, cited by Hughes *et al.* 1995: 106). In this sense, they may be different from private sector organizations since, inasmuch as the latter are motivated by the goal of profit, they are by definition instrumentally rational: profit is their practical, organizational purpose.

Jeavons (1992) has suggested that voluntary organizations are distinctive from government and the private sector in this 'value expressive function' in which 'they have usually come into being and exist primarily to give expression to the social, philosophical, moral or religious values of their founders and supporters'. Similarly, for Paton, small and medium-sized voluntary organizations in particular are often 'value-based organisations founded on commitment (arising from devotion, compassion, enthusiasm, solidarity, defiance, etc) and working for a common or public benefit' (1991: 7). As with functional analyses of the role of professionals, these aggregate level arguments can be applied at the level of the individual managers or employees in these organizations. For example, both Mirvis (1992) and Onyx (1993) have argued that their survey data from America and Australia show that employees in the voluntary sector appear to be less cynical and gain more satisfaction than their counterparts in the government and private sectors. Finally, both government and the voluntary sector itself have described voluntary bodies as especially innovative, cost-effective and participative because of their assumed proximity to need, access to volunteers and flexible working practices.

However, the images of commitment and benevolence that emerge from these commentaries have been counterbalanced by accounts which project a less sympathetic view of voluntary bodies. The 'amateurism' identified with voluntary organizations at the end of Chapter 4 has been identified alongside particularism, paternalism and insufficiency as theoretical aspects of 'voluntary failure' (Salamon 1987). Theorists have also identified voluntary organizations with less benevolent goals and activities, including those of status enhancement and the pursuit of political power (James and Rose-Ackerman 1986). Furthermore, it should be recognized that there is little *systematic* evidence that voluntary agencies in general have all the comparative advantages over other organizational forms that rhetoric has attributed to them (Knapp 1995). In addition, inasmuch as voluntary organizations are operating in the same markets and institutional contexts as private and statutory sector agencies, they may be vulnerable to 'isomorphic' forces (DiMaggio and Powell 1983). This may be a 'good thing' if, for example, we accept the premise that the adoption of 'professional' interpretations of need are appropriate in contexts in which amateurism or a lack of appropriate training is deemed to be dangerous. However, such developments may also be damaging if they tend to undermine the distinctiveness of organizations that prompted support for them in the first place.

Sociological analyses of small, private sector businesses

Most private sector residential care providers, both in our sample and in the country as a whole, are recognizable as small businesses (see Appendix). There was therefore a prima facie case for considering the literature on the motivations of small businesses for additional perspectives. For example, Scase and Goffee's study found little evidence to support the stereotype of 'rational economic man' we described as the mainstream economic approach:

> although most [business people] regarded profitability as a primary goal, this is often conditioned by a number of non-economic factors. Among many small employers, for example, a personal obligation to customers and a desire to provide a good service not only determine price levels but also attitudes towards expansion.
>
> (1982: 161)

The same authors also argued that the reasons for the establishment and growth of small businesses were not the outcome of personal characteristics associated with the entrepreneurial stereotype such as drive, determination and ambition but 'a function of various forms of personal discontent and random occurrence' (Scase and Goffee 1982: 37–8). They concluded that the conventional view of entrepreneurial motivations gave 'insufficient attention to the highly variable non-monetary factors that are often central to the formation of business enterprises' (Scase and Goffee 1982: 37–8). Other sources have emphasized that the critical motivating factor explaining the formation of small businesses is the desire for independence. For example, the Wilson Committee reported that the 'main advantages of being a small firm are felt to be the independence and freedom offered' (Wilson Committee 1979: 55).

An earlier study had identified the relevance of the small business literature in the social care field. In his analysis of a survey of private sector residential homes conducted in the early 1980s, Judge (1984) drew attention to what he described as 'the false ideology of entrepreneurship' based on stereotypes of businessmen as 'highly successful ruthless profit-maximizers'. As evidence, he pointed to the premium that home owners tended to place on independence and control over their own business, together with the substantial amounts of personal commitment to their homes.

Summary

Our overview of these literatures offers a starting point from which we may begin to examine the motivations and behaviour of residential care providers. It enables us to identify a number of 'ideal types' with which to structure our examination of the data, while cautioning against taking these formulations at face value.

The overwhelming message of both the modified economic approach and the small business literature is that we might expect to find significant departures from rational profit maximization in the case of private sector providers in general (as argued by the former), and among small-scale homes in particular (as argued by the latter). Other orientations of the sort we have noted are anticipated to be relevant, particularly those consistent with the existence of value-rational behaviour, and reflecting the impact of professional influences. Providers with similar training and backgrounds might be expected to have similarities in motivations and behaviour, in whichever 'sector' their current organization is located.

The final twist to the analysis emerges from the qualifications we noted concerning the claims that 'other regarding' behaviour dominates both in voluntary organizations in general, and as a result of professionalization processes across sectors. While we have identified plausible arguments why these claims are likely to have some validity, we have also noted reasons to challenge their deterministic and functionalist character. Agencies and individuals may have been adept at promoting favourable images to structure perceptions of their operations, and it is clear that they have made a considerable impact on local authorities. However, our aim is not to take this rhetoric at face value, but to examine the extent to which it has some basis in reality.

Research questions and empirical methods

The Appendix describes both the methodology employed in studying residential care providers and the characteristics of the sample. In seeking to acquire information about providers' 'motivations for being in this business' we were addressing the following key questions:

- Are proprietors and managers of private homes primarily motivated by profit maximization?
- Do home owners and managers seek satisfactory incomes rather than maximum profit?
- Are voluntary sector managers motivated by their duty to the community to a greater extent than their counterparts in the private sector?
- Do small private sector proprietors and managers give particular weight to independence in comparison with other providers?
- Do professional values appear to be of relevance in the independent sector?
- Are home owners and managers *without* backgrounds in the caring professions profit maximizers?

In face-to-face interviews, providers were first asked to identify from eight given motives those which they judged to be important for them as individuals (rather than for the organization as a whole or some grouping within it). They were then asked to identify and rank the three most important motives. The listed motives were:

- income and profit maximizing
- a satisfactory level of personal income

- duty/responsibility to society as a whole
- duty/responsibility to a particular section of society
- to meet the needs of elderly people
- independence and autonomy
- professional accomplishment or creative achievement
- to develop or use skills and expertise.

Three points should be borne in mind in interpreting what follows. First, our questions were brief and simply expressed. Second, the relatively small sample means that we should be cautious about subcategories which account for a minority of providers.[1] Third, although our target interviewees were home owners (in the case of private sector homes), in practice it was sometimes the home's managers we met. On some occasions we interviewed both together. Conducting only one interview for each organization meant that we were unable to capture systematically any differences in motivation that might have existed *within* agencies. However, we did ask about potential divergences between personal motivations and the home or organization's aims and activities, and relatively few interviewees identified this as being the case (94 per cent thought their organization's aims reflected their own personal motivations).

These examinations of motivations rely upon the subjective valuation of providers themselves. We also adopted what economists refer to as a 'revealed preference' approach where providers' motivations and generic types are inferred from what they *do* rather than what they say. Ideally, this is achieved by comparing the behaviour expected from an *ideal type* provider in particular contexts with observed behaviour. In this vein we sought to examine providers' *behavioural processes* – with regard to, for example, price-setting, advertising strategies and resident selection criteria. We relied on both responses in our interviews and postal questionnaire data. We systematically examined the impact of environmental or 'exogenous' factors on providers' behaviour to explore the relationship between behaviour and market structure in terms of the prevalent level of competition, as well as input costs. We utilized the rational maximizer/perfect market as a benchmark ideal type. In particular, we wished to ascertain providers' 'market awareness' and the extent to which their behavioural processes appeared 'business-like' or 'commercial'. The fundamental premise was that rational maximizers would be both highly aware of their market environment, and commercial in their behaviour. Our aim was then to establish how far different providers approximated to this model.[2]

Empirical findings on providers' motivations

To what extent were providers' declared motives consistent with the bodies of theory described above? Table 6.1 shows the proportion of respondents by sector, indicating each of the motives important to them, while Table 6.2 shows those motives which were ranked first by respondents in each sector.

Table 6.1 Number of interviewees registering motive, by sector

| Motive | Current sector of ownership | | | | | |
	Private (N)	(%)	Voluntary or not-for-profit (N)	(%)	All sectors (N)	(%)
Income and profit maximizing	8	20	0	0	8	14
Satisfactory level of personal income	28	68	7	42	35	60
Duty/responsibility to society as a whole	10	24	5	29	15	26
Duty/responsibility to particular section of society	15	37	12	71	24	47
To meet the needs of elderly people	38	92	16	94	54	93
Independence and autonomy	29	71	8	47	37	64
Professional accomplishment and creative achievement	34	83	8	47	42	72
To develop or use skills and expertise	26	63	9	53	35	60

N = 58: 41 private, 17 voluntary or not-for-profit.

Motives

One of the most important findings was the relatively small proportion of providers who registered profit and income maximization as motives at all: only eight (14 per cent) across all sectors, of which only three rated this as their most important motive (5 per cent of the whole sample; 7 per cent of the private sector subsample). These responses provide prima facie evidence that the majority of providers do not have profit or income *maximization* as a goal, especially not as a primary goal. None of the providers outside the private sector admitted to this objective.

The findings also provide a preliminary answer to the income satisficing question. Most interviewees in the private sector (68 per cent) reported that the attainment of a *satisfactory* level of income was important, apparently offering some support for the 'watered down' version of *homo economicus* (as suggested by behaviourist theory). However, a handful of those in the private sector who ranked satisfactory income as important, without prompting, went on to qualify this observation. Their responses suggested that the generation of income was sometimes conceptualized as allowing the achievement of other goals, rather than as a primary goal or objective *per se*. It appeared that non-maximization of income was less to do with the informational or computational limitations emphasized by the behaviourists than with the

Table 6.2 Number of interviewees ranking each motive first, by sector

Motive	Sector					
	Private		Voluntary or not-for-profit		All sectors	
	(N)	(%)	(N)	(%)	(N)	(%)
Income and profit maximizing	3	7	0	0	3	5
Satisfactory level of personal income	3	7	1	7	4	7
Duty/responsibility to society as a whole	1	2	2	13	3	5
Duty/responsibility to particular section of society	2	5	4	27	6	11
To meet the needs of elderly people	14	34	5	33	19	34
Independence and autonomy	6	15	1	7	7	13
Professional accomplishment and creative achievement	9	22	1	7	10	18
To develop or use skills and expertise	3	7	1	7	4	7

N = 56: 41 private, 15 voluntary or not-for-profit.

importance of other goals. One interviewee remarked simply that 'income has got to come into it; if [we] weren't making money, [we] couldn't operate'. An almost identical unprompted remark came from a second interviewee, while another pointed out that it was the *combination* of factors that was important to them: '[While] income is important, just to have income without meeting the needs [of elderly people] wouldn't be satisfactory.' The message that securing satisfactory income was regarded as a subsidiary goal is reinforced by the figures in Table 6.2. This shows that only a very small proportion of providers who rated satisfactory income as important ranked it as their *most* important motive: of the twenty-eight private sector providers who said it was important, only three (7 per cent) ranked it higher than the other motives listed.

This finding begs the question why some providers did not identify income as important at all. After all, we might expect its generation to be a necessary condition for organizations' survival in the market place. One possible interpretation was that earnings were perceived as being too low to qualify meaningfully as even 'satisfactory'. One of the private sector respondents who did not admit to any income motive remarked: 'it definitely wasn't that . . . [if it was] I'd be doing something else'.

Monetary rewards are regarded as less important by providers in the voluntary and not-for-profit sectors (although we did not collect remuneration data, so we do not know if this would be reflected in a remuneration differential between sectors). None registered a profit or income maximizing motive and only two-fifths regarded satisfactory income as a motive, compared with over two-thirds in the private sector. There were differences between the sectors with respect to other motives. Positive responses to the motive of duty/responsibility to particular sections of society were concentrated markedly in the voluntary and not-for-profit sectors, as expected given the particularistic character of many voluntary sector services. In addition, while 40 per cent of providers in the latter sector rated duty and responsibility (to society as a whole, or to parts of society) above all other motives, only 7 per cent of private sector providers did so (Table 6.2).

If voluntary and not-for-profit organizations were 'other regarding', we might expect to see significantly higher proportions of these agencies oriented towards the meeting of needs of elderly people. In fact, our data show that the vast majority of providers across *all* independent sectors claim to rank this as an important priority (Table 6.1), and it was also the single most highly ranked priority across all sectors. While this can be explained on the grounds that 'other regarding' or altruistic behaviour is in fact to be found across all sectors, it could be explained differently: meeting the needs of elderly people could be fully consistent with the pursuit of self-interest, since *not* to meet client needs might result in a loss of custom and of revenue.

Small businesses and independence

While 'sector' was the most useful way of looking at providers when considering our initial three questions, alternative categorizations are implied as more relevant by the other key questions that we posed. Tables 6.1 and 6.2 confirm the importance of the remaining motives which the literature suggested were likely to be relevant – independence and autonomy, professional accomplishment and creative achievement, and the development or use of skills and expertise – but do not link them explicitly to factors which we might expect to be important *across*, rather than between, sectors. We can interpret the small business literature as suggesting that the motive of 'independence and autonomy' is likely to be more evident within those private sector homes regarded as effectively 'small businesses' rather than homes affiliated to 'corporate chains' with separate ownership and control. The apparent differential in the importance of this motive between the private and voluntary sectors may simply reflect the greater number of 'corporate' homes in our sample in the voluntary sector (reflecting the national pattern, as described in the Appendix).

Simple cross-tabulation of our data provided limited evidence in support of this thesis. While nearly twice as many single-home as multiple-home interviewees ranked independence first, this ranking still only accounted for 15 per cent of single-home providers. A slightly larger proportion of single-home interviewees also registered independence as important at all: 67 per cent as compared to 58 per cent of multiple-home interviewees.

Significance of background

Our final question emerged from the suggestion that professional socialization experiences were likely to be relevant in shaping motives. The existence of a professional caring background might tend to underplay self-interest and monetary goals, while stressing the importance of professional accomplishment and meeting clients' needs. We have already suggested that individuals working in voluntary organizations might be less interested in monetary rewards. The implication of this argument is that providers *without* either a caring *or* voluntary sector background would be more likely to emphasize income and profit-related goals.

Tables 6.3 and 6.4 show how motives were linked to provider background in our sample. To make our analysis more manageable, we have reduced the number of provider categories from that described in the Appendix by collapsing all those with a health and/or social care public sector professional background into a single category: 'public sector caring professionals'. The data suggest that provider background *is* important. Six of the eight providers in this subsample who indicated that profit or income maximizing was a motive had a non-care background. Caution must be exercised when generalizing because of the small numbers, but it is noteworthy that while half of the non-care and mixed partnerships acknowledged profit as important, only two interviewees with public sector backgrounds indicated that this was the case for them, and none of the six with voluntary sector backgrounds did so. The three providers who did rank profit as their primary motive had non-care or mixed backgrounds.

We are on safer ground statistically when considering the former public sector caring professionals who accounted for the majority of providers in the sample. 'Meeting the needs of elderly people' and 'professional accomplishment' were the most frequently cited motives. Their importance is reinforced by Table 6.4, which shows that these two motives accounted for two-thirds of the first-ranked motives of all providers with this background. It is noticeable that both in terms of the listing and the ranking of motives, 'professional accomplishment' tended to be associated with providers from caring professional or mixed backgrounds.

Independence and autonomy, as we have already noted, tend to be ranked highest in free-standing, single-home units in the private sector. How important was the previous experience of these providers? A small number of interviewees, unprompted, referred to a perceived *lack* of autonomy they had experienced in the public sector. One former nurse described how she 'was frustrated with the whole NHS set up', and several of those with a local authority background had seen the opportunity to operate independently in these sorts of terms. A housing trust manager who had formerly been an

Table 6.3 Percentage of homes registering motive, by background

Motive	Background category									
	PSCP (N)	(%)	VSB (N)	(%)	Non-care (N)	(%)	Mixed (N)	(%)	All type (N)	(%)
Income and profit maximizing	2	7	0	0	4	50	2	50	8	16
Satisfactory level of personal income	20	65	3	50	4	50	3	75	30	62
Duty/responsibility to society as a whole	5	16	3	50	4	50	1	25	13	27
Duty/responsibility to particular section of society	14	45	3	50	5	63	2	50	24	49
To meet the needs of elderly people	29	94	5	83	8	100	3	75	45	92
Independence and autonomy	22	71	2	33	5	63	3	75	32	65
Professional accomplishment and creative achievement	24	77	3	50	5	63	3	75	35	71
To develop or use skills and expertise	19	61	2	33	5	63	3	75	29	60

N = 49: 31 public sector caring professionals (PSCP), 6 voluntary sector background (VSB), 8 providers with non-care professional backgrounds (non-care), and 4 partnerships known to comprise a caring professional and a person with a non-care background (mixed).

Assistant Director of Social Services described how he had got 'fed up with being behind a desk . . . listening to claptrap while services were deteriorating'; a former Officer-in-charge of a Part III home suggested that levels of administration were becoming too onerous, and this had prompted him to set up a partnership with his wife. Another former Part III home manager, who had purchased the home he previously managed, referred to his experience of 'inertia and bureaucracy'. A caveat is due here because while these remarks suggest that independence and autonomy was important for these interviewees, the other motives were also of relevance.

Links between motivations and other variables

The above discussion suggests that profit maximization in the private sector is relatively rare, and that income satisficing goals are more common, although even these were often rated behind other objectives. Sector, size and background each have relevance in explaining provider motivation. However, we need to explore the *relative* importance of these factors. Multivariate statistical analyses (probit and logit regression) were therefore undertaken to

Table 6.4   First ranked motive, by background

Motive	PSCP (N)	(%)	VSB (N)	(%)	Non-care (N)	(%)	Mixed (N)	(%)	All types (N)	(%)
Income and profit maximizing	0	0	0	0	2	25	1	20	3	6
Satisfactory level of personal income	2	7	0	0	1	13	0	0	3	6
Duty/responsibility to society as a whole	0	0	2	40	0	0	0	0	2	4
Duty/responsibility to particular section of society	2	7	0	0	2	25	0	0	4	9
To meet the needs of elderly people	13	45	2	40	1	13	2	40	18	38
Independence and autonomy	3	10	1	20	1	13	1	20	6	13
Professional accomplishment and creative achievement	6	21	0	0	0	0	1	20	7	15
To develop or use skills and expertise	3	10	0	0	1	13	0	0	4	9

N = 47: 29 PSCP, 5 VSB, 8 non-care, 5 mixed. The note to Table 6.3 explains the abbreviations used.

assess simultaneously the relationships between home characteristics and expressed motivations. Alongside sector and background, we sought to assess the relevance of other provider and wider market characteristics.[3]

The overall message to emerge from these analyses was that caution should be exercised in adopting too deterministic a view about some of the results described thus far. While the expected relationships between each of the sector, size, background categories and motivations often emerged, their impact was frequently swamped when considered alongside each of these other categories, and when market characteristics were also considered. Indeed, the expected relationship between sector and profit maximization was not statistically significant. Size of homes (number of places) appeared to be a key factor, conceivably because larger homes tend to be more profitable and so perhaps tend to attract people oriented towards profit. Moreover, we found a significant positive relationship between these motives and multi-home organizations, and also the extent of competition. Taken together, this would suggest that in deciding what sorts of home 'fit the bill' as small businesses, size of home, as well as organizational status may be important. The latter finding also suggests the significance of market environment, an issue to which we now turn in our analyses of behavioural process.

Providers' behavioural processes

In looking at providers' behaviour we sought to gauge their proximity to the economic stereotype by examining three issues using multivariate regression analysis:[4] first, market awareness in terms of the extent of formal market analysis and market perceptions; and second, commercial orientation in terms of selectivity of clients, advertising and pricing.

Extent of market awareness

Only 23 per cent of the sample had undertaken formal market analysis, around half of these because it was a condition of obtaining a mortgage. The multivariate analysis revealed a number of significant relationships between home and market characteristics and providers' propensity to undertake such an analysis. First, voluntary sector homes and smaller homes were less likely to undertake formal market analysis, which is perhaps consistent with the view that voluntary homes tend to be less commercial by their very nature. It is also relevant that, as we note in the Appendix, voluntary homes were often longer-established than private homes, and market analysis might be less relevant simply because it is a relatively modern notion. The analysis also revealed a lower likelihood of small homes undertaking market analysis. This could be due to their general non-business orientation, but it could also be that larger homes simply have greater capacity to undertake such an exercise.

Two other interesting relationships were found. Other things being equal, homes which were started from scratch were more likely to undertake market analysis than those purchased when already operating. This has a straightforward explanation: established homes have a track record and the existence of this source of information reduces the need for formal market analysis. Second, providers in less competitive markets were more likely to undertake market analysis. This may be explained by the theory that the existence of a large number of providers in the local market is an indicator of a healthy level of demand.

Another way in which we considered market awareness was to analyse the extent to which providers considered themselves to be 'in a market', and the amount of information they had on other providers. 'Awareness' was high, with 72 per cent of providers responding positively. The analyses provided further evidence of voluntary homes' non-commercial orientation; they were less likely than private homes to see themselves in this way. It could also be symptomatic of their inherently particularistic focus in terms of clients: they might conceivably not regard themselves as being part of 'a market' because their specialist niche in terms of an identity-based clientele effectively affords them a monopoly (see also the discussion of selectivity below). Large rather than small homes, and homes that were part of a group rather than single-ownership, were more likely to see themselves as operating in a market place, other things being equal. This finding is consistent with the hypothesized non-commercial character of small businesses.

Around two-thirds (65 per cent) of all providers had some information on other providers operating in their (self-defined) local market, while 36 per cent claimed to have complete knowledge. Interestingly, conceiving provider size as measured by whether the organization was a single-home or part of a multiple-home chain, small businesses were *more* likely to have information about other providers. This may reflect a more intimate knowledge of local conditions, whether acquired for commercial purposes or not. The analysis also revealed a positive relationship between level of competition and likelihood of information about competitors, consistent with an expectation of greater value of such information for homes in vigorous competition.

Commercial orientation

Seventy-one per cent of homes advertised to the general public (that is, to prospective clients and their relatives). 'Proactive' methods used for advertising included press (used by 44 per cent) and local TV or radio (7 per cent). What might be referred to as 'non-active' formats were also deployed: 85 per cent used *Yellow Pages*, 21 per cent left pamphlets in GPs' and dentists' surgeries, and 19 per cent held open days. Forty-six per cent of providers also advertised to statutory authorities (as purchasers). 'Word of mouth' was said to be the most frequent method of attracting clients among those providers who had not advertised, and, indeed, was regarded as important by many who were advertising.

Proactive advertising is the more obviously 'commercial' behaviour, and the anticipated association with private sector operators was statistically significant, although there was no significant link to organizational size. Unsurprisingly, the propensity to advertise either proactively or through more passive methods was negatively related to home age. It appears plausible that older homes had less reason to advertise perhaps because of the existence of a track record or reputation accumulated over time. Also of interest was the strong positive relationship between the probability of advertising and the degree of competition, which is in keeping with the profit-maximizing model: theoretically, the value of advertising relative to its cost is positively related to the level of competition.

By far the most common method of discriminating between or targeting clients was their level of dependency. Sixty per cent of providers indicated that they had formal or informal admissions policies of this nature. Client selection on the basis of their membership of a professional, religious or ethnic group, or their geographical origins, was characteristic of only 15 per cent of providers. Even rarer were providers who chose between clients on the basis of how they were funded: just one in twenty adopted this approach.

Perhaps the most obvious behaviour to be suggested by theory arises from the particularism of voluntary organizations, and their origins and purpose in terms of catering for identity-based groups, linked to religious or professional affiliation, and ethnicity. While theory suggests that profit-maximizing firms might be neutral to these factors, the roots of voluntary organizations in these communities would suggest they might be more likely to select on the basis of such criteria. The data revealed that while some individual identity-based organizations made a point of emphasizing they were open 'to all' but, overall, voluntary organizations were indeed more likely to differentiate between clients on these grounds.

A relationship emerged which suggested that small homes were more likely to select clients on a geographical basis. This may reflect the deliberate targeting of local residents: perhaps another example of local 'nous' also manifested by higher levels of awareness about other local providers. Finally, voluntary sector homes had on average slightly more dependent clients than private sector homes, after accounting for a host of factors, in particular price differences. Again, this is consistent with a greater profit orientation in the private sector (see also Chapter 8).

We leave the detailed task of linking pricing strategies to home and market characteristics to Chapter 8. Here we simply summarize some overall findings. We asked providers to identify and rank in order of importance the factors they consider in setting prices (Table 6.5).

First-ranked factors were dominated by two criteria: operating costs (ranked first by 54 per cent of providers) and local authorities' preferred prices (ranked highest by 30 per cent). Other factors which emerged as important (ranked second or third by at least a quarter of providers) included repayment burdens, service characteristics, client characteristics and competitors' prices. Occupancy levels, home demand and area demand were mentioned by few

Table 6.5 Principal factors affecting pricing decisions: rankings

Factor	Ranked first (N)	(%)	Ranked second (N)	(%)	Ranked third (N)	(%)
Operating costs	29	53.7	6	15.4	3	11.1
Repayment burdens	1	1.9	7	17.9	2	7.4
Occupancy levels	2	3.7	2	5.1	5	18.5
Service characteristics	1	1.9	6	15.4	3	11.1
Client characteristics	3	5.6	7	17.9	3	11.1
LA preferred prices	16	29.6	3	7.7	3	11.1
Competitors' prices	0	0	5	12.8	4	14.8
Home demand	0	0	0	0	4	14.8
Area demand	0	0	1	2.6	0	0
Advice from associations	0	0	0	0	0	0
Future expectations	0	0	0	0	0	0
Other	2	3.7	2	5.1	0	0
Number of responses	54		39		27	

providers, while none suggested that advice from associations or future expectations made any impact on their pricing policy.[5] We would expect the profit-maximizing provider to take account of competitors' prices and local demand conditions. Using multivariate techniques we found that multiple-home organizations were less likely to incorporate these two factors in their price. This may be explained in part by noting that most chain organizations have prices set at head office, so that their prices do not always reflect local conditions, and large organizations tend to be market 'leaders' anyway. This also implies that there may be more profit-oriented homes than suggested by the small numbers in Table 6.5.

Only a third of the sample reported that local authority prices exceeded costs. When asked about the effects of local authority pricing, the most common responses were that the imposed prices decreased their profitability (50 per cent) or viability (30 per cent), while 29 per cent indicated that imposed prices had or would prompt them to diversify (see below). Only a small minority suggested that their selection of clients was affected by these prices, and just 12 per cent said that it already had, or would prompt them to leave the market.

Diversification and potential market exit

One of the prime concerns of the government has been to encourage independent sector residential care providers to diversify into other areas of social care. As we noted in earlier chapters, the twin purposes of this policy have been to buttress proprietors in a shrinking residential care market and to increase the volume of independent sector provision of non-residential services, where local authorities have largely maintained their historically dominant market share.

It is important to note that in asking residential home proprietors about diversification we were asking about firm plans, not just considerations. One-third said that they planned to diversify into domiciliary care, 38 per cent into day care and 28 per cent into respite care. Fewer than one in five were planning to operate new services in other areas, most often nursing care and sheltered housing. We also asked home owners about planned changes, if any, to residential provision: 61 per cent were planning no change, 32 per cent were planning some increase in the number of places, and only 7 per cent planned to reduce them.

In analysing such behaviour (albeit conjectured or expected behaviour, rather than observed behaviour), we examined the likelihood of diversification into domiciliary, day and respite care in terms of home and market characteristics. We also employed two 'interaction' variables: time in business for those homes which were *purchased*, and time in business for homes which were *inherited*. Three key findings emerged from these analyses:

- Homes *purchased recently* were less likely to plan to diversify than homes acquired in other ways or purchased less recently. One explanation for this is that such homes were likely to have a reasonably healthy current demand for places – otherwise there would have been little incentive – and so *less* of an imperative to diversify in a given market context because, by definition, there exists adequate demand for residential care.

- Homes located in markets characterized by *competition* were *more* likely to intend to diversify. A possible explanation is that, since homes in competitive environments are less sure of relying on sustained demand for residential care services, diversification is relatively more attractive.

- Plans to diversify in *domiciliary care* (but not day or respite care) tended to be associated either with *small* or *large* homes. This may be linked to a greater *imperative* to diversify for small homes due to less favourable cost conditions in residential care (lack of access to scale economies), and a greater *ability* to diversify in the case of large homes (in terms of the capacity to cover the fixed costs of diversification).

Conclusion

The principal aim in this chapter has been to explore provider motivations systematically and, in so doing, to reflect upon the assumptions about motivations which appear to permeate existing thinking by local authorities, particularly about the profit-seeking motives of private sector providers and the non-financial goals of voluntary bodies. At one level, our task has been to explore this proposition empirically. But it is also more general. We would argue that if commissioners are to be in a position to manage the market, they must understand and, as far as possible, be able to predict the likely behavioural responses of both current and potential new providers to changes in commissioning arrangements and regulation. An essential precondition for this is an understanding of the motivations, values and beliefs of providers. But motivations are not directly observable, and so a means of linking motivations with more readily discovered characteristics – such as sector, home size and organization – would greatly facilitate the commissioners' task. This chapter has provided some statistical description of these linkages.

Human behaviour is of course governed by a complex mixture of motivating forces which interact with an array of constraints and regulations, making the task of *systematic* prediction of behaviour from first principles highly exacting. In order to reduce this problem to a manageable size we constructed a number of *ideal types* drawn from economic theory, the sociology of professions, theories relating to the distinctiveness of voluntary organizations, and sociological analyses of small businesses. Our aim was to see if the providers in our sample exhibited a propensity to mirror any of these ideal types. We sought to ascertain such motivations not only by asking providers directly, but also by inference from an analysis of behaviour.

The first approach has some obvious limitations in being vulnerable to interviewees' misrepresenting their true motivations. Falsification may be deliberate, and may conceivably reflect 'socialization' effects. For example, providers may regard profit-seeking as in some sense inconsistent with the professional or caring norms with which many identify and to which many purport to adhere. They may, therefore, be tempted to give the response they think they 'should', rather than the one which reveals their true motives. The second approach is less susceptible to this problem, but requires us to make untested assumptions about the linkages between behavioural process and motivation. This may generate problems of *context specificity*: that is, because behaviour is sensitive to environmental and market conditions, we may either misconstrue relationships or constrain ourselves in generalizing to other contexts. Strictly speaking, this is a difficult problem to preclude completely, although it can be partially arrested by collecting information to control for the prevailing context. None the less it is an important caveat which advises caution when interpreting the data.

The interviews provided direct observations about motivation which we interpreted with respect to our ideal types. Because stake-holders' assumptive worlds were themselves relatively crude and unsophisticated, our questions were themselves quite simple, not needing to go very far to challenge stake-holders' assumptions. The evidence from our provider interviews on motivations, taken together with the evidence on purchasers' perceptions of provider motivations (Chapter 4), reveal some significant gaps in understanding between purchasers and providers. A number of the latter – especially small private and voluntary homes – appear to be markedly non-commercial in their expressed motivations. Some owners even described themselves as 'not business-like' or 'not really in a business', and professional goals which were related to user welfare, as well as norms of duty and responsibility, all appeared to be highly relevant. At best, recognition of these qualities appeared often to be understated in the crude conceptual maps developed by purchasers (and outlined in Chapter 4).

The data revealed wide variation in provider behaviour, particularly when interpreted with respect to market awareness and commerical orientation. A minority of organizations did appear highly aware and orientated in a fashion that is consistent with the profit-maximizing ideal type. But most organizations displayed rather crude behavioural processes. In this respect, the profit-maximizing model was found wanting, and by implication the relevance of our other ideal types was suggested. It is difficult and often misleading to interpret specific behaviours as indicating that providers fall into particular ideal type categorizations. None the less, this relatively crude behaviour by some providers – particularly the statement that they took little account of demand factors in pricing – strongly discounts the profit-maximizing ideal type in these cases. While it is easy to reject ideal types according to specific behaviour, it is more difficult to go further and say which of our other ideal types, if any, is more appropriate. But the rejection of the profit-maximizing model in some cases is important because much policy rhetoric and associated guidance is based on this. Allowing different behavioural responses in markets characterized by imperfections will often mean quite different policy and regulation (see Chapter 8).

We also found that the homes with the most noticeable market awareness and commercial orientation (along our range of dimensions) tended to be from the private sector, relatively large, part of a multi-home organization, of intermediate age, and purchased rather than inherited. One of the clearest findings, however, was the enormously wide range of provider behaviour related to the considerable variety of home characteristics. We found that for almost all facets of behaviour considered there was a significant relationship between the likelihood of such behaviour being commercially orientated and the extent of local competition.

In order to shape and manage the developing market sensitively, local authorities need to develop a richer understanding not only of the relationships between homes and market characteristics, but also of the diverse patterns of motivations and behaviours which we have identified. They need at least to acknowledge the complexity of this market and the dangers of proceeding on the basis of what we have shown to be ill-informed stereotypes of providers.

Notes

1 In particular, discussion of motives outside the private sector, and of those providers without a public sector background (see below) should be treated as providing indicative evidence at best.

2 In adopting this revealed preference methodology, a problem exists in determining what idealized behaviour would be in 'real' social care markets. In particular, the extent to which idealized behaviour is 'business-like' or commercial in orientation is context-specific. That is, the behaviour of any provider, including those to whom this model applies, will be contingent upon many factors, most obviously the prevailing demand and supply conditions. Under certain conditions, it is conceivable that strategies usually regarded as business-like, or commercial in character — such as undertaking more advertising rather than less, or purposefully selecting clients according to their dependency characteristics — are actually *not* consistent with profit maximization. For example, strictly speaking, a profit-maximizing firm will advertise to the point that the marginal revenue from so doing equals the marginal cost. But this marginal revenue will itself depend on a number of contextual factors, including, among other things, the intensity of competitors' advertising. In some circumstances, the optimal strategy from such a provider's point of view may actually be not to advertise, or to advertise *less* than other providers.

3 Details of these analyses are available from Julien Forder at the PSSRU.

4 All the findings we report with regard to categories of provider were statistically significant at the 5 per cent level. In our limited dependent variable analysis of the behaviour data from the interview schedule we drew upon a core of home characteristics variables. These variables fall broadly into two types: categorical and continuous. The first set of variables related to the sector of each home; whether they were run as a single home, or part of an organization or chain with two or more homes; and whether they were inherited, started from scratch or purchased as a going

concern (see Appendix for details). Also included in this set is a categorical variable relating to whether the principal purchasing authority has a fixed or flexible pricing regime. The second set of variables includes: the size of home (the number of places) and its time in business (in years) (see Appendix). The market characteristics variables, described in the text, are also continuous. We drew on data from two sources. First, we created indicators on the extent of competition using data on average local authority occupancy rates or number of places per head of population at retirement age or above from Department of Health RA statistics. Second, we used an index of property prices derived from OPCS data as a proxy for input costs. Further details of the regressions are available from the authors on request.

5 We did not explicitly ask about DSS rates in all our interviews, but this was undoubtedly also a major factor for many homes.

Part II
Is the market working?

7

Is the market working?
Policy perspectives

Introduction

The satisfactory working of the new social care market is fundamental to the overall success of the government's community care reforms. Whether or not the market 'works' will profoundly affect the nature, range and quality of services provided to users and their carers. From the perspectives of these stake-holders, the crucial question is whether the new arrangements deliver a better match between needs and resources within a framework of eligibility criteria which at least does not significantly reduce opportunities for service access. At the same time, expectations and concerns about the market vary between other parties, especially between central government, local authorities and providers in the independent sectors. Each has a stake in its operation, although views will inevitably differ about the ultimate shape of the market and what constitutes success. Inevitably, therefore, the evaluation of the mixed economy must be a pluralistic one which takes account of the differing expectations, criteria and timescales of a wide range of stake-holders.

In addition to this range of perspectives on the relative success or failure of the market, it is important to note that there are at least two approaches to such an evaluation and that they produce different but potentially overlapping definitions of success and failure. The first approach focuses on the criteria by which the outcomes of social care markets should be judged in terms of the service patterns and opportunities for users that the market produces. The second is concerned with the conditions necessary to create and sustain a market structure which, in the long run, is capable of delivering outcomes consistent with those criteria. We call the first the policy-related criteria, and the second the market economics criteria.

Thus, in this and the next chapter, we analyse our fieldwork data in the light of these different but overlapping sets of criteria. Here we examine our data from the perspective of what we may term the *social policy goals* which the market is expected to serve and promote. In the following chapter we review them in the light of the *market failure* framework. We must emphasize, however, the incomplete and imperfect nature of the information on which we are drawing here. Two limitations are particularly significant. First, at this early stage of policy implementation and associated data collection it would be inappropriate to draw any firm conclusions about success or failure against *any* criteria. Second, this stage of data collection was designed to capture shifts in attitudes, motivations and preparations for implementing the community care changes rather than to evaluate their outcomes. None the less, our data do enable us to report on the extent to which authorities were planning for different outcomes and also the kinds of outcomes they anticipated would emerge in the short and longer term. In addition, they allow us to speculate about the potential consequences of different approaches to shaping the market. Finally and most importantly, they enable us to ground a theoretical framework in the particular context of social care and thus to structure more targeted data collections in the focused studies which form subsequent stages in our research programme.

There are a number of levels at which the success or failure of market outcomes may be assessed. At the most general level, we may distinguish between its political, social and economic goals.

Political goals

The political goals of the community care reforms include the suitability or acceptability of the market as an allocation mechanism. Is it acceptable to key stake-holders, particularly the electorate? Too many business failures, displaced service users and transparently unmet needs might not be consistent with the Government's political goals for social care markets. On the other hand, well-managed closures of some independent residential and nursing homes might, nationally if not locally, be considered a political achievement, as well as being a significant success by the criteria of social goals. At another level of analysis, however, these and similar market-based reforms may be examined in terms of their appropriateness as alternative forms of governance. We refer to such an analysis in the final chapter.

Social goals

Within the context of the current changes, social goals concern the benefits of markets in terms of the genuine (and informed) choices which they offer purchasers, users and carers; the quality of life which they promote; and the innovations in service type and organization which they encourage. In a much broader context, other social criteria would include equity and a targeting of resources which is generally considered both fair and effective. Perhaps most fundamentally, however, they concern the extent to which they increase, limit or even decrease social cohesion. However, such a meta-analysis of the community care changes falls outside the focus of the present study.

Economic goals

The economic goals of markets would be expressed in terms of different interpretations or facets of efficiency (including targeting, and therefore also equity). Economists emphasize that efficiency should be seen as a broad concept which includes choice and innovation, good targeting and promotion of quality of life. This emphasizes that the social and economic goals are not independent.

Within this general framework, we may identify more specific groups of criteria derived from the Government's policy objectives in the field of community care. *Caring for People* expressed these objectives in various ways.

First, and in the most general terms, it defined community care as 'providing the services and support which people . . . need to be able to live as independently as possible in their own homes, or in "homely" settings in the community' (Secretaries of State 1989: para. 1.1). Elsewhere, it stated that 'promoting choice and independence underlies all the Government's proposals' (Secretaries of State 1989: para. 1.8). These core aims were reflected in 'six key objectives for service delivery', among which was included 'the development of a flourishing independent sector alongside good quality public services' (Secretaries of State 1989: para. 1.11). All these objectives provide, therefore, an over-arching set of criteria against which to assess the market's contributions to meeting the objectives of community care policy.

Second, however, the White Paper also specified a number of goals which were to be served directly by the stimulation of providers in the independent sector. These comprised: a wider range of choice for users and carers; more flexible and innovatory ways of meeting individual needs; and better value for money resulting from competition between providers (Secretaries of State 1989: para. 3.43). Thus, the promotion of choice, innovation and cost-effectiveness constitutes a further set of criteria for assessing the operation of the market.

Lastly, whether or not the market 'works' is a question which can be asked at the apparently more mundane – but ultimately critical – level of organizational maintenance. As preparations for implementation advanced, Department of Health guidance was designed to ensure a 'smooth transition' from the social security funding arrangements. In particular, it sought to ensure that the resources transferred would be used in ways that minimized disruption to independent sector providers, to hospital throughput and to the continuity of care for existing residents in residential and nursing homes. Thus, another approach to judging the success of the market in the medium to short term revolves around the degree of turbulence surrounding its introduction and the effectiveness with which that change process is managed.

The smooth transition criterion focuses attention on the more immediate consequences of introducing the market, including those associated with the management of the change process itself. The criteria linked to choice, cost–effectiveness and innovation concern the extent to which the operation of the market promotes what may be considered intermediate outcomes associated with process and systems characteristics. By contrast, the independent living criteria relate to (some) final outcomes for users and carers.

These sets of criteria are not necessarily mutually consistent or mutually reinforcing, at least in the short term. In particular, the smooth transition objective is potentially inconsistent with what may be regarded as the ultimate goal of community care policy, that of promoting independent living. At least during 1993/94, local authorities were required to regard the previous year's pattern of social security expenditure as 'an implied commitment' (Department of Health 1992a). In other words, they were to purchase broadly the same volume of residential and nursing home provision as had been supported through the social security system in the previous year. This guidance reflected two core objectives for the Department of Health in its management of the implementation process which, in turn, were closely associated with political imperatives surrounding the introduction of the reforms. The first was to avoid destabilizing the supply side of the new community care market. Such disruption would threaten both the continuity of care received by existing residents and also the business prospects of residential and nursing home proprietors, many of whom were considered to be natural government supporters. Its second objective was to avoid destabilizing the NHS market, an area of high political vulnerability for Ministers. The Department of Health was thus especially concerned that local authorities should not reduce the level of nursing home placements for patients discharged from hospital or otherwise slow down throughput in hospitals. Any action which led to blocked beds threatened to undermine the capacity of hospitals to meet waiting list or other activity targets and, thereby, call into question the success of the NHS reforms.

A further potential implementation difficulty was that the greater the success of care managers in diverting users from inappropriate institutional placements, the greater the risk that they would compromise the objective of minimizing disruption to existing patterns of supply. At the same time, however, a strategy of ensuring 'minimal turbulence in the market' could be expected to restrict the exercise of choice since the policy's underlying assumption was that larger numbers of users and their carers would opt for packages of support in their own homes following the removal of the 'perverse incentive' provided by the former social security arrangements.

In what follows, we summarize the evidence from our fieldwork which casts light on whether the market will 'work' in respect of any of the three policy perspectives identified above.

Smooth transition

The issue of 'smooth transition' has two aspects: the extent to which the overall reforms were bedding down without undue turbulence or disruption; and the arrangements for managing what, in most authorities, was expected to be a significant reduction in the scale of residential and/or nursing home services. We found no evidence of major problems in the introduction of the basic community care changes, at least from the perspective of local authorities. In terms of the two most fundamental implementation requirements, assessments were being made and care arranged in response to them. Nor were any *major* supply-side disruptions reported. This view was broadly endorsed by the small number of interviews carried out with providers in the private sector. Examples were cited of homes closing or being on the verge of closure. Wholesale collapses were not evident, however, and we have no information about how the volume of such difficulties compared with those experienced before April 1993. Similarly, we were not made aware of any significant difficulties about hospital discharge arrangements. Our interview schedule was not designed to focus closely on immediate post-implementation issues, but the overall impression we gained was of minimal turbulence and no significant discontinuities to services.

Many authorities did, however, report differences in demand and placement patterns from those they had anticipated. These most commonly comprised higher numbers of assessments and/or lower numbers of placements in residential/nursing homes. Thus, in one of the first interviews we conducted in early May 1993 (in a London borough), the Director noted that:

> the [market] that we anticipated bore absolutely no relation to the demand since 1 April which is a bit of a shock to everybody really . . . We haven't made a nursing home placement since 1 April . . . [and] we have been able to create some quite interesting packages for people to remain in their own homes.

This pattern was maintained: in late July, the Director of a shire county reported that 'the demand that we have been led to anticipate based on a steady state . . . has just not materialized', although he went on to note that the demand for respite care for people with physical disabilities had 'shot through the roof'. Similarly, our final interview in August (which had been rearranged from an earlier date) produced the same surprised reaction, this time in a metropolitan district:

> We are stumped by what we have experienced so far. I had a very high anxiety level about what might happen in the first few weeks of community care . . . but four months on our admissions are 50 per cent less than we anticipated [and] the admissions are primarily into the nursing home sector, not residential care, by an enormous margin.

However, surprise was accompanied by caution about the future. First, authorities were conscious that levels of demand had been distorted by unusually large numbers of admissions to independent sector homes in the period before 31 March, motivated by a desire to secure protected rights status for residents; indeed, some authorities suggested that unusually large numbers of patients had been 'cleared' from hospital beds during March in order to beat the 1 April deadline. In addition, home owners, uncertain about local authority purchasing intentions and behaviours, were reported to have been active in seeking to fill unoccupied beds over this period. In one locality, for example, a home had advertised free accommodation for a limited period for new residents during the month of March.

A second area of uncertainty was that authorities were commonly waiting for the winter months in the expectation that demand would increase: in the meantime, many recognized that independent sector residential and/or nursing home providers were under pressure. One Director emphasized that:

> the biggest single issue that I think we are addressing today [June 1993] is that the market is under strain because it is overprovided and that is why we are getting this bitter in-fighting now [within the private sector]. It is survival.

In other localities, the lower-than-expected number of placements was affecting attitudes towards the local authority with the result that the independent sector was described as 'feeling very nervous, very suspicious and pretty ill at ease with us'.

The vast majority of authorities expected an over-supply of residential and/or nursing home places during the year. Only three authorities – all in London – anticipated that there would be insufficient supply, while a further two reported that supply and demand would be in balance. However, some of the authorities anticipating surplus capacity overall also identified local shortages owing to the uneven geographical distribution of existing provision. Even so, seventeen authorities expected there to be business failures, compared with only one which did not and eight in which the situation was not clear. The anticipated scale of such failures varied. A county authority did not expect 'a major destabilising of the market . . . no wholesale closures'. Other authorities had calculated expected 'failure rates' which ranged from 15 to 50 per cent. Others were unable to quantify the size of the problem they would face: 'I can't give you the scale – all I can say is it is going to be a reality and providers are now talking to us about really being very concerned'. In the case of many counties, predicting the potential level of business failures was made more difficult by uncertainty about the purchasing behaviour of neighbouring and other authorities from whom the private sector had traditionally 'imported' residents. As one of those interviewed noted:

> I don't yet know whether there is over-provision. There still might not be an over-provision because, after all . . . London boroughs are not replete with independent provision.

Such authorities were also concerned about the impact on the local economy of business failures, with several drawing the following analogy:

> If there is a substantial collapse of the market in [this authority] . . . it is like a pit village really . . . there are no other real areas of employment.

The lower-than-anticipated number of placements had reinforced such concerns, leaving some interviewees to predict a more rapid process of failure and retrenchment than they had originally expected. Against this background, we sought to establish what kinds of contingency arrangements, if any, authorities were putting in place. Nine authorities had arrangements to intervene to pre-empt failure; thirteen had arrangements to rescue after failure; and twelve proposed to promote diversification to prevent failure. In two cases, the interview did not provide any information relating to this issue and, in a further two, the authority did not have any contingency arrangements for responding to home failures. (In one case because there was 'no effective local supply'; in the other, the contingency plan was to have enough community care in place when the market failed.)

Early intervention

The ability to intervene in advance depends upon authorities having information systems which provide early warning of potential difficulties. One interviewee described establishing 'an embryonic computer mapping system' for this purpose. Another referred to the need for 'smart monitoring' through a process of contract monitoring which would ensure that providers could not 'get into a position where they are vulnerable before we know what is going on'. Some of the indicators they would look for were the absence of staff training and high levels of staff turnover. The latter, in particular, was seen as 'an early warning sign about a company that is not really happy and hasn't really got its act together'. However, few authorities described such early warning arrangements.

Interventions designed to forestall failure were of two broad types: financial and managerial support. One authority reported that it had entered into block contracts in order to prevent market destabilization, and three others indicated a preparedness to use block contracts in future to prevent the failure of homes they wished to keep open because of their quality of care, their location or size. Another authority referred to the possibility of 'guiding' users to homes of proven quality as a strategy for underpinning their financial viability. The second broad category of assistance included the role of purchasing officers in one authority providing 'honest feedback' to individual homes about why they were not being chosen by users. Other authorities were prepared to offer advice on costs and charging issues, in at least one case drawing on previous experience of such work with the voluntary sector.

Post-failure rescue

The dividing line between assisting homes in advance of or following failure is not entirely clear. It is most obvious at the point when a home closes, and a number of authorities referred to their responsibilities for relocating residents in such cases. Their general attitude was that such action would not prove difficult against a background of over-capacity: 'the private sector can consume its own smoke' was a view which reflected their general position. One authority described an explicit process of contract letting which would avoid localized monopolies and thus ensure that an alternative provider would be available to meet the consequences of failure. Two authorities also referred to contract provisions which would specify continuity of care in the event of closure and other ways in which residents should be treated in such an event.

At least three authorities were also geared up to manage homes in the period between failure and closure. One said it had staff earmarked for this purpose and had already used them twice. Another described how it had established 'an escape line' for local banks and had made it clear to them that they would be prepared to 'put in management while you close or dispose of [homes]'. Its model was that of the hotel industry where individual businesses changed hands without residents being aware of their commercial failure. Finally, a number of authorities justified their decision to retain some in-house provision partly on the grounds that it was needed to meet the consequences of home closures.

Diversification

Although authorities were generally interested in diversification as a strategy for extending the range of services, a smaller number explicitly described it as a strategy for preventing business failure. One Director described himself as 'peddling the diversification message for all its worth'. He continued:

> If you are a private home proprietor who is telling me that you are going bust, I'll say to you, 'Look, I'm going to be letting contracts for home care. Why don't you use some of your care assistants for home care? Why don't you use your kitchens for meals on wheels?' . . . I would hope they would be wise enough to change their business plans.

Another interviewee said that he had talked to home owners about diversification and that he had quoted the Minister of Health to underline that he was 'responsible for community care, not community care providers'. Two other authorities also stressed their responsibility to secure diversification on the supply side to prevent market failure: it was said that 'the medium-term viability will be very poor if we only continue to provide what we purchase now. There are not enough resources to maintain the residential market.'

Which homes should succeed or fail?

Many Directors were becoming increasingly aware that the market might operate in ways which meant preferred providers would go out of business. References were commonly made to the 'big boys' succeeding because of their lower unit costs and to smaller homes failing. Such concerns were founded on a belief that the quality of the small homes was higher, and that competition would be reduced in the longer run.

Such concerns were leading some authorities to think more systematically about their market shaping role. For example, one spoke of 'cultivating suppliers to encourage high-quality care'. We return to issues relating to market shaping and competition policy below. However, it is worth noting that parallel concerns were expressed by private sector proprietors: one, for example, argued that 'smaller more personal, intimate, caring establishments such as this one are going to have to give way to the big independent market leaders'.

Similar views were expressed in our study of independent sector providers (see Chapter 6). However, it is worth recording here that the immediate post-implementation concerns of both local authorities and small home owners were borne out by Laing & Buisson's findings that in the year to mid-1993 the average size of new nursing homes increased from thirty-eight to forty beds (compared with twenty-eight beds in 1988–89). Moreover, and within that total, homes opened by major providers that year averaged sixty-three beds, about double the average size for the existing stock of nursing homes. A small rise in the average size of residential homes was also reported (Laing & Buisson 1994: 31). Alongside this continuing increase in home size, the same source also reported further small increases in the larger providers' share of the market: by October 1993, providers with three or more homes owned 22.5 per cent of nursing beds but only 4.5 per cent of residential beds (Laing & Buisson 1994: 34). A final indicator which supports the concerns of those interviewed is that the home closures in the year to August 1993 were concentrated among the smaller homes (Laing & Buisson 1994: 31). If, however, statistical data support these views about the emerging shape of the supply in the independent sector, fears of a major wave of home closures were not borne out. Indeed, Laing & Buisson report that the number of closures had remained constant for four years in the case of nursing homes and for two years in the rate of residential home closures (although there had been an acceleration in closure rates for residential homes over the previous four years). Moreover, this pattern of relative stability in the overall volume of provision in the independent sector was maintained over the following year (1993/94) with a small reduction in overall residential placements being concentrated in the local authority sector. There was no significant increase in the number of nursing home de-registrations and closures of residential homes were significantly lower. In addition, the trend to larger-scale nursing homes continued (average size up from forty to forty-six places), although the average size of residential homes fell slightly (Laing & Buisson 1995).

Some localized disruptions to the continuity of supply would, of course, be consistent with the overall picture. None the less, our findings that a smooth transition to the new market arrangements was being negotiated during the months after April 1993 was borne out by a wide range of governmental and independent sources during the first year of the reforms (see Wistow 1995a). As the Audit Commission concluded in late 1993:

> So far implementation has proceeded smoothly – a major achievement for all concerned given the many forecasts of disaster made before 1 April and the heavy agenda of change ... Most authorities appear to have made a sound if somewhat cautious start.
>
> (Audit Commission 1993: para. 2)

Such initial judgements are not necessarily indicative of the longer-term robustness of the reforms as, for example, the Department of Health's (1994a) own initial monitoring report made clear. However, there was a broad consensus consistent with our findings that the basic 'smooth transition' criterion of successful implementation was met during the immediate implementation period and thereafter. Such findings were widely seen to mean that the basic organizational building blocks of the reforms were successfully being put into place during their first year. However, they were not to be confused with improvements in the range or quality of services available to users and carers, a dimension of the reforms to which we now turn.

Choice, cost-effectiveness and innovation

The creation of social care markets was primarily advocated in the White Paper on the grounds that it would promote gains in choice, cost-effectiveness and innovation. These criteria of success are essentially features of service systems believed to improve outcomes for users. As such, they are best regarded as intermediate rather than final outcomes and, thus, as proxy rather than real indicators of the successful operation of social care markets in terms of their social goals. In addition, both the cost-effectiveness and innovation criteria are associated with key economic goals in terms of the belief that innovatory forms of service delivery will enable more value to be squeezed out of fixed resource levels at a time when upward pressures of demand are increasingly meeting downward pressures on taxation and public expenditure.

Perhaps not surprisingly, there was a range of views about the extent to which the social care market was achieving, or would achieve, improvements in choice, cost-effectiveness and innovation. Most Directors (sixteen of the twenty-five) identified improvements in choice compared with six who did not; and fifteen Directors identified improvements in cost-effectiveness while three did not. However, only seven reported improvements in innovation. In each case, a small number identified both positive and negative features of developments in the market along each dimension; these figures therefore contain an element of double-counting.

Choice

The concept of choice – and its extension – is fundamental to the advocacy of market-based reforms in the public sector, which is seen traditionally to have been inflexible and unresponsive to the needs and demands of consumers. A small number of those interviewed were critical of, or pessimistic about, the impact of the community care reforms on choice: one argued that the situation was one of

> Hobson's choice for many because, although formally you go through the [assessment] process, is there any possibility that they would be getting anything different? For lots of people the answer is no . . . Certainly, when it comes to purchasing domiciliary care, there isn't any choice.

Another suggested that choice was:

> Fine for those people who can make it and provided they've got the tools to make it. But frankly I don't see very many people being able to make the choice or having the tools to make the choice.

Whether the market would respond in specialist areas like services for people who were severely disabled was another perceived limitation on the ability to exercise choice. However, the great majority of responses were either broadly positive or combined both positive and negative elements. In the first group were those who compared users' capacities to exercise choice now with the position before April 1993. Factors identified included 'genuinely independent assessment', especially when compared with the situation in which NHS employees were perceived to have a direct interest in placement decisions as owners of, or part-time employees in, private homes. Changes in the practices of social services staff were also identified:

> Pre-April 1st our staff were motivated not to enable people to go into the private sector . . . There is a whole area of choice which has become available to service users and we are facilitating that.

A number of interviewees identified the role of the new systems in helping to enable users and carers to make *informed* choices. Assessment processes, the development of professional practice and the statutory directive on choice were, therefore, clearly seen as positive enhancements to the exercise of choice.

Others felt that the new situation was less clear-cut. For example, one pointed out that the new arrangements both restricted 'millions of choices by stopping them going into residential care' while, at the same time, extending choice to those who had previously not had any opportunity to access packages of domiciliary care which would enable them to remain in their own homes. Elsewhere, the objective of ensuring a steady state was seen to be a constraint on the exercise of choice, although some authorities had earmarked small percentages of the STG to fund innovatory packages of care. Again, however, the implications for choice were not unambiguous. In an authority which intended to achieve a 5 per cent switch from residential to other forms of care, it was said to be paradoxical that a failure to achieve steady state could mean 'it was difficult to respond to people's choices' for residential or nursing care if local homes closed. Equally, the greater the number of Part III homes which became resource centres for day, domiciliary and respite care, the smaller the number of people who would be able to exercise a choice in favour of public sector residential care. Private sector providers were also concerned about the consequences of home closures for the exercise of choice. The widely anticipated concentration of closures on smaller homes was perceived to mean that:

> The element of choice is going out of the window . . . Residents will have a choice but they will have the choice of moving to one 50 or 60 bedded nursing home or another 50 or 60 bedded nursing home. Purpose-built places really haven't been designed to offer the warmth and welcoming of the small independent living environment.

Finally, interviewees in several large rural counties suggested that 'choice depended on where you live' because of the geographically uneven distribution of residential services in the independent sector. In that context, 'steady state' implied the reverse of choice since it meant:

> managing the users . . . rather than managing the market. I don't think it is right to be managing the users to keep the market in a stable state.

In addition to geographical limitations on the ability to exercise choice, variations by user group were also identified. Some authorities, for example, contrasted the need to 'start from scratch' with drugs and alcohol services with the 'strong choice' available to the very elderly. There were also reservations about the set of choices generally available to people from ethnic minority backgrounds. In one ethnically mixed locality, the position in drugs and alcohol services was contrasted unfavourably with services for elderly people where choice had been enhanced by the entry into the market of home proprietors from culturally diverse backgrounds.

Although actual or potential limitations to the exercise of choice were frequently identified, perhaps the most striking finding from our interviews was the extent to which the term was employed. We have not systematically reanalysed our 1991 interviews, but it was clear that unprompted references to the concept of choice were considerably fewer than in 1993. While we cannot tell from our data what effect this had on the day-to-day practice of local authority care managers, our impressions of attitudinal change taking place are confirmed by evidence from elsewhere. For example, the Audit Commission (1993: para. 13) found that nearly all authorities (92 per cent) in a sample covering four-fifths of social services departments provided potential residents with a list of options and allowed them to visit homes before making a final decision. In addition, 84 per cent of authorities provided staff with guidelines on how to offer choice. The Commission concluded that such developments showed 'an impressive commitment by authorities to the principle of choice, which should continue to be developed to include an increasing range of options that allow people to stay at home' (Audit Commission 1993: para. 13).

Opportunities for exercising choice between individual nursing and residential homes were also reinforced by the dominance of 'spot' (and, to a lesser extent, cost and volume) contracts within our sample (see Chapter 5) and also more generally (Audit Commission 1993: para. 42). Compared with block contracts, such arrangements enhance the capacity of social services departments to purchase places best suited to individual needs and to specify that care is delivered according to the requirements of individual care plans. (On the other hand, as we shall argue in Chapter 8, they might also leave providers too vulnerable to the vagaries of market forces to invest in innovation or other longer-term quality- or efficiency-enhancing arrangements.) Other sources suggest that new opportunities were being offered, even in the initial post-implementation period, to enable people to remain at home (Department of Health 1993a; Association of Directors of Social Services 1994) and that individual users were increasingly being involved in care planning decisions (Department of Health 1994a). However, the latter developments were recognized to be limited in scope and the difficulties of changing professional and other organizational practices to enable users and carers to make informed choices about their future lives should not be under-estimated (Ellis 1993; Stevenson and Parsloe 1993). Moreover, the potential impact of resource constraints on the exercise of choice has become increasingly apparent during the second year of the reforms, as we show below (Department of Health 1994b; Wistow 1995a).

Cost-effectiveness

Interviewees rarely used the term cost-effectiveness in the correct technical sense and most simply equated it with reducing costs (cf. Knapp 1984). Several argued that there was scope to use purchasing power 'to drive prices down' including, in one case, through the select list mechanism. Some were surprised that they had been able to secure prices lower than they had anticipated – without obviously compromising quality – and had come to recognize that the cost structures of some private homes enabled them to continue operating with higher vacancy rates and lower income streams than they had expected. However, and perhaps reflecting local variations in market conditions, there was concern that only the larger providers had the scope to reduce prices and that the effects of price competition would have undesirable consequences for the pattern of supply.

It is worth emphasizing that, in some authorities, this concern was a contributory factor in the growing recognition that 'we may need to push up prices to get quality'. One authority expressed its approach in terms of first establishing 'quality thresholds' and then seeking 'to get the best price' above them. By contrast, another authority suggested that private sector companies would not be:

> hard-nosed about costs . . . but about quality and reputation. It is a bit like Sainsbury's where you don't pare down prices to capture every last customer. You have a strong commitment to quality and reputation.

Finally, two authorities expressed concern that the scope for cost-effectiveness gains was being limited by providers' capacities to organize cartels. Typically, however, local authorities reported the lack of cohesiveness and the extent of competition between providers in the private sector. One noted that it was:

> important to remember that private homes are already in competition with one another. So this gives me an edge.

Ministers had been explicit about their expectations that local authorities should use their purchasing power in this way to exert a downward pressure on the prices charged by the independent sector (House of Commons Health Committee 1993b: para. 71). The evidence suggests that, in the main, social services departments were successful in containing price increases. As we showed in Chapters 5 and 6, most authorities and providers reported using fixed, rather than floating, prices linked to DSS rates for existing residents with 'preserved rights' status. More generally, the Audit Commission found that the prices paid by local authorities remained stable throughout 1993/94 and that 'if anything prices stabilised after fluctuating somewhat initially as authorities got used to the market' (Audit Commission 1994: para. 44). A further study of 44 English authorities also found that average prices paid for both nursing and residential home care were within or close to the relevant DSS rates (London Research Centre 1994: 18).

In addition to price, there are two other noteworthy dimensions of cost-effectiveness: the relative costs to local authorities of services in domiciliary and institutional settings; and the development of targeting. Although neither dimension was prominent in our 1993 interviews, both have subsequently become more explicit. Thus, at the time of our fieldwork, constraints on developing domiciliary alternatives to residential and nursing home care were predominantly seen to lie in the absence of sufficient supply in the independent sector. More recently, however, cost constraints have been emphasized as a result of the growing recognition that, after taking into account contributions to the costs of residential and nursing home places from social security benefits, the net cost to social services departments may be less than that of an equivalent domiciliary care package (Wistow 1995a). Indeed, the head of the Social Services Inspectorate has publicly expressed concern that 'the expense of some community-based packages might lead social services departments to arrange residential places which were not the choice of the user' (Department of Health 1994b: 46). Subsequent advice from the Department of Health's Finance Division to Berkshire stated that authorities were expected to take financial considerations into account where the net cost of day and domiciliary care exceeded the net cost to an authority of a residential care place (Downey 1994). Where independent living is significantly more expensive than residential or nursing home care and resources are under pressure, it is difficult to see how authorities could avoid adopting such an approach (Wistow 1995a).

The cost-effectiveness of different strategies for targeting has also begun to be questioned since our fieldwork was conducted. Essentially, there is a trade-off to be made between focusing resources on those who currently have the most intensive care needs and those at risk of developing such needs in the future. This issue is inextricably bound up with how and at what levels eligibility criteria are set for access to different kinds of services. The unexpectedly low level of initial demand meant that authorities were little concerned about such questions at the time our interviews were conducted. Since then, however, funding constraints appear to have been met by the tightening of eligibility criteria in ways which focus resources on those with greatest need and by withdrawing them from users and carers with lower levels of need (Robinson and Wistow 1994; Henwood 1995). To the extent that this approach leads to restrictions on preventive care for those at risk, its longer-term cost-effectiveness must be in question.

Innovation

Innovation was sought in terms of change in the design and composition of services. It was especially associated with the need to develop a wider range of options which enabled more people to remain in their own homes. In particular, the policy expectation was that the injection of competitive forces would stimulate the emergence of a wider range of both providers and provision.

Most interviewees who discussed innovation did so simply in terms of identifying early indications of new developments. Only one was straightforwardly dismissive of this criterion, arguing that the market was:

a diversion that swallows up an awful lot of practitioner, operational, managerial, political energy . . . that could be used in developing actual innovative practice.

For the most part, there was cautious optimism about the scope for innovation. One Director suggested that innovation was already evident in the work that care managers were doing and that 'on the provider side people are beginning to think quite imaginatively both in-house and certainly externally.'

The importance of the market in stimulating innovation within the public sector was recognized by a number of authorities, including one which had 'floated off' substantial parts of its direct services to an arm's-length trust and another which was introducing internal trading accounts. As we have previously noted, however, the relative absence of alternative services and potential suppliers of such services in the independent sector, coupled with the requirement that social services departments spent 85 per cent of their special transitional grant in that sector, were considered major constraints on authorities' capacities to innovate. By the end of the first year the Association of Directors of Social Services (1994) was calling for a relaxation of the 85 per cent requirement. Early Department of Health monitoring suggested that only 'a small minority of users' received care packages that were 'genuinely more flexible and imaginative' than those available before April 1993 (Department of Health 1993a: para. 4.4). It is possible that the level of such innovatory packages increased after we completed our fieldwork.

A study of patterns of STG expenditure in a third of all authorities found that the slow demand for residential placements at the beginning of 1993/94 had the effect of modifying their initially cautious focus on maintaining a 'steady state' in the residential and nursing home markets. As a result, there was an increase during the final quarter of the year in the use of STG for non-residential services, often in the form of one-off payments to prevent underspending. However, only 17 per cent of the grant was allocated to such services during the whole year: 12 and 5 per cent in the independent and local authority sectors, respectively (London Research Centre 1994: 21–3). The latter study also found that the majority of authorities 'felt that constrained budgets were not conducive to innovation' (London Research Centre 1994: 23). A particular issue was the inappropriateness of using short-term underspendings in circumstances where longer-term investments were needed to establish services with sound foundations. As we argue below, the capacity to deliver innovative service packages is crucial to the achievement of the most fundamental aspects of the reforms.

Independent living

From the perspective of the White Paper's over-arching objectives, the success of the market will be judged by the extent to which it enables people to live as independently as possible in their own homes or in 'homely' settings in the community. That objective was expressed in terms of the capacity of social services departments to 'divert' users from residential to community-based settings. Early successes in meeting this goal were claimed by the Association of Directors of Social Services which identified diversion rates of 20 per cent 'on a conservative estimate' (1994: 4). Initial Department of Health monitoring reported that rates of 10 per cent and above were being quoted by social services departments (1994a: para. 4.3), although it also emphasized the difficulty of making precise estimates. Meeting this diversion objective in the context of a developing mixed economy implies a greatly expanded role for independent sector providers of day, domiciliary and respite care. At this stage in the development of the social care market, however, the independent sector is making only the most limited contributions to such provision, especially in the case of domiciliary services. To some extent, this outcome may be regarded as an intended rather than an unintended one. The concept of an 'implied commitment' to purchase residential and nursing home places at the 1992/93 level necessarily had the effect of restricting the scope for diversion into alternative care settings in 1993/94. None the less, the STG was resourced at a level above the 'implied commitment' level (House of Commons Health Committee 1993b), thereby giving some room for the development of new service patterns. In practice, however, supply-side constraints have made it impossible for authorities to purchase such services from the private and voluntary sectors, and the 85 per cent requirement has constrained their ability to extend the public sector contribution to innovative service patterns.

None of our interviewees thought that there was sufficient supply or suppliers of services designed to promote independent living, although it is important to recall the incompleteness of their supply mappings (Chapter 4). As the Director in a traditionally Conservative – but now hung – council noted: 'day and domiciliary services are only just beginning to develop' in the independent sectors. Other authorities referred to the 'marginal level' of such provision and described it as 'small beer'. The Director in one of the 'market enthusiast' authorities succinctly summed up the overall situation in the following terms:

> There simply isn't a ready-made provider sector for parts of the services . . . and if we wish to externalize services, we need to find new ways of developing the market.

However, we have indicated that not all authorities were eager to develop this part of the market (Chapter 3). In particular, there was markedly greater caution about using the private sector to provide services in people's own homes than in the case of other forms of supply. For example, a market enthusiast referred to:

> the limits on proceeding because of the lack of regulation . . . People are more vulnerable in their own homes.

Similarly, but from the other end of the spectrum of approaches towards market development, one interviewee – voicing a 'resigned scepticism' common to a small group of authorities – suggested that attitudes would change 'at a stroke if the government changed its position on the regulation of non-residential services'. Consistent with this view, at least three (Labour) authorities were 'not actively encouraging diversification' because, as one said, it was 'not politically feasible' to extend the operation of private sector providers in domiciliary settings. Another described the 'resistance from politicians to the development of contracts' for domiciliary care. Although this general approach was tempered – in this instance – by a preparedness to agree the purchase of such care on a 'case-by-case' basis, there was an underlying reluctance to use public funds to give an unregulated independent sector access to the homes of vulnerable people to provide a service which was necessarily difficult to monitor and inspect.

In contrast to such attitudes, a second group of authorities was actively promoting the growth of independent sector provision in non-residential services. A number were involved in the Department of Health's Caring for People Who Live at Home initiative. Others, as we have previously indicated, were encouraging home proprietors to diversify in order to sustain their financial viability: according to one authority 'the message is diversify or go under'. Such authorities were among those employing a wide range of methods to encourage diversification (see Chapter 6); but even those most positive about market development were sceptical about the scope for diversification, largely because of the substantial differences between residential services and other sectors of the market:

> You need . . . different staff, maybe different skills or retraining . . . Even providing respite care is not the same as providing residential care . . . people are looking for shared care and relief care.

Size was also seen to be a factor affecting the capacity of homes to move into other areas of the market:

> The more vulnerable, smaller homes have found it difficult to change. They work on a fixed income and their potential for being innovative and creative is limited. It is the bigger organisations that phone up and say they want to expand.

Such differences between services were seen to have substantial implications for the extent to which the independent sector could increase its market share. As one interviewee emphasized:

> You have got to grow new suppliers or bring (established suppliers) in from elsewhere. That is a very different activity from just bolting it onto existing suppliers. It is not realistic to expect completely new people to come off the wall and start running five elderly people's homes and a home help service.

The limited capacity of existing residential suppliers to diversify was evident in reports from a number of Directors that they had 'very few' or 'a very small number of approaches' from home proprietors about this issue. In addition, at least two Directors were sceptical about diversification proposals they had received. One said he had been 'put off by one or two ill-thought-out schemes'. Another had 'not met anyone who had formulated a model which looked as though it could be taken up and worked with'. Another sceptic said that there had been more 'talking than doing' and that the time had now come to meet existing providers to 'differentiate between those who were serious [about diversification] and those who were not'.

We have deliberately emphasized perceptions about the problematic nature of extending non-statutory supply outside the residential sector for two reasons: first, they contrast with the more positive attitudes to market development overall and may be significant as a reflection of the difficulties authorities must confront as they take practical steps to translate aims and aspirations into reality; second, the need to stimulate a greater diversity of provision is fundamental to the long-term success of the market in delivering community care objectives. We should, however, note that authorities were also seeing progress in this area; for example, diversification into respite and day care was more frequently identified than diversification into domiciliary services. In addition, there appeared to be a greater tendency for authorities to deal with and encourage diversification within the voluntary sector than the private sector. For example, one market enthusiast authority reported that:

> The voluntary sector is diversifying quickly. It is a major provider of home and day care. The private sector is slower but there are numerous [home owners] who ought to be persuaded to move into other forms of care.

Another authority similarly reported the growing strength and confidence of the voluntary sector as a result of a shift three years ago from grants to service agreements. This initiative had left the voluntary sector 'healthier and fitter' and better able managerially to take on an expanded role in service delivery. A number of other authorities referred to the ability of national voluntary organizations, most frequently Age Concern and Anchor, to import the necessary expertise.

Finally, it was evident from the number of Directors who reported receiving phone calls about diversification from local as well as national organizations in both the private and voluntary sectors that potential suppliers were becoming increasingly aware of the market opportunities in this area. Moreover, a small number of authorities admitted it was they who were not yet ready to respond to such initiatives. Whatever the root causes of the currently slow development of alternatives to residential services, it is fundamental to the success of the market that they be understood and overcome. As one Director noted bluntly:

> If it is difficult to find provision to meet identified needs, we will have failed in managing the market.

It is equally clear that diversification is only one mechanism for achieving such ends, and in all probability has a relatively small role to play. The 1993 KPMG/Department of Health study emphasized the problems of diversification in terms of the entirely different nature of the residential and domiciliary care businesses, and the experiences of our sample authorities appear to be consistent with those findings. As indicated in the previous chapter, our more recent study of residential care providers found that only 38 per cent were planning to diversify into day care services and only 31 per cent were planning to diversify into domiciliary care services. In addition, a survey conducted by the United Kingdom Home Care Association in January 1995 found that only 16 per cent of respondents had diversified from residential or nursing home services (Young and Wistow 1995). Thus, the route to promoting more independent living would appear to lie more in the direction of establishing new providers.

The findings from this study, together with those of the subsequent national monitoring exercises, suggest that some policy objectives were more fully achieved in the initial implementation period than others. The replacement of social security funding by local authority assessment and purchasing arrangements took place with minimal disruption to supply in the independent sectors or to throughput in the NHS. The basic organizational systems and processes were put in place and began to bed down. A commitment to the concept of extending choice for users and carers was also evident within social services departments. Significant levels of diversion were claimed (see above). However, our interviewees also highlighted resource and supply-side constraints on increasing such diversion rates and enabling individuals to exercise a choice to live in their own homes, supported by innovative care packages.

None the less, it is clear that not only was the basic 'smooth transition' objective being realized at the time of our fieldwork, but also that this success was maintained throughout the first year and into the second. If that criterion of success now seems modest, it is only because it was met. Unlike some other areas of policy, central and local government agencies succeeded in working together to implement major change without the whole policy framework being called into question within months of its coming into effect (Wistow 1995a,b). Having successfully negotiated that early implementation phase without the anticipated 'disasters', the focus must now move up the hierarchy of policy objectives we identified at the beginning of this chapter and which provided the framework for our subsequent analysis. Subsequent phases of this research will seek to establish how far they can be realized, although it is already clear that a continuing 'smooth transition' to the twin goals of 'choice and independence' cannot be assumed. Indeed, they are increasingly in tension with changes in the role of acute hospital services which place growing pressures on community care as well as with the imperative to control public expenditure which provided much of the stimulus for ending the former social security arrangements (Wistow 1995a,c).

At the time of our fieldwork, Directors had mixed views about longer-term market prospects. As indicated previously (see Chapter 2) there was more support in 1993 than in 1991 for the introduction of a market in social care, based in part on a developing recognition of its potential advantages. Sixteen Directors thought the market would have overall advantages rather than disadvantages; however, when we sought to explore expectations about whether the market would succeed or fail in practice, a different picture emerged. Only nine Directors clearly expected the market to succeed compared with four who did not and twelve who were either unsure or did not provide an answer. Among those who were pessimistic, one argued:

> There are real dangers about this free market philosophy and I think that part of the White Paper was ill-thought out, ill-conceived and doesn't bear any analysis whatsoever . . . because of the political drive which is behind it. [It] didn't analyse sufficiently skilfully the medium- to long-term consequences of embarking down this road.

Another Director similarly referred to:

> being tied up with a lot of political rhetoric which wasn't needed . . . Developing a market in some abstract sense is not good for anybody.

At the other end of the spectrum, one Director expected that in four years' time the authority would score 'quite heavily on the simple criteria' of choice, cost-effectiveness and innovation. He concluded that as long as all providers:

> were operating to the specifications we've set, that they are producing services from a value base that we want, then I think [the market] will have proved itself. I think we have to wait and see on that, but I feel reasonably optimistic about that, actually.

Others similarly had 'no great anxieties' in the medium term although in one case this assessment was accompanied by concern whether by year four the allocation formula would enable it to continue 'to develop the market to good effect'. Finally, a small number of those interviewed were more cautious in their assessment. One felt the market would succeed 'with difficulty' and emphasized the need for managers to become 'more adaptive' and 'flexible'. Another suggested that it would succeed in terms of the White Paper criteria 'but at a price . . . in relation to the current size of the market'. He further questioned whether the government would allow the market to work because the pressures from home owners might be 'too great . . . to let that level of collapse be sustained'. Another interviewee was positive about the way that 'ideas about competition are gaining hold much more quickly than we anticipated', but was concerned that the market 'could all go wrong very quickly'.

Conclusion

At the beginning of this chapter we distinguished two perspectives on the operation of the social care market. In our discussion thus far we have concentrated on the social policy perspective, employing criteria derived from the objectives set out in *Caring for People* and subsequent policy guidance. There was evidence of optimism about the potential for these objectives to be met by market mechanisms. However, there was also anxiety about the operation of social care markets which formed part of a wider concern that authorities must learn to manage the market both to avoid its collapse and to influence its emerging shape. Our second perspective, drawn from economic theory about the structure and operation of markets, enables us to address these concerns and forms the subject matter of Chapter 8. In the final chapter we draw on both perspectives to consider how the market might better be harnessed to serve social ends.

8

Is the market working? Economic perspectives

Introduction

In the previous chapter we addressed questions about how well the market is 'working' by reference to criteria based on the main policy goals set out in *Caring for People*. Such criteria are, of course, highly context-specific in the sense that they derive from the analysis of community and social care. Their starting point lies in the substance of social policy rather than the more technical analysis of market economics. Yet the latter approach also has an important part to play in evaluating the operation of the market. We have already employed it in Chapter 5 to explore the implications of service specification and contracting processes. Its particular contribution is to provide generally applicable propositions about the conditions under which markets succeed or fail, and which are not, therefore, rooted in a particular policy sphere or type of product. Thus, it provides a broader meta framework within which to structure and analyse empirical data.

As earlier chapters make plain, *Caring for People* advocated the creation of social care markets as mechanisms for promoting choice, cost-effectiveness and innovation, and our interviewees were increasingly becoming attuned to a market culture. However, they were also conscious of potential disadvantages and barriers to social care markets. Some of the latter concerns had ideological and cultural roots, or reflected financial and other resource pressures. Others were based not only upon perceptions of differences between the social care and other commodities usually traded in markets but also upon imperfections in the social care system (see Chapters 2 and 3). To the extent that such perceptions are validated, they demonstrate that the changing attitudes towards the market culture may be a necessary condition for market success, but they will not provide a sufficient condition.

The policy objectives described in *Caring for People* imply a more flexible approach to shaping the market so that it can deliver better outcomes for users. The concept of 'managing the market' emerged relatively late in the implementation timetable, and then largely – and narrowly – in the context of the smooth transition objective (Department of Health 1992a).

With the minimum requirements now apparently met, central and local government must give even more attention to the future shape and structure of social care markets. It is therefore vital to gain a better understanding of the implications of local authorities' commissioning and other market arrangements for performance and for the achievement of the various social, political and economic goals set out in the previous chapter. We now examine these local arrangements and their longer-term implications. We are not looking at local authorities' decisions about appropriate target *levels* of provision, but the mechanisms they use to translate intentions into practice: how do they use their commissioning responsibilities to move from supply targets to actual allocations of services to users?

Assessment criteria

In order to assess local authorities' actions and intentions we need to define the criteria for judging purchasing arrangements, and we need a framework to guide the evaluation. At the most general level, the core objectives of social care are usually couched in terms of the improvement or maintenance of user and carer quality of life. Other objectives – linked to these core aims – might include expanding user choice, delivering high-quality care, keeping within available budgets, and – in some cases – protecting the public. In Chapter 7 we discussed objectives of this kind under the heads of political, social and economic goals. Many of these aims are connected with efficiency and equity, which are the primary concerns of an economic analysis.

It is relatively straightforward to couch efficiency and equity in terms of concepts and criteria which are familiar to social services providers and purchasers (Knapp 1984). The *production of welfare* framework distinguishes the main components in the delivery and utilization of social care, and the linkages between them (see Box 8.1). For example, purchasers would ideally like to secure high levels of final outcome – better improvements in user and carer welfare – at low cost, which is one interpretation of an efficiency improvement. Or, given a purchasing budget for the coming year, purchasers would like to meet as many assessed needs as possible, or to achieve the greatest possible gains in user quality of life. Efficiency can also embrace notions of choice and quality of care, although neither tends to be seen as an end in itself, and efficiency embodies innovation and technical change, being dynamic in nature. Social services authorities seek to target their available resources on assessed

---

Box 8.1   Production of welfare

The production of welfare framework clarifies how the main elements of social care delivery are linked together. The framework's main components are:

- *resource inputs*, mainly staff, buildings, other capital and consumables;
- *costs*, which are the resource inputs expressed in monetary terms;
- *non-resource inputs*, which are influences on the achievement of outcomes for users or carers (see below) which have no identifiable price or are not currently marketed (such as the quality of a care environment, staff attitudes, users' experiences);
- *intermediate outcomes*, which are services of a given quality, produced by the resource and non-resource inputs; and
- *final outcomes*, which are changes over time in the health, welfare and quality of life of users, carers and other members of society (if relevant).

The production of welfare: Final outcomes are achieved by combining resource and non-resource inputs, in the context of user and other circumstances and characteristics.

Source: Davies and Knapp (1981); Knapp (1984).

---

needs according to their *equity* principles and values. Resources are commonly allocated disproportionately in favour of those people adjudged to be priority cases, that is, whose needs are perceived to be greater. These desired allocations of resources involve specific value judgements. Social services arrangements can be assessed according to their *target efficiency*, that is, the degree to which the desired allocations are met, offset against the associated cost (Bebbington and Davies 1983). These criteria of efficiency and equity, used to assess the workings of markets, have as much relevance in social care as elsewhere.

A framework for evaluating markets

Our evaluation of social care markets is based upon a theoretical framework drawn from 'new institutional economics' (Williamson 1975, 1985). Only a brief and simplified account can be provided here; further details are given by Forder (1995a).[1] The central element in the analysis is the transaction – the exchange of goods, services, money or other forms of currency – between the *principal* and the *agent*. The principal is one party to a transaction who commissions another party (the agent) to produce goods or services. In the present context, the local authority purchaser or commissioner is most appropriately thought of as the principal. The identity of the principal may change: it could be a single care manager or it could be a senior management placement panel. But while the identity may change, the defining characteristic does not: principals make decisions as to how public money should be spent to secure provision. The agent in social care is the provider, whether an in-house public sector provider or an independent organization or individual.

A transaction can be characterized in terms of three interconnected elements – regulatory framework, imperfections and benefits – and it is the interplay between them which influences the success of a given market according to the criteria set out earlier. The *regulatory framework* (or governance structure), in this social care context, describes the degree of control over agents exerted by local authorities and other parts of the state and the legal system. Indeed, the regulatory framework governing a particular set of transactions in practice can be seen as a point on a spectrum of distributions of control, with pure hierarchy at one end (bureaucratic, top-down control by the principal) and pure market at the other (agents entering into voluntary exchange with the principal, without coercion or hindrance). Different regulatory frameworks embody different sets of incentives, including those created by the commissioning party to persuade the agent to act in certain ways. Together, then, the rules, protocols and conventions which define regulatory frameworks imply particular distributions of control and incentive structures.

The second characteristic of a transaction is the nature and extent of imperfections (or hazards) associated with exchange. If the agent has better information than the principal regarding the characteristics of a transaction, or if either party is uncertain about some future aspects or issues pertinent to the exchange, there are said to be *information imperfections*. When competition is limited, between either principals or agents, there are *structural imperfections* (Le Grand and Bartlett 1993; Forder et al. 1996). These are the two main economic hazards facing social care markets. In the absence of regulation, one or both of these imperfections will cause market failure.

The third element of a transaction is the set of resource consequences or *benefits*, both for the principal (on behalf of users and carers) and the agent. The scale and distribution of these benefits will depend on the incidence of imperfections and the regulatory framework in operation. If there are no imperfections (which is a purely hypothetical position) and a minimal regulatory framework, benefits will be maximized. We can call this the benchmark case. More realistically, the existence of imperfections will mean lower benefits, and it is the role of regulation – through accreditation systems, fixed prices, and trade and industry policies of various kinds – to ameliorate these adverse consequences. The difference between the benefits (net of costs) flowing from the benchmark case and the actual net benefits in any real world case can be defined as the level of transactions costs.

Arrow defines transactions costs as the 'costs of running the economic system' (1969: 48), and they should be distinguished from production costs, the costs of transforming resources into goods and services. Williamson claims that 'transactions costs are the equivalent of friction in physical systems' (1985: 19). They can be broken down into five categories (see Box 8.2)

> **Box 8.2** Transactions costs
>
> 1 Structural losses
>
> 2 Informational losses
>
> 3 Bargaining costs
>
> 4 Costs of selective intervention
>
> 5 Costs of implementing and operating regulation

to operationalize the concept for policy purposes (Forder 1995b). We now consider each in turn.

Structural losses accrue when one party to a transaction has market power, because of the existence of structural imperfections. An obvious example is when market power is exercised by a monopoly provider in pursuit of their own interests, to the detriment of purchasers. Structural losses may take two forms: first, where market power is used to inflate prices beyond the costs of production (to give excessive profits); and second, where costs are allowed to grow beyond their minimum technically attainable level.

Informational losses, the second category of transactions costs, may be incurred when relevant information is incomplete or distributed asymmetrically between parties. The party with the better information could then mislead the other party and benefit accordingly (Rasmusen 1992). One example is *moral hazard of hidden information*, where one party receives better or more precise information but misinforms the other. For example, a provider might misreport a client's dependency characteristics to the purchaser, prompting the purchaser to pay for a higher level of care than is actually needed. Another example is *moral hazard of hidden actions,* where one party puts less effort into the job than was previously agreed for the transaction. The purchaser and user may not realize that 'shirking' is occurring because they only see the resource inputs or intermediate outcomes, and the provider's efforts can be obscured among the myriad other (uncertain) contributory factors. An example is where the provider misrepresents the quality of care. A third form of informational loss is *adverse selection*, where one party possesses characteristics which may influence how well the transaction is carried out, but does not reveal them to the other party. An example would be where a nursing home only accepts as residents those elderly people who are not too dependent or too confused (so-called 'cream skimming'). In each example, the party with the better information is able to alter the allocation of resources in such a way that the total benefit of the transaction is reduced. Informational losses also accrue if inappropriate responses are made to uncertainty (Rees 1989).

Bargaining costs arise because, in practice, contracts cannot be so complete as to be able to cover every contingency. (This incompleteness stems partly from information imperfections and partly from the limits of human cognitive ability.) The principal and agent will have to negotiate a solution, generating additional transactions costs, which in market systems fall on both parties. The problem is not the cost of gathering information *per se*, which is obviously required, but rather that *both* parties go to this expense, often collecting the same information. In hierarchical systems only the principal may need to gather the required information (because they make the relevant decisions) and so transactions costs will be lower. However, in hierarchical systems, problems can arise because the principal could take (distorted) decisions that are in his/her best interests, regardless of whether they harm the agent. This problem is called *selective intervention* and is the fourth transactions costs element. Even where there are no personal (financial) interests at stake because, for example, the principal is paid a pre-specified salary, the temptation to intervene may be too great. Managers may feel the imperative to manage, believing their interventions will be beneficial even when this is unlikely (Milgrom and Roberts 1990). Costs of selective intervention may also arise as *influence costs*, because individuals and groups expend time, effort and ingenuity attempting to affect the decisions of others.

Finally, account must be taken of the costs of actually *implementing and operating regulation*. We need to distinguish between this cost component and transactions costs more generally, the latter being the costs of governing the allocation of resources using the regulatory framework. Thus, these operating and implementation costs would be incurred even if no transaction was undertaken.

This theoretical framework serves to highlight key facets of the *economic* consequences of operating different systems of regulation or governance. A change in regulatory framework, given prevailing structural and informational imperfections, will change the level of total transactions costs, and their distribution between the five categories. It then follows that a market might perhaps be 'managed' in order to change its regulatory framework and to reduce these losses, that is, to minimize total transactions costs. In practice this entails choosing commissioning and purchasing arrangements, installing rules and protocols, and operating 'trade and industry' policies. At a more general level, this framework addresses the question of the circumstances in which markets or hierarchies/bureaucracies are more appropriate than markets. In evaluating social care commissioning or purchasing, therefore, we should examine how alternative arrangements might reduce transactions costs, and how they might influence structural and informational imperfections. First, we consider the significance of these imperfections and the size of the structural and informational losses which they might imply.

The scale of the problem

Information imperfections

Commissioners need various kinds of information for various reasons:

- to map current supply (quantity, characteristics, prices), and to predict future market supply dynamics;
- to describe providers' characteristics (particularly motivations and probable responses to commissioners' actions);
- to map current population needs, and to estimate future patterns of need;
- to move from assessed needs to coherent service demands, including the specification of desired services;
- to elicit users' and carers' preferences and choices regarding services, and their views on services received;
- to check that product or service specifications are being met (in terms of quality of care or user and carer quality of life); and
- to monitor cross-boundary flows, capacity and occupancy levels, user flows between different services, and provider efficiency.

Information holdings are both incomplete and asymmetrically distributed between purchaser and provider. For example, few local authorities in our sample had made headway with the mapping of need, information on the quantity of supply was still patchy (especially for non-residential services), and information on motivations often either lacking or misinterpreted. Of particular concern to authorities was their lack of information about the 'product' – the characteristics of services (cost, quality, staffing, coverage) and how those characteristics related to user and carer needs and outcomes.

If information imperfections exist, we should find evidence of informational *losses*. Using the data gathered in our study of the residential care market for elderly people, described in Chapter 6, we can gauge the possible extent of some of these losses.

One of the questions we addressed in that study was the misrepresentation of dependency characteristics, with average client dependency levels being hypothesized to be related to the incentive structures faced by homes. Dependency was measured using an index of four physical elements (mobility; incontinence; performance of basic tasks, including dressing and washing; and toileting) and one mental functioning element (confused mental state). We found that where homes did *not* operate with a single price for any local authority contract placements (which was the case for 42 per cent of sample homes) – that is, they differentiated their prices on a per client basis – the average dependency was significantly lower than for homes which *did* operate with a single price. This was the case after controlling for other factors, including staffing levels, size of home, the nature of accommodation, sector, proxies for input prices and competition, and, especially, average revenue accrued. This finding is consistent with our hypothesis that, where they are not constrained by a fixed or single price, *some* homes will exaggerate a client's level of dependency to the buyer and thereby secure a higher price. Such homes, after accounting for differences in revenue across all homes, would then have lower dependency clients. Indeed, the data suggest that identical homes in identical circumstances – except that they face a single price – have clients with higher average dependency for the same price: that is, a higher ratio of dependency to price. The simplest explanation for this observed difference in behaviour is homes which do not differentiate their prices on a per-client basis have no opportunity to exaggerate dependency levels.

Next we examined the data to assess whether this difference in behaviour varied according to the ownership of the home, and specifically whether provision was undertaken in the private or voluntary sector. The data suggested that, on average, private sector providers operating with a variable price had residents with significantly lower average dependencies for the same price than voluntary sector providers in the same circumstances. This is consistent with the hypothesis that, even where they have the same opportunities/ circumstances as private homes, voluntary sector providers are not motivated to behave in the same way. We next examined this same difference in behaviour in respect to a measure of competition in the local market. We found that the data supported the hypothesis that this difference in reported dependencies per price charged would be smaller in areas of high competition compared with areas of low competition.

Despite data limitations, therefore, we found evidence of information losses. Furthermore, the data support our underlying message that authorities may be able to select regulatory structures (specifically incentive structures in this case) that minimize the adverse consequences and lower the transactions costs.

Structural imperfections

During our research with local authorities, many reported underprovision of domiciliary services and some specialist residential services. This supply deficit can be explained either by the 'natural' time lag in responding to new levels or compositions of demand, or by structural imperfections. In Chapter 5 we reported that authorities expressed mixed opinions regarding the possible extent of structural imperfections. Half the sample had set up dedicated budgets to stimulate supply, suggesting that they saw value in helping new organizations to overcome the market entry barriers associated with acquiring expertise, recruiting good-quality care staff, and achieving a viable (economical) scale of operation. As one interviewee explained:

> To diversify from residential to domiciliary care takes a long time. It doesn't happen overnight. There are different types of expertise and you cannot just assume that because somebody can run an old people's home or a nursing home, they can suddenly run a good care agency . . . So we have gone [forward] in a fairly cautious way in order to ensure quality . . . They are quite vulnerable, people in their own homes.

Some other interviewees took the view that potential suppliers were keen and able to enter the market should authorities express reasonably certain demands. This was in part supported by interviews with providers. Limitations

---

Box 8.3   Commissioning arrangements

1 Balancing in-house and external provision

2 Choosing the balance between case-level and strategic purchasing

3 Provider selection

4 Pricing arrangements

5 Contract reimbursement

6 Contract types: spot or block

7 Specification and monitoring.

---

on supply were not so much due to the costs of market entry as to the lack of local authority commitment in making sufficient funds available, paying reasonable rates, or making their purchasing intentions known. One Director explained:

> The [profit] margins on domiciliary care are between 6 and 8 per cent. Margins for residential care are between 14 and 18 per cent, and for nursing homes between 18 and 26 per cent. So there isn't the same incentive.

Another told us of American companies 'sniffing around four years ago', but 'They went off, didn't they? They weren't daft!' Other evidence of structural imperfections emerged from our survey of residential care providers. There was a significant negative relationship between the degree of competition and prices. Product differentiation – particularly on a geographical basis – may be a root cause.

Assessing authorities' commissioning arrangements

In seeking to commission social care markets for people assessed to be in need, local authorities face a great many options. In the remainder of this chapter we focus on seven of them, selected to reflect major issues confronting authorities in 1993 (see Box 8.3). How did authorities' chosen commissioning arrangements stand up to the criteria for successful markets? We will examine these arrangements in the context of the transactions cost framework developed earlier in the chapter. Elsewhere, we have examined a somewhat wider set of commissioning arrangements and in more detail than is possible here (Knapp and Forder 1996). A more technical analysis can be found in Forder (1995b). For each of the seven issues, we now discuss the attendant information and structural imperfections, and transactions costs.

In-house or external provision

As we saw in Chapter 5, local authorities had chosen widely different balances between in-house and external provision. Steps had been taken in a few authorities to prepare in-house units for the rigours of the market: formulating business plans, developing costing models, extending non-residential service coverage beyond the standard working week, and so on. In one or two cases, widespread 'externalization' was underway, whereas some other authorities were intent on continuing to be large-scale providers.

The problems arising as a result of informational imperfections should be lessened somewhat if services are purchased from in-house providers, not only because they may be more likely than independent providers to share the values and motivations of purchasers, but also because they do not have the same incentives to be selective about the information that they make available. In-house providers may then have a closer, more trusting relationship with purchasers. While there is a danger that 'cosy' relationships of this kind may encourage slack and complacency, there may be offsetting advantages in the sense that better information can flow between purchasers and providers.

With a significant level of structural imperfections, providers may have market power which they can use to their benefit but to the detriment of purchasers (and so clients). With hierarchical 'in-house' provider systems, such problems may not occur. However, we risk replacing the costs of market power with the costs of selective intervention. Also, it may be difficult to create the right incentives in hierarchical systems. Evidence from the tendering of ancillary services within the NHS and elsewhere in local authorities suggests that the threat of external competition can induce productive efficiency gains and cost savings within directly-managed units. A competitive market environment might be more responsive, flexible and efficient. Some US evidence points to perverse managerial incentives and significant organizational rigidities in public sector provision which could potentially be rectified by the introduction of competitive pressures (Ferris and Graddy 1988). In the UK, there is some research on services for people with long-term mental health problems which suggests that health and local authority accommodation was more highly staffed than private and voluntary accommodation, even when residents' needs did not appear to warrant it, and residents' outcomes were not always superior (Beecham et al. 1991; Donnelly et al. 1994). There is also some older evidence of an independent sector cost advantage over the public sector, after standardizing for user characteristics, although not measuring a full span of outcomes (Judge and Knapp 1985; Knapp 1986). This research evidence is patchy, and some of it is outdated, but it is consistent with the expectations of some local authority officers and members that there could be cost savings and gains in flexibility and quality if they 'externalized' some of their services. One Director argued:

> Social services have got this huge rising demand curve and the ceiling on public expenditure pressing down. Now in that scenario, Directors

of social services are going to have to look hard at first defining what they want by way of standards, but then asking themselves whether they can achieve that standard more cost-effectively by doing things internally or externally. The job is to get as many bangs for our bucks.

It is difficult to say whether operating with in-house providers will mean lower transactions costs than when 'external' markets dominate. With markets there ought to be lower selective intervention costs, and competition among independent providers could improve productive efficiency. However, if the potential for competition is low in external markets, monopolistic behaviour can arise. Also, bargaining costs will be high, as will the potential for information problems unless trust can be substituted for explicit monitoring.

Case-level or strategic purchasing

In Chapter 5 we noted that most authorities had opted for a fairly cautious approach to devolution: the majority held purchasing budgets at team manager level, even though many of them recognized advantages with lower-level purchasing. What are the likely transactions cost consequences of the different arrangements?

In principle, devolved powers allow purchasing to be more sensitive to the needs and preferences of users. This reduces the impact of information asymmetry because care managers have the incentive to acquire information about providers and about the progress of individual users through their services. They also have the statutory obligation to share much of that information with users and carers. Almost all of our interviewees recognized this advantage. As one officer put it:

> The idea was [to devolve] budgetary control down to group manager level. They are the ones who are seeing the reasons for individual placements and will have the opportunity to agree novel arrangements, if you like, for keeping people at home.

This sentiment was echoed by many others, including the committee Chair who said:

> It seems to me that people will take more care in the way they spend the money and the way they manage the client's affairs if they're actually responsible for what they're doing.

Another wanted to 'marry up professional with financial decision-making'. Clearly, devolving purchasing power was perceived to reduce the inefficiencies and inequities that can follow from information imperfections. At a local level, services could be more effectively targeted on assessed needs with a greater impact on user and carer well-being than would be the case with centralized purchasing. On the other hand, of course, the individual care manager may not have the broader view necessary for strategic efficiency and equity. As one Director explained:

> I cannot see . . . that [devolving purchasing to care managers] could be a terribly useful way forward when we are trying to provide consistency of care, and when we are trying to make sure that resources are equitably distributed across the whole community.

Related anxieties expressed by others concerned a potential loss of information to purchasers, for providers can contribute significantly to the ongoing assessment of needs and the tailoring of services to meet them. They also feared that care managers would no longer be able to provide counselling, advice or advocacy.

Care managers with budgets to buy services on behalf of users *potentially* lose some of the financial cushion of a large organization, as well as the ability and technical resources to process information and make financial decisions. Decentralized purchasing is thus associated with greater risk where information imperfections exist. Purchasers might therefore choose to avoid risky but innovative care packages, opting instead for something more reliable but maybe less suitable. There are many implications, but we will mention just two. First, a large organization with centralized purchasing can engage in risk pooling and risk spreading, and, in principle, secure lower contract prices. Second, because wrong decisions by care managers can put budgets under strain and upset financial planning, authorities need excellent information systems and central control over purchasers' spending. A typical comment from our interviews was:

> Until staff lower in the organization understand the financial conse-quences of decisions, we are not likely to generate the value for money that is required.

Devolved purchasing may therefore imply lower efficiency as purchasers must spend more to avoid risk which they cannot internalize.

A centralized purchaser, with monopsony power, is usually thought to be incompatible with the development of an efficient local market. Excessive and irresponsible use of purchasing power could ultimately drive good providers out of the market, generating long-term structural losses. However, if this buying power is used to counterbalance market power on the provider side (power that grew from significant structural imperfections), it offers the potential for efficiency improvements. This partly explains the moves among some London authorities to form purchasing consortia. Centralized purchasing also facilitates strategic commissioning, investment and market shaping generally. For example, if potential new providers face difficulties securing sufficient quantities of capital or skilled staff, a relatively centralized purchasing system could be better placed than a decentralized system to offer subsidies, contracts linked to investments, and so on.

Decentralized purchasers, having less market purchasing power, will more often find themselves engaged in a series of one-to-one bilateral relationships with providers. This means that the potential for coordination problems is higher and so may increase the costs of bargaining compared with centralized purchasing arrangements. Decentralized purchasers will also have less authority *individually* and so the problems of selective intervention may be reduced. This is particularly stark when compared with a centralized purchaser who intervenes inappropriately by, for example, imposing non-sustainable prices or specifications which damage relationships, motivation, innovation and quality of service. As one Director emphasized, 'this arms-length separation by the purchaser has drawbacks in terms of attitudes to providers'. Decentralized purchasers do not have the authority to intervene, whether in an inappropriate or other fashion, and so should generate relatively lower transactions costs.

With good information, greater centralization of purchasing powers should reduce the problems stemming from markets which are characterized by limited supply-side competition. But the costs of acquiring sufficient information and the potential for distortionary intervention may undermine this advantage. Decentralized purchasing arrangements are likely to reduce the transactions costs associated with informational losses. This also has downsides: many local authorities are worried that the costs of operating devolved purchasing systems may themselves offset the relative benefits of such systems, especially when account is taken of the costs of reorganization and training.

Provider selection

The third commissioning arrangement which warrants particular attention is the choice between a preferred provider selection mechanism – a so-called 'select list' system – and open purchasing. A preferred provider list is a way in which authorities can assume additional control and facilitate the implementation of different incentive structures. In their extreme form, preferred provider systems are actually partnership arrangements: local authorities maintain trading relationships with current suppliers to the immediate exclusion of all others. Once again, therefore, it is appropriate to use our economics framework to interpret authorities' decisions and their implications.

A preferred provider list is likely to encourage closer working relationships between purchasers and providers, including mutual trust and improved, shared knowledge about price, quality and the motivations of the different parties. This should reduce informational losses by limiting the capacity of providers to exploit private information to their own advantage. The alternative – open purchasing – may alienate providers and actually exacerbate information problems. It will certainly limit mutual understanding. One social services Director summarized it thus: 'We have been particularly concerned about maintaining relationships where we've got them, and not getting into confrontation.' Where there is some competition and where quality cannot easily be determined by the buyer, a preferred provider system gives providers the incentive to develop and maintain a good reputation for high-quality provision. The reason for this is that the costs of being 'caught cheating' – of delivering lower-quality care than the level specified in the contract – are higher, for the result would be the loss of 'select list' status, while the benefits of honesty are not totally eroded by competition (Forder et al. 1996). Not only will a purchaser feel more secure against the risks of exploitation, but may accumulate experience and apply expertise. A preferred provider system is thus consistent with a climate of 'obligational contracting'.

In using a select list rather than open purchasing, local authorities are setting conditions which providers are obliged to meet. If the market is characterized by structural imperfections, this can be advantageous because it limits the scope for providers to wield market power by removing key variables from provider control. For example, select lists often require providers to meet local authority price and quality specifications. The potential disadvantages of a select list system are the costs of operating select lists and the 'blunting' of incentives because providers are somewhat insulated from the rigours of competition. It is possible (if not always easy) to create incentives in other ways, not just by competition (for example, by tying reimbursement to outputs). However, non-market incentives tend to be very demanding on information, and are thus more costly. If there are few incentives, complacency and productive inefficiency may go unchecked, and may manifest as restricted choice. Indeed, many local authority interviewees expressed structural concerns about select lists in this latter respect. For example, one Director commented:

> The drive . . . that we took most seriously to heart was the notion of choice. If we had a select list and it didn't correlate with individual choices, did it have a value? What were we achieving by having a select list?

Another Director simply said that their authority's rationale for using open purchasing was that 'we wanted to maintain maximum choice'.

Preferred provider arrangements can be problematic when conducting cross-boundary transactions, because different authorities may require providers to meet different criteria to be eligible for list membership. For providers to become accredited in two or more authorities they must therefore simultaneously uphold two or more sets of specifications, which can quickly become infeasible or expensive, and could certainly deter them from marketing their services more widely. There could be similar difficulties with block contracts with different purchasers if each requires different specifications (see below). Difficulties of this kind could encourage the localization of markets, leading ultimately to local monopoly.

Select lists shift some control over service characteristics to purchasers, reducing bargaining costs, but perhaps pushing up the costs of distortionary intervention. Providers have little choice but to accept the conditions for list membership and, individually at least, they cannot easily negotiate different terms. This lack of flexibility may reduce productive efficiency and choice, and is especially disadvantageous if select list conditions constitute inappropriate interventions into the market (for example, by imposing unrealistic and irrelevant standards on to providers). Moreover, producers may expend significant resources on 'influence activities' to try to change clauses and conditions (Milgrom and Roberts 1990).

On the face of it, a preferred provider list appears to generate higher transactions costs: essentially, it is another layer of bureaucracy. However, many conditions of service delivery can be agreed at an early stage when providers apply for preferred status and hence do not need to appear again in the final contract. Consequently, if there are significant economies of scale in transaction activities undertaken centrally, a select list may actually reduce transactions costs. It can certainly shift some of the burden from care managers and other devolved purchasers. There seems to be a case for arguing that a preferred provider list generates lower *total* transactions costs than open tendering, for there are fewer informational and structural problems. However, as we have noted, by insulating providers from the rigours of competition, a select list system also dilutes the benefits of market incentives. This could mean either low productive efficiency or high operating costs of non-market incentive schemes. None the less, on balance, it is perhaps not surprising that we found that the majority of local authorities in our sample (twenty-one of the twenty-five) were using a form of list system to purchase residential and some non-residential services.

Pricing arrangements

In the purchase of residential care the majority of the local authorities in our sample used *pre-specified* arrangements with a fixed price closely tied to DSS rates and case-by-case contracts (see Chapter 5). Our present task is to consider the strengths and weaknesses of these pre-specified arrangements compared with spot purchasing. In the next two subsections we consider the relative merits of different contract reimbursement structures and contract types.

If certain conditions prevail, the main virtue of a floating price system – and the key defining characteristic of a market – is that price transmits information on both quality and available capacity (slack capacity will cause the price to fall, excess demand will push price up). Information on quality as experienced by users of a service will give a provider a good or bad reputation within those users' social networks. In theory, this will either push demand up or down and hence influence the local market price. Others may feel that they need only look at price to form conclusions about quality. Price movements therefore mean that purchasers may not have to collect information about capacity or aspects of quality directly. If it is particularly difficult or costly to monitor quality, this could be a useful, low-cost signalling device. These advantages are lost with pre-specifed reimbursement (such as fixed prices) and therefore, in theory, informational losses are likely to be higher. This relative advantage is conditional on imperfections being minimal, however. Otherwise, the informational benefits of floating price systems will not be so high because inherent information or structural imperfections can hinder the ability of prices to act as accurate signals of scarcity and quality.

If local authorities employ a system of fixed prices – that is, if they assume price-setting control – provider market power and its *potential* abuses will be at least partially contained. By imposing a ceiling on prices, providers will be limited in their ability to secure excess profits. This is a strong argument supporting the use of regulatory responses. With residential care markets, in particular, penetration by a few very large corporate providers could create structural problems (oligopolization) of increasing significance.

By imposing prices on providers, local authority regulators are removing a major source of bargaining costs, but we must weigh this saving against the increased costs of selective intervention. Indeed, we have already mentioned the dangers of imposing *non-sustainable* prices. If the 'wrong' price is imposed, the market will be characterized by either excess supply or excess demand. One Director explained:

> The process that we have engaged in and begun over the first six months it to try to appraise what effect that [fixed price] is having and whether there is a case for adjusting that price . . . We thought we should start where the system was rather than make too many ill-informed estimates of what it might be. Now we may have made a very ill-informed estimate and, if we have, we'll be adjusting that rather dramatically.

Strong providers might exploit their market power in other ways, or they might try to persuade the price setter to choose a higher pre-specified fixed price. These are examples of influence costs, and represent unproductive uses of resources.

Turning to other transactions costs, we might expect problems with a fixed price system because of the costs of determining relative scarcity in the market and thus the 'correct' fixed price. Floating prices have their own transactions costs, especially if price bargaining is protracted. We noted that an advantage of a fixed price is that much of this negotiation can be avoided, or repeated less frequently. Fixed prices could also offset costly structural losses. Overall, the size of total transactions costs for fixed rather than floating price systems will depend crucially on how much of a threat is posed by structural imperfections, and on whether commissioners can find appropriate fixed price levels to deal with this problem.

Contract reimbursement

Most contracts employed by the authorities in our sample were reimbursed using a single fixed price agreed at or before the time the contract was signed. This was certainly the case in the majority of authorities with pre-specified arrangements because the price was fixed irrespective of individual contracts. Even where the price of individual contracts was negotiated on a spot basis, and some account of potential costs was made by assessing client dependency characteristics, the price was still fixed at the beginning of the contract period and not affected retrospectively by providers' actual costs.

Alternative reimbursement mechanisms – or, in keeping with our terminology, alternative incentive structures – could be used. One is *cost-plus* reimbursement where payment is made according to the actual cost of the contracted service, plus a profit mark-up. In this case, the exact payment is finalized after the contract has been served. True cost-plus arrangements generally involve the provider submitting audited cost accounts and being reimbursed on that basis according to a formula agreed in advance. Another possibility is *incentive* contract reimbursement, which uses a combination of fixed-price and cost-plus elements (Laffont and Tirole 1993). How do these different reimbursement methods compare?

The use of fixed price reimbursement will reduce the likelihood of moral hazard problems (see page 141). Providers have no leeway to push up price based on the claim that costs were higher than anticipated (regardless of whether costs were *actually* higher). This reimbursement system encourages them to reduce costs so as to maximize the difference between costs and the fixed price (i.e. profit). If output levels are sustained, there is a net efficiency gain. However, fixed-price reimbursement could also leave the way open for providers to cut corners on aspects of quality which are difficult to monitor, and may encourage 'cream-skimming', for providers have a financial incentive to seek to admit only low-cost clients. Without close monitoring, clients' characteristics may not be readily apparent to purchasers, so that cream-skimming could occur without their knowledge.

Cost-plus reimbursement has its own difficulties. It does not encourage providers to pare down the costs of achieving given quality standards or user outcomes (poor productive efficiency), although it does have the potential to limit cream-skimming and shirking on quality. In regard to cost inflation providers could justify higher costs by claiming that clients were of higher-than-expected dependency. Yet this might not actually be the case; these additional costs could in fact arise because of a penchant for higher management emoluments, larger dividends for share-holders or other expenditures unrelated to care.

Difficulties of this kind might make incentive contracts attractive, for they allow purchasers (or regulators) to adjust the ratio of fixed-price to cost-plus reimbursement components, and so hopefully establish a favourable balance of consequences. No authority in our sample was yet using an incentive contract, but a number were aware of the benefits of mixing reimbursement schemes. One Director said:

> As far as a straight purchase of a bed is concerned there is the contract, full stop, and that is [priced] at DSS rates. But the care managers have a fair amount of discretion to spot-purchase *additional* things and that's the way we will try to do it.

Other authorities were using discretion in regard to additional payments to compensate providers with high dependency clients. For example, some purchasers were willing to pay higher rates after some time where clients were found to be more dependent than originally expected.

The choice of reimbursement mechanism has implications for how purchasers and providers approach uncertainties about future levels of need and cost. Purchasers will not know for sure the number and characteristics of people who may require services in the future, and providers will not know their future costs. Both will be able to make informed predictions, but both will be looking to agree contracts which do not expose them to too much risk.[2] Uncertainty about costs could be tackled by using some degree of cost-plus reimbursement. Regardless of the actual cost of providing the service, the provider receives the fixed and certain mark-up, and in return for this reduction of risk, the purchaser should be able to reduce the mark-up payment so that, if costs work out as expected, payment is lower than would be the case under a fixed-price contract.

In contrast to these various implications for informational imperfections, the choice of reimbursement mechanism is unlikely to have implications for market structure. When structural imperfections give providers market power they are generally able to command higher levels of payment irrespective of the reimbursement mechanism used. Furthermore, the choice of reimbursement does not have direct implications for the scale of bargaining costs or the costs of selective intervention. However, looking at transactions costs more broadly, fixed-price contracts are less costly to implement – purchasers can just shop around for the best price – whereas cost-plus arrangements need audited financial accounts. Perhaps the most costly are incentive arrangements because of the complexity of having fixed-price and cost-plus elements. These operating costs must be set against the potentially large transactions costs savings – through reduced informational losses – expected from the use of an appropriate incentive contract arrangement.

Spot or block contracts

Contracts are distinguished by whether payment is made for units of services (day places, residential beds, domiciliary care hours) or for clients. Block contracts buy units of particular types of service at an agreed price regardless of whether services are used. Case-by-case contracts usually link payment directly to clients while they are using the service (see Chapter 5).

Choice of contract has no direct bearing on the adverse consequences of any information imperfections, except through the constraints it imposes on the reimbursement mechanisms. Case-by-case contracts can be reimbursed in any of the ways set out in the previous subsection. But strict cost-plus reimbursement is incompatible with block contracts. This means that block contracts are not vulnerable to misrepresentation of costs linked to client (dependency) characteristics, because payment is linked only to the quantity and quality of services. They are, however, open to the problems of shirking and cream-skimming.

Contract choice has consequences for dealing with uncertainty. Because block contracts guarantee a level of revenue, small or risk-averse providers may be prepared to accept smaller payments in return for this insurance. One independent sector provider echoed this, saying:

> My instinct is that you are better off having the certainty than making a profit. I have tried to make a profit and to do entrepreneurial things, but the entrepreneurial things for me are setting up different formats. Making the last cent out of things is not very clever.

At the same time, block contracts leave purchasers with the risk of having either too few or too many places in the facilities that clients want to use. The Department of Health directive on choice obviously exacerbates this risk. One interviewee's rationale for not using block contracts was:

> because we cannot direct people to go to a particular home. It is only working through their personal choice . . . [Thus], we cannot guarantee that we will take up ten places a year in a particular home, even if it is the cheapest home and provides the best care.

If purchasers are dealing with a large number of clients and buying a wide variety of places under block contracts, then the chances of being wrong are lessened. They might therefore be more willing to take the risk of letting block contracts if they believe they can secure a lower rate than the spot purchase price (which will be the case if *providers* are not prepared to take much risk). Moreover, protecting valued, small providers from risk may be a sensible strategy for purchasers if it keeps the market viable in the future. A Director noted this instability or uncertainty problem. With block contracts, there is:

> the kind of information that the providers require in order to plan and have some medium-term security – you are not going to take on extra staff if you think or know you are going out of business. So that is why I think we might need to move towards block purchasing rather than spot purchasing.

The risk to purchasers in using block contracts comes from price fluctuations. If future spot prices are higher than the agreed price for the block contract, the authority can save money but at the risk of undermining the viability of smaller providers. If future spot prices are lower than the agreed price, public money may appear to have been wasted. Despite the benefits of certainty, one Director expressed a common concern when he said:

> There is a lot of reluctance here in the authority to sign these [block] contracts in case we are paying for something which we could have got for half price two years down the road.

It is sometimes claimed that block contracts can install local monopolies, but this need not be the case unless a purchaser deliberately negotiates large block contracts with just one or a few large providers (in which case the contract holder has the opportunity to exploit market power and to destroy potential future competition). The trade-off, clearly, is between the insurance benefits generated by large block contracts and the dangers of excessive market power.

In general, block contracts should be cheaper to operate than case-by-case contracts because they offer economies of scale in drafting and negotiation. Moreover, they should reduce informational losses associated with uncertainty because they provide insurance opportunities. On the other hand, block contracts restrict choice, and they require more careful consideration and investment in estimating expected patterns of demand, and may later need to involve more negotiation and bargaining over some of the details of placements or reimbursements. By contrast, case-by-case arrangements give authorities more opportunity to be proactive. Whether block contracts will reduce total transactions costs is difficult to calculate because of the degree of conflict between the individual components of total transactions costs.

A number of authorities in our sample had floated off sizeable proportions of their own services to trusts or other bodies and were buying places under block contract. The independent sector providers in these areas had expressed concern that this practice was undermining competition or tilting the playing field, especially because in many cases these former local authority homes were more expensive by virtue of operating with staff on local authority conditions of service. Representatives of independent sector providers – who argued that the rationale for offering these block contracts was largely political – wanted these trusts to compete with them for *spot* contracts. In fact, a few of these authorities made it clear that their choice of contract was a question of transactions costs. They were singly or jointly responsible (with other purchasers such as health authorities) for a certain number of clients who were destined for these homes, and were tied into these agreements. It was therefore easier and less costly to place these clients en bloc. Moreover, a level playing field would be partially restored if an authority was willing to let block contracts with independent sector providers (as long as they met the appropriate specifications).

Specification and monitoring

Earlier in the chapter we set out the production of welfare framework, showing the links between resources, services and their qualities, and the various outcomes for users. Purchasers' ultimate aims are to secure high levels of final outcome at least cost. Difficulties arise because the links between resources, needs, service characteristics and outcomes are unknown, unclear or hidden from view. If there were clear and well-defined relationships between intermediate and final outcomes – for example, between quality of care and user quality of life – it might be sufficient to specify contracts (and to undertake monitoring) in terms of intermediate outputs. But this is rarely or un-equivocally the case. We would thus expect informational losses in the form of cream-skimming or shirking.

Contracts (even block contracts) thus need some form of outcome specification even if reimbursement is not made on an outcome basis. Most authorities had barely started to plan the development of final outcome measures at the time of our study. One social services Director gave the example of a small home which had three or four staff on duty at any time. That number was perfectly adequate, but, he noted, the home had thirty or more different staff 'going in and out in the course of a week', generating confusion for the elderly residents. 'I think when you talk about outcomes we are a long way from having real outcomes.'

Should authorities be striving to set up contracts with complete specifications or should they work with loose specifications? A loose or incomplete specification could exacerbate problems of asymmetric information, for providers have greater freedom to pursue their own interests rather than those of the purchaser or user. On the other hand, a loose specification may be more conducive to the establishment of *trust relationships* and so-called *obligational contracts* (Sako 1992). In its simplest form, the argument about obligational contracts suggests that if parties to a transaction can be trusted to behave appropriately then the need for close monitoring is reduced. Because obligational contracts are embedded in more particularistic social relations between trading partners who entertain a sense of mutual trust, transactions can take place without prior agreement on all the terms and conditions of trade. In other words, contracts can be incomplete, and contingencies which are not fully specified can be overcome without recourse to protracted bargaining and arbitration in the form of universalistic legal or normative rules, as would be the case for more highly-specified 'classical' contracts (what Sako calls arm's-length relationships). Trust has long been seen as a lubricant for contractual relations (Arrow 1974), and is widely recognized in social care. One Director explained that they were going to avoid contracts which had complex intermediate output and input specifications:

> We do not want to tie people down . . . It is a genuine partnership. If it does not work, we will have a look at it again but I think that is the way to approach it.

A task for local authorities is to develop strategies which can promote and sustain trust between trading partners, and indeed to shape this trust so that it lubricates transactions and generates desired outcomes. Other things being equal, strategies should be encouraged which economize on transactions costs. This is likely to be the case in what has been called 'contractual trust', which rests on the moral norms of honesty and keeping promises which are inculcated in people through socialization and education (Sako 1992). To perpetuate a relationship based on contractual trust, parties must endorse moral integrity in transactions, and move away from total or default reliance on legal sanctions. Trust of this kind might also develop out of the cultivation of personal networks.

The choice of specification has no direct ramifications for the incidence of structural losses. Provider market power could be exploited to influence prices or push up profit margins whether the contract is tightly or loosely specified. However, the requirement to meet highly detailed specifications is clearly a barrier to entry – a structural imperfection – so that looser specifications might encourage competition. In addition, they might lead to higher bargaining costs but lower problems of selective intervention. The incidence of bargaining is higher because loose specification covers fewer contingencies. However, even bargaining costs may not be prohibitive if each party to a transaction trusts the other to reveal pertinent information truthfully. There may still be problems as to how spoils should be divided when bargaining, but the growing literature on trust highlights norms and conventions that provide clear, if implicit, guidelines to overcome difficulties of this kind.

Generally, tightly-specified contracts will be more costly to draft and monitor. One local authority Director stated:

> We have got service specifications for residential care and that was a tortuous exercise. It was very salutary. We started out with specifications which were far too complex and actually scrapped these for much, much simpler ones. We worked out that we could not manage the process with overcomplex specifications, let alone pay for it. We certainly could not manage the evaluation process, so we have drawn back from that.

Overall, it is readily apparent that the obligational mode of working has the potential to reduce total transactions costs quite significantly. However, in some ways obligational contracting is a high-risk strategy, for there are relatively few safeguards if things go wrong. Thus it might be more accurate to say that *expected* total transactions costs are probably lower, and to note that the collapse of trust relationships *could* produce seriously inefficient resource allocations.

Conclusion

This chapter has used an economic framework to analyse some of the principal features of social care markets and, in particular, to examine the choices open to local authorities in their arrangements for commissioning. The analysis has been based upon a theoretical framework derived from 'new institutional economics'. Five categories of transactions costs have been identified, and the differential impact on each of alternative regulatory frameworks has been posited. At the time of our fieldwork, most local authorities were giving little consideration as to how markets might be shaped to achieve the range of social, political and economic goals which we have previously outlined. As they increasingly turn their attention to such market-shaping activities, they need to bear in mind the transactions costs outlined here in their choice of commissioning arrangements. In addition, it is imperative that the arrangements they design are sensitive to their own local market contexts. Governance arrangements that seem appropriate in one market context may be entirely inappropriate in others. In the final chapter we further explore the implication of this and our other analyses for the continuing process of shaping social care markets.

Notes

1 This framework is more general than the simpler 'market failure' approach employed in the first phase of our research (Knapp *et al.* 1994; Wistow *et al.* 1994).
2 Where one party is more averse to risk than the other, the contract could be structured such that both parties benefit. If, for example, purchasers have less aversion to risk than providers (because of their scale), uncertainty about numbers of clients could be dealt with by changing contract types from case-by-case to block contracts.

9

Conclusion: harnessing and developing the market

Introduction

The community care reforms were designed to achieve the most far-reaching and complex changes in the funding, organization and delivery of social care services since the creation of the post-war welfare state. It was not expected that such fundamental changes would be secured overnight and, indeed, the *Caring for People* agenda was described as one for 'a decade and beyond'. Accordingly, the Department of Health's implementation programme focused on ensuring that local authorities had in place the minimum requirements implied by the shift in responsibilities from the social security system to social services departments.

These requirements were specified in Departmental guidance as, first, establishing arrangements for assessing individual care needs, especially of those who would previously have been supported through the social security system; and, second, arranging the provision of care in response to such assessments (Department of Health 1992a). These requirements were further elaborated as a series of eight 'key tasks' on which local authorities, in collaboration with other agencies, would need to concentrate in order to reach a minimum state of preparedness by April 1993. Thus, our fieldwork evidence – gathered predominantly in the months immediately following that date – must be seen against the background of those limited implementation targets and also as a consequence, at least in part, of that implementation focus.

This is not to suggest that the government's implementation strategy was in some sense deficient: as we have shown in previous chapters, its strategy generally succeeded in achieving the necessary minimal state of preparedness across the country as a whole. Rather, we simply wish to emphasize that the findings from this study must be assessed in the light of both the initial tasks which local authorities were set and also their understanding of the roles and responsibilities implicit in those tasks. More particularly, local authorities were called upon not to take over the operation of established social care markets but to create a largely new market structure capable *in the long run* of meeting a set of challenging policy objectives. Moreover, the creation of social care markets was only one element of the community care reforms (Wistow *et al.* 1994: 24–5). In our initial study, we sought to simplify the complexity of the reforms through the identification of four core strategic dimensions of policy change (reproduced in Box 9.1).

Box 9.1   Strategic dimensions of change

Institutional services   _ _ _ _ _ _ _ _ _ _ _ _ _   Community services

Supply-led services   _ _ _ _ _ _ _ _ _ _ _ _ _   Needs-led services

Public sector provision   _ _ _ _ _ _ _ _ _   Independent sector provision

NHS auspices   _ _ _ _ _ _ _ _ _ _ _ _   Local government auspices

---

This process of disaggregating the overall policy into its component parts also provides a format for depicting the essential features of what may be termed the 'old' and the 'new' community care. Thus, the nature of community care in at least the last two decades can be represented by the characteristics shown on the left-hand side of the figure: supply-led, provider-dominated services, often delivered in 'institutional' settings, delivered predominantly by the public sector and – for some user groups – with an inappropriately large role for services based on medical and nursing models. By contrast, the right-hand side of the figure encapsulates the features of community care to which current policy is directed: needs-led, purchaser-dominated services, often based at home or in homely settings, delivered through a pluralistic system of supply and organized under the auspices of the local authority lead role.

Broadly speaking, therefore, the underlying purpose of *Caring for People* may be seen as encouraging shifts along each dimension from left to right. However, concerted movement along those dimensions implies not only a substantial change agenda but also the need to manage change in ways which ensure a smooth transition and continuity of provision for existing users. Such tasks are complicated by variations at local level in the starting points for change on each dimension, views about how far along them the respective endpoints should lie, and the speed at which change can be made in the light of local resource constraints, political preferences and other circumstances.

Further complications arise from the potential tensions, if not contradictions, between the four dimensions themselves, and also between those dimensions and the smooth transition imperative. There is a fundamental issue about the relative weight to be given to each dimension of change and especially the relative priority to be accorded to the objectives of creating a mixed economy and community-based needs-led services. In particular, the underdeveloped nature of the independent domiciliary care sector seriously constrains the pace of development of alternatives to hospital, residential and nursing home care. This inherent difficulty is further compounded by the smooth transition objective as reflected in the requirement for local authorities to spend 85 per cent of the social security transfer on independent sector provision.

Local authorities were, therefore, seeking to implement the changes in a context of complex and potentially competing objectives. Our work since 1990 has enabled us to understand more about the opportunities and barriers associated with the creation of social care markets and a more mixed economy of supply within the framework of policy objectives described above. In the next section, we summarize the findings reported in previous chapters about the key characteristics of the social care markets which began to emerge largely during 1993 and 1994.

Summary findings: characteristics of social care

Our findings may be grouped in two main categories: those concerned with market characteristics and those concerned with the motivations and perceptions of key stake-holders. In respect of the latter, we saw in Chapters 2, 3 and 7 that some important differences existed in local authorities' approaches to commissioning, although there had been significant changes in attitudes and beliefs since 1991. In particular, social services departments were increasingly describing their task as that of managing 'the market' rather than managing a mixed economy of care. Although 'market enthusiasts' remained in a minority in 1993, most authorities could be described as 'market pragmatists'. A crude anti-commercialism was being replaced by a more cautious recognition that social care markets could offer potential benefits and opportunities for users and carers as well as problems which would still need to be overcome. Thus sixteen of our twenty-five authorities saw overall advantages in developing markets. Although only nine directors clearly expected markets to succeed, sixteen identified actual or emerging improvements in choice, associated with the introduction of assessment processes and related changes in professional practice by frontline staff. Similarly, fifteen identified improvements in cost-effectiveness, which were associated with local authorities using their purchasing power 'to drive down prices'.

Turning to provider perspectives, we showed in Chapter 6 that sector, size and background were all relevant to an understanding of provider motivations. Our study of residential homes in the independent sector suggested that motivations were far less homogeneous than purchasers apparently assumed. Although we found a significant relationship between commercially-oriented behaviour and the extent of local competition, private sector providers tended not to be profit-maximizers. In addition, professional goals were more highly ranked than commercial ones. Only a minority of providers appeared close to the profit-maximizing ideal type; usually these were relatively large homes in the private sector and part of multi-home organizations. In this respect, there was some correspondence between local authority perceptions of the motivations of 'the big boys' and our evidence. For the most part, however, purchasers misunderstood the diversity of attitudes and motivations among providers. Different motivations are likely to lead to different behavioural outcomes, and these outcomes will be influenced by the degree of structural and informational imperfections that prevail. Ultimately this will affect the degree of success in achieving the policy goals mentioned above.

The structural and informational characteristics of the emerging social care markets were discussed in Chapter 8, where we identified significant imperfections compared with textbook benchmarks. In Chapters 4 and 8 we indicated the sort of information that local authorities need. However, we also showed that such information was not only incomplete but also asymmetrically distributed between purchasers and providers. For the former, the purchasing function remains underdeveloped in regard to basic market analysis and market mapping. For example, in most authorities needs mapping was still in its infancy. It was widely regarded as complex and costly, and typically was limited to identifying current usage rather than mapping latent or future needs.

In addition, almost all authorities in our sample raised the issue of underdevelopment of supply, particularly independent domiciliary services. Many directors expected that some of their preferred providers (especially small homes) would go out of business, but few authorities were systematically seeking to shape the supply side. No local authority interviewee expected there to be sufficient independent sector non-residential services; and even 'market enthusiasts' were cautious about expanding such services in the private sector because of the lack of a statutory framework for regulation. There were also doubts among local authorities about the scope for diversification by residential providers because it represented a shift into fundamentally different types of business for which many were ill-equipped. For providers, deterrents to diversification included: uncertainty about patterns of demand and purchasers' intentions; a recognition that day and domiciliary care were significantly different businesses from residential care and could be intrusive to residents; small profit margins; and the need for different types of staff when such staff are difficult to recruit.

We found no evidence of major supply-side difficulties arising from such structural weaknesses during the immediate post-implementation period. However, the numbers of residential and nursing home placements were lower than expected and the vast majority of authorities were anticipating oversupply during the year. Seventeen authorities expected there to be business failures: only one did not. Anticipated failure rates ranged from 15 to 50 per cent. All but four authorities were developing contingency arrangements to prevent or to cope with business failures.

In 1991, the vast majority of local authorities had few direct contacts with the private sector as social care providers. In 1993, however, the private sector was on authorities' policy and purchasing maps as an accepted part of the mixed economy. Nevertheless, the development of genuine partnerships between local authorities and the private sector remained very uneven. Two authorities reported provider cartels but most said that, currently, the private sector either lacks coherence or is genuinely competitive.

Although there was an awareness of informational and structural weaknesses, thinking about market shapes, structures and forms of regulation and governance was limited to two areas. First concerns existed about the perceived dangers of monopoly or oligopoly supply. Second, purchasers often expressed preferences for preserving a multiplicity of small providers in residential and nursing home markets. Both preferences were associated with concerns to maintain quality and to work with voluntary rather than private providers in the domiciliary market. The latter preference can be seen to derive from purchasers' views about the lack of statutory regulation in this field, together with the risks associated with the delivery of care to vulnerable people in their own homes. While these two lines of thinking indicate an awareness of structural and informational imperfections, such considerations seldom went any further. As such, this example illustrates a more fundamental limitation in the conceptual frameworks, perceptions and beliefs held by local authority purchasers about how to coordinate the social care system using market mechanisms. In Chapter 7 we described attitudes and expectations regarding the degree of choice, cost-effectiveness and innovation that local markets would deliver, based upon authorities' assumptive worlds and understandings of the implications of using markets to allocate social care. However, the economic perspective of Chapter 8 suggests that decisions concerning regulatory and commissioning frameworks were not based on an assessment of the full range of potential transactions costs. Indeed, there seemed to be a tendency to place greater emphasis on certain aspects of transactions costs, and less or none on others. For example, many purchasers reported the perceived benefits of markets in creating strong incentives for providers to be cost-effective and responsive, but appeared to be less aware of the informational problems associated with the use of markets or the costs of negotiation to resolve unforeseen contingencies. These findings reinforce the view that purchasers were implicitly working with a somewhat unsophisticated market model and there was little evidence that authorities were striving to broaden their conceptual frameworks and understanding of the kinds developed in Chapter 8. In what follows, we consider the implications of our findings for the roles which local authorities have been given in managing social care markets.

Market management and regulation

Symptomatic of the lack of sophistication in some purchasers' thinking was their conception of 'the market' as though it were a single, undifferentiated entity. Rather, a market can be thought of as a mechanism to allocate resources, the features of which vary according to both its regulatory framework – that is, the distribution of legally and contractually defined control and its incentive/reimbursement structures – and also the institutional context, which embraces political, cultural and historical factors. A whole range of market types is possible, therefore, from a pure, textbook model to a highly managed, quasi-market. Moreover, they are likely to differ not only from authority to authority but also across client groups and service types. Furthermore, as behaviour is contingent on incentive structures and the distribution of control of key decisions between purchaser and provider (for example, about pricing, reimbursement arrangements, contract compliance and so forth) different market systems can produce very different outcomes. In fact, it is often useful to think, more generally, of a market as being a particular *governance structure* that includes non-market, hierarchical structures and also networks (Williamson 1985; Rhodes 1995). This concept is slightly more general than the term *regulatory framework* used in Chapter 8 because it explicitly recognizes social embeddedness (for example, the impact of norms and values of key stakeholders; see Smeltzer and Swedberg 1994; Granovetter 1995).

The theoretical framework presented in Chapter 8 suggests that, given a particular governance arrangement, structural and informational imperfections are key determinants of the size of total transactions costs in a mixed economy. In principle, such imperfections could lead to inefficiently high transactions costs within pure markets (Le Grand and Bartlett 1993; Forder *et al.* 1996). We argued in Chapter 8 that the choice of appropriate commissioning arrangements could reduce transactions costs, given the level of imperfections, by modifying governance structures so that they deal better with prevailing imperfections. The essence of this market management strategy is ensuring that regulatory forms match prevailing imperfections (see Chapter 8). In addition to modifying governance, local authorities could also attempt to tackle the root causes of these structural and information imperfections. Although there can be no presumption that *reducing* imperfections will necessarily lower transactions costs, authorities should also be aware that it may be more cost-effective for them to change the nature of the prevailing *imperfections* rather than to change the existing forms of *regulation*.

The kinds of information needed by local authority commissioners were set out earlier, ranging over current and future needs, supply, costs and users' and carers' preferences. Action to improve the availability of information – and thus to directly tackle information imperfections – could take a number of forms as indicated in Box 9.2. We should note that our evidence suggests that relatively few of these measures had been developed across the sample authorities.

Box 9.2   Improving available information

A   Legal removal of constraints on the provision of information by providers, including financial information.

B   Financial and quality audits of providers as part of the contract negotiation.

C   Openness in contract bidding (contract details available publicly).

D   Monitoring and review mechanisms to check provider performance in meeting contract specifications.

E   Joint initiatives between commissioners and groups of providers (including associations).

F   Joint consultative forums with providers.

G   Regular surveys of providers in a given market.

H   Analysis of the financial security of providers.

I   Development of better techniques for measuring user and carer needs and outcomes, and their utilization in routine settings.

J   Development of better information systems, information technology (ISIT), and wider access to data.

K   Dissemination of medium- and long-term purchasing plans.

L   Dissemination of authorities' current and predicted purchasing arrangements.

M   Dissemination of details of authority's methods of: contracting, payment, monitoring and market management (such as rescue packages and protocols for safeguarding residents).

Where structural imperfections exist, there is a case for local authorities adopting some combination of subsidies, franchising and competition policies. Offering subsidies to new organizations to help them overcome entry barriers (or offering them to current providers who are otherwise unable to expand or diversify) could take the form of training and advice, legal advocacy and simple financial transfers. Local authorities could support franchising by established providers to circumvent some of the problems of high costs of market entry. In addition, local authorities could be empowered to develop local 'trade and industry' policies to maintain or improve market competitiveness (see Box 9.3). For example, they could support providers in the private capital market by offering collateral and supplying low-cost finance.

In practice, efforts to reduce imperfections can only be partially effective; there is no doubt that the main social care markets do and will continue to

---

Box 9.3   Trade and industry (competition) policies

- Overcome entry barriers by subsidies (grants and financial incentives), assistance with staff training, or other means.

- Regulate provision of venture capital, and support providers in the private capital market (by providing collateral and supplying low-cost finance).

- Ensure that potential providers can easily access the information they need in order to enter a market (such as information on purchasers' plans, openness on current contracts, details of accreditation requirements, and so on).

- Lower the artificial barriers stemming from government legislation, such as preferred provider relations, streamline registration and accreditation procedures.

- Exercise legal powers to block anti-competitive behaviour, such as some mergers, brand proliferation, predatory pricing.

- Exercise legal powers of disintegration to break up monopolies.

- Resist the opportunities to exploit monopsony powers to drive prices down if this could undermine the viability (and quality) of providers.

---

exhibit significant degrees of informational and structural imperfections. Moreover, many social care needs are such that they imply long-term contact between users and providers in which the quality and continuity of personal relationships are key features of the social care services as economic goods that local authorities wish to buy. As we have stated, such imperfections and the nature of social care services will mean inefficiently high transactions costs in pure markets trading with classical contracts. However, it is clear that the main social care markets are significantly removed from the pure market model and that considerable scope exists for local authorities to adapt existing governance structures; that is, to employ alternative commissioning arrangements, regulatory policies and so forth. There may, for example, be gains from using incentive contracts, especially those that employ subjective performance assessment and those embedded in trust relationships. There might also be advantages in using systems of 'managed floating' prices rather than fixed prices (especially as the latter are often *ad hoc*). Preferred provider lists could help to control the transactions costs associated with informational imperfections. Some authorities were beginning to appreciate that their purchasing power could be used to force down prices.

The relative merits of alternative commissioning arrangements were discussed in the last chapter. We considered not only advantages but also the problems: for example, the threatening of provider viability and potential exacerbation of information problems. Low prices not only attract organizations that are likely to cut corners, but also endanger trust relationships that otherwise could operate very effectively at minimizing information problems.

At this early stage of the development of social care markets, authorities were understandably cautious in choosing their purchasing and other arrangements. It is premature and dangerous to generalize, especially since the relationships between the whole array of commissioning arrangements and regulatory structures is complex and multidimensional; but it is questionable whether the commissioning arrangements that are currently being developed lead to regulatory frameworks that are too hierarchical and thus too costly. On the other hand, it is also arguable that the rhetoric and expressed understandings of our local authority respondents are located too close to the pure market endpoint. The optimum lies somewhere between the endpoints of hierarchy and pure markets though its identification may be as difficult in practice as it is in principle. In the next section we consider these issues further in our analysis of local authorities' purchasing role.

Developing the purchasing role

Local authorities are called upon to perform a range of roles in the market, which may be summarized under three broad headings: purchasing (including creating and shaping the supply side); providing; and monitoring. Each of these roles in the new market implies a changed or different approach from that carried out by social services departments in the pre–1993 mixed economy. Thus, monitoring is not only given greater prominence as part of an outcomes-oriented culture, but becomes more significant in a context where a greater volume of care is purchased from external providers. Similarly, the scale and scope of the provider role is not only being redefined, often very considerably, but the development of internal cost centres and trading accounts are substantially changing the relationships between in-house service providers, local politicians and other parts of the local authority, which are themselves now in the process of being market-tested. In particular, public accountability is now to be exercised more frequently through the arm's-length process of service specification and contract monitoring than day-to-day operational management through the traditional hierarchies of local authority departments and their committees.

It is, however, the purchasing role which represents the largest departure from established ways of working in social services departments. In the past, developmental and financial processes have been dominated by the allocation of resources to in-house services, generally in response to provider-led definitions of need. In future, departments will increasingly be expected to purchase externally, on behalf of users and carers, and with greater degrees of responsiveness to their needs and preferences. It is worth recalling at this point the rationale for the separation of purchaser and provider roles, which lies at the heart of the concept of enabling as market development. Indeed, this is the fundamental organizational principle of market-orientated reforms more generally in the public sector.

- First, dissaggregating these functions enables a greater degree of functional specialization. In particular, it strengthens functions which have hitherto been weak or ill-defined: needs identification; service specifications; clarifying the financial implications of decision-making; and performance review. Such functions have traditionally tended to be subordinated to the day-to-day demands of provider management.
- Second, the separation is intended to weaken the influence of providers' vested interests in the identification of needs and service responses, thereby better enabling the creation of a needs-led system of care. As the Audit Commission has argued, 'it allows commissioners to concentrate on and listen to the user without the pressure to favour their own service provision' (1992b: 20).
- Third, and by the same token, the purchaser/provider separation is designed to achieve change on the supply side. Providers become more responsive to need when resources cease to be allocated to them automatically and instead are held by those responsible for needs assessment and service specification. The introduction of competition between suppliers is similarly expected to promote gains in responsiveness to need, choice, cost-effectiveness and innovation.

This purchasing role is technically, politically and organizationally demanding. It is technically demanding because it requires a substantial development of skills in the areas of needs identification, service specification and quality assurance, as we have already outlined in Chapter 1. It is politically demanding in requiring a shift from the traditional local authority culture of civic pride in provision to a less tangible form of civic pride in the outcomes secured on behalf of users and carers. Finally, it may be considered organizationally demanding because the purchasing role requires collaboration as well as competition. Thus, effective purchasing depends upon a recognition that purchasing and providing are interdependent rather than separate activities. Mature purchasers should focus, first, on what they wish to buy and for whom; second, on how it is best coordinated and supplied; and third, with what longer-term implications for providers and the market. This task requires them to secure suppliers with the value base and organizational capacity to deliver the outcomes for users that policy objectives demand. In addition, mature purchasers need to be sensitive to the needs, motivations and vulnerabilities of suppliers, including the impact on them of purchasing decisions and behaviours.

In our initial study, we found that local authorities' attitudes towards the market were predominantly based on a crude anti-commercialism. Now that the social care market is beginning to operate, a central issue is whether this anti-commercialism will be translated into a no less crude form of 'macho purchasing', as some of our empirical evidence appeared to suggest (Chapters 2 and 7). Purchasers have a power to undermine as well as to create markets. In Chapters 2 and 6, for example, we described the concern of providers that the process of managing down residential and nursing home markets would lead to the 'wrong' homes closing, a view which both purchasers and providers generally equated with the demise of small homes offering high-quality care in homely settings. Such an outcome could either be accelerated or prevented by the different ways in which authorities exercise their purchasing powers. Earlier research argued that local authorities got the voluntary sector they 'deserve' in the sense that local voluntary sectors reflected the level of resources and the degree of skill which authorities invested in their development (Challis et al. 1988). The findings from our work with both purchasers and providers suggest a similar message for local authorities in respect of their relationships with the private sector: that it is essential for them to be aware of and responsive to the needs and vulnerabilities of providers no less than those of users and carers. Indeed, an effective response to the latter largely depends upon fostering secure and appropriately motivated suppliers. A key market management task for local authorities is, therefore, to relate with equal sensitivity to both the supply and demand sides of the market. Thus, the strategic skills and sensitivities which authorities develop and deploy in their purchasing role will determine how far they achieve the market structures that will produce the service outcomes demanded by the Caring for People objectives.

The introduction of the NHS market was similarly characterized by concern that the new purchasing authorities were adopting stances towards providers based on stereotypical understandings of roles within 'commercial' markets. The then Minister of Health warned that such behaviours reflected misconceived notions of purchaser/provider relationships in other sectors and advocated an approach which placed more emphasis on collaboration.

> References to the 'purchaser/provider split' . . . convey an image of 'stand off' relationships. That is not what we want . . . Market relationships in the private sector . . . are built on partnership and long-term agreements. I believe we can learn a lot from private sector experiences in this area.
>
> (Mawhinney 1993: 19)

In practice, the respective roles of competition and collaboration within markets are more complex than this formulation allows (Wistow and Hardy 1996; and Chapter 8). None the less, the literature on trust and obligational contracts alluded to in the previous chapter provides some degree of theoretical underpinning for the ministerial advice. As Chapter 8 argues, governance arrangements which promote trust and obligational relationships may be effective in mitigating imperfections in social care markets. A further foundation for the Minister's approach is provided by the notion that 'social care is different'. Perhaps most especially, many social care needs are such that they imply long-term contacts between service users and service providers in which the quality and continuity of personal relationships, no less than the environment in which care is provided, are important aspects of their effectiveness. Only in respect of the most simple needs and solutions do user/provider relationships approximate to the pre-defined, self-liquidating transactions of classical contracts in which the identities of the parties concerned are largely irrelevant considerations. Such characteristics of social care needs and service delivery processes are also consistent with contracts between purchasers and providers based on trust, long-term relationships and an understanding of provider vulnerabilities to changes in market conditions and purchasing behaviours.

Such collaborative relationships do, of course, carry with them the danger of purchasers becoming too close to their providers and thereby undermining the rationale for separating the two functions (what we called 'influence transactions costs' in Chapter 8). However, an awareness that the needs of both users and providers may best be served through long-term relationships does not inevitably lead to what is termed 'provider capture', the process by which purchasers succumb to the influence and interests of providers. If they are to avoid this outcome, purchasers need not only to display *sensitivity* in their relationships with providers: they also need to be *robust* and *business-like* in their dealings with them.

As was argued above, purchasing and providing functions are being separated in order that the former may provide a challenge on behalf of users to the vested interests of the latter. That role requires the determined exercise of responsibilities for defining outcomes, identifying need, specifying the volume, mix and quality of services to meet those needs, and monitoring provider performance against identified needs, desired outcomes and available budgets. In effect, purchasers have to maintain a delicate balance between robust performance management, on the one hand, and sensitivity to the potential consequences of that robustness for provider viability, on the other. Excessively macho purchasing is no more in the interests of end users than the re-establishment of excessively cosy relationships between purchasers and providers. We identify below more specific actions that social services departments may need to take if they are to be successful in shaping the markets in ways which meet users' needs.

Implications for local authorities

The general tenor of the argument in this book is that neither pure market nor pure hierarchy is an appropriate governance structure for the successful operation of the mixed economy of social care. Instead, some intermediate form of quasi-market (embedded in a social network) where relationships are more integrated and collaborative appears more desirable. Even then, for quasi-markets to be workable, local authorities will need to acquire both a better understanding of the impact of different forms of governance or regulation on the mixed economy of social care and the skills appropriate to their new roles as regulators. In particular, it is essential that they exercise their purchasing responsibilities in the light of the potential for market failures, to help the development of new providers and sustain existing providers of proven quality and reliability. Leaving the allocation of community care to Adam Smith's 'invisible hand of the market' could be seriously damaging. Indeed, local authorities should use two very visible hands – as service commissioners and market managers – to shape the new markets. Above, and in the last two chapters, we have discussed ways in which local authorities could manage the mixed economy of social care, to install appropriate governance arrangements to address imperfections, and problems that stem from the special nature of social care. Generalizing from across our sample – and recognizing the need for local variations as appropriate – a number of examples of tasks for local authorities implied by our research are:

- Local authorities should encourage new providers – particularly in domiciliary and day care – and diversification by some existing providers. They should also protect others. Many are keen to encourage *small* providers – even if they are more costly – because of an assumed or observed quality premium.
- Most authorities are being cautious about *price* competition: currently there is little. But if social care markets are to function fully and properly to achieve the efficiencies which the government expects, authorities will need more flexible pricing policies.
- Authorities should be sensitive to the motivations, needs, interests, strengths and weaknesses of providers. In particular, they may need to give special consideration to ways in which local voluntary organizations can compete on a level playing field with other sectors.
- There is also a clear need to improve the information flows from authorities to current and potential providers. This may be achieved by attacking information imperfections directly and/or by using governance arrangements that blunt incentives to misuse information.
- Standardized contracts cut operating and implementation (transactions) costs but increase the (transactions) costs of dealing with information imperfections (for example, the need for adequate monitoring). There were some inordinately complex contracts in use in some authorities. Over time, authorities and providers need to promote greater trust across the purchaser/provider divide: to act collaboratively as well as competitively. The common preference for voluntary over private sector providers, and for traditional over new providers, is often built on familiarity and trust.
- Authorities should encourage a range of market behaviours by current and potential providers. However, they should beware of aggressive price-cutting and other ploys to protect or expand market share such that, in the longer term, market power can be exploited to the benefit of a provider and to the detriment of purchasers and users.

- There are dangers in allowing local authorities' provider roles to be determined *only* by market forces; in particular, they should not be solely defined in residual terms − that is, by whatever private and voluntary agencies do not supply. Authorities have to provide a safety net − as 'providers of the last resort' − but generally they should choose their niches proactively not reactively, and be informed by an awareness of comparative advantage.

- There is a need to tackle market structure imperfections. A variety of local *trade and industry* policies may be used to stimulate greater competition and regulate the emerging markets. In addition, authorities could use commissioning arrangements whose successful operation is not sensitive to the existence of market structure imperfections (for example, partnership arrangements).

- Local authorities should give more *voice* to users and utilize their perceptions of quality and outcomes alongside, or maybe even in lieu of, complex/ expensive monitoring.

Conclusion

In our initial study, we suggested that, from one perspective, the *Caring for People* changes should be seen as the introduction of the 'new public management' (Hood 1991) into the fields of community and social care. Like community care itself, 'new public management' is in many respects a portmanteau term, the meaning of which continues to evolve. Rhodes (1995: 5) usefully distinguishes two strands in its development − managerialism and new institutional economics. He further argues that the former was a dominant strand before 1988 while the latter became 'the main influence' thereafter (Rhodes 1995). We have demonstrated here the influence of the 'new institutional economics' in prescribing what might constitute appropriate governance structures in social care, whether markets or not. At the same time, however, *Caring for People* reflected the influence of a further theoretical framework − that of normalization theory − which provided the sources of its underlying social care goals. It is the relevant weight of these two approaches which have formed a central tension in local authorities' implementation of the changes, a tension which was most centrally reflected in their notion that 'social care is different' from other goods and services. In our analysis here, we recognized the relevance of such differences and have been concerned to highlight the importance of ensuring that the new market mechanisms serve − and do not displace or erode − the social care outcomes which the White Paper claimed to advance.

A further problematic feature of the changes from the perspective of local government is their challenge to the traditional hierarchical forms of organization in which responsibility for funding and providing services are integrated. While not, at this stage, questioning the basis of the separation of purchaser and provider functions, our analysis has been concerned with the inappropriateness in social care of market mechanisms based upon a 'text book' or neo-classical model. While the Government has not proposed such a 'purist' model, the predominant source of initial unease about the changes within local authorities grew from their concern that such an approach was intended. What our analysis has demonstrated is that – left to themselves – there are dangers of local social care markets producing outcomes inconsistent with core social care objectives. In practice, we have found no support for the notion that such markets should be self-regulating. However, the continuing task – and debate – is to establish the most appropriate forms of regulation consistent with local circumstances and national policy objectives.

This book has been concerned to identify some of the key dimensions and implications of such an approach. One of the principal themes to have emerged from the analysis is that of 'mature purchasing' based upon the development of long-term relationships, founded on trust, but operating within a regulatory framework which is robust in both its commitment to social goals and to the underlying discipline provided by the possibility of market entry by alternative suppliers. What clearly emerges is an approach which is neither pure hierarchy nor pure market. Its essence is in some respects captured by such terms as 'managing' or 'shaping' the market. However, a more appropriate metaphor may be that of managing inter-organizational networks in which, to adapt Rhodes (1995: 17) 'facilitating, accommodating and bargaining' are among the key roles for social services departments. As Brooke (1989) has also argued, the core role of local authorities in the contract culture is that of the management of influence. It follows from this analysis, therefore, that traditional political skills are no less important than tools of economic analysis as underpinnings for purchasing authorities (Wistow and Hardy 1996).

Finally, we have been cautious about analysing social care markets from too narrow an economic perspective. We have emphasized that the markets were said to have been introduced to promote social care ends and these apparent intentions provide a clear set of non-market criteria for evaluating the success of the community care changes. We have also made clear that resolving the tension between markets and social care objectives is the core element of the continuing management task for local authorities within the current national policy framework. At the same time, however, markets need to be approached from a much broader governance perspective. As we noted in Chapter 1, the introduction of market mechanisms into social care is part of a wider strategy for reducing the role of government – for taking government into the market. However, as Walsh (1995: 256) has argued, the role of government in making judgements between competing values and interests, as well as judgements about the balance between individual and collective interests, remains an essential one.

That such judgements lie at the heart of the purchasing function demonstrates the essentially political nature of this role, whether undertaken by local or central government. In a publicly-funded 'market', purchasers are necessarily accountable for its outcomes in terms of the distribution of resources and, in the case of social care, the quality of life secured for users and carers. It is precisely because 'social care is different' that the extent and form of market regulation is so important.

Appendix
Research methodology

Methods and samples: the 1993 purchaser and provider studies

Sample selection

Much of the empirical material reported in this book was gathered from twenty-five local authorities across England, both in 1991 and 1993. These authorities were selected in 1990 and were representative of all English authorities at that time in relation to:

- political control, May 1990;
- total expenditure on personal social services (PSS) per head of population, 1987–88;
- percentage of total PSS expenditure going to services provided by voluntary organizations and registered private persons, 1987–88 (approximation to contracting out);
- percentage of total PSS expenditure going to general contributions to voluntary organizations and registered private persons, 1987–88; and
- percentage of places in residential care accommodation for elderly people in voluntary and private homes, 1986–87.

We also sampled a small number of voluntary and private organizations across service types and client groups in five of these twenty-five areas in 1993, obtaining general information on their impressions of the developing mixed economy. The collections of information from local authorities and providers were both quantitative and qualitative, and based on: (a) examination of relevant documentation, supplemented with telephone interviews; (b) face-to-face interviews with officers and councillors; and (c) face-to-face interviews with a small number of providers across client groups and service types. We briefly describe each of these components in turn.

1993 pre-interview data collections from sample authorities
The specific questions addressed in the pre-interview activities were:

- What steps has the authority taken to map needs, demands and resources as a basis for formulating purchasing strategies: that is, how well does it understand the local market?
- How is the authority planning to use its special transitional grant and social security transfer: that is, what services is it intending to purchase and in what sectors?
- How is the authority encouraging alternative non-residential service providers?
- What organizational arrangements has the authority established to manage its purchasing function, in particular the extent of budgetary devolution to care managers?
- Do information systems allow expenditure to be adequately monitored?
- What contracting and tendering procedures have been established?
- What arrangements have been made for monitoring/reviewing market developments?
- What contingency arrangements have been made to cope with business/ market 'failure'?

Our first source of information was local documentary sources: principally the community care plans and authorities' written purchasing plans. We also completed a *pro forma* during a telephone interview with (usually) a principal officer in each authority to get a picture of some elements of the mixed economy, and also valuable descriptions of current and intended developments. It was on the basis of this telephone-interview description of *what* authorities were doing that we then conducted the semi-structured face-to-face interviews with Directors and Chairs. In the latter we were asking *why* authorities were developing their commissioning and purchasing functions in particular ways. In this way we were able to gather quite detailed information from a number of sources within each authority.

The telephone interview *pro forma* had three sections: market analysis (mapping needs and demands, mapping supply); market creation (use of the special transitional grant, STG, encouraging supply); and market management and regulation (organizational arrangements for purchasing, service specifications, selection of providers, contracting procedures, involvement of other stake-holders, performance monitoring and review, contingency planning and risk management).

Sample authority interviews

Central to our research was the interviewing of key people in each of the twenty-five sample areas. We aimed to chart authorities' early reactions to the full implementation of the community care changes, including their perceptions of the barriers and opportunities for developing a mixed economy, and their longer-term aspirations, concerns and plans, particularly in relation to markets. Some direct comparisons were made with their perceptions and plans in 1991.

Two interviews were planned in each authority, one with the Director of Social Services or his/her nominee, and the other with an elected member, usually the Chair of the social services committee. In authorities with hung councils we generally interviewed the social services spokesperson for each of the main parties. These interviews were conducted between late April and August 1993. The interview schedules were tested in four local authorities in April and May 1993 and slightly amended after this pilot. The schedule bore many similarities to the framework used for our 1990–91 interviews and covered: enabling; market analysis and understanding; market creation; market management and regulation; and future market prospects. The officer and member interviews covered similar ground.

Interviews were semi-structured and tape-recorded. The shortest took forty-five minutes, the longest nearly four hours. Directors and Chairs (or their designates) were usually interviewed separately. Taped interviews were transcribed verbatim, from which we have extracted the quotes from officers and members in subsequent chapters. In all, we conducted nearly fifty face-to-face local authority interviews, twenty-five interviews with officers (one per authority) and twenty-three with Chairs or spokespersons (eighteen of the twenty-five). Less-than-full coverage was achieved because the interviews were conducted close to county council elections which produced major changes in political control. This often meant that we were interviewing – or in some cases unable to interview – new Chairs or spokespersons. In 1992, seven of the sample authorities had been Conservative-controlled, four of them shire counties. By 1993, only three of the twenty-five authorities were Conservative-controlled, none of which was a shire county. Eleven of the twenty-five officers interviewed were employed in the same authorities in 1993 as in 1991, and most had been interviewed on both occasions. Because a minority of our officer and member interviewees were women, gender-specific personal pronouns have been used carefully in the book so as not to allow identification of individuals or authorities: female pronouns do not necessarily indicate women, and male pronouns do not necessarily indicate men.

1993 private and voluntary sector interviews

Interviews were also conducted with a small number of key people in the private and voluntary sectors in twelve organizations spread over five areas: two voluntary day and residential care providers for people with learning disabilities and mental health problems; five residential or nursing care home owners and representatives across both the voluntary and private sectors; two domiciliary care providers; two Councils for Voluntary Service; and the manager of a carers' support scheme. The semi-structured questionnaire covered:

- provider opinions on local authorities' understanding of needs, supply and motivations of suppliers;
- the potential for increased private and voluntary supply in each provider's own area of activity;
- the opportunities and barriers to the development of a mixed economy of care;
- providers' comments on the purchasing arrangements that local authorities have put in place; and
- issues concerning the success or failure of markets and their medium-term viability.

Sample local authority characteristics

The tables which follow provide broad statistical summaries of the mixed economy of care in 1993, the year in which the final parts of the NHS and Community Care Act were implemented. The tables offer comparisons between all local authorities in England, our sample of twenty-five and the subsample of eight in which we conducted the provider study. We focused on services for elderly people because this client group accounted for the majority of total spending, represented the key social care market for strategic management, and was the subject of our provider study.

Where possible, the weighted mean for each characteristic covered by the statistics is reported for each of the three samples (109, twenty-five and eight authorities), along with the median percentage. By and large, the differences between sample and population are small, so that it is reasonable to generalize from our samples.

Table A.1 gives data on percentage market share of places. We see that the sample and the national figures correspond closely. The median share of local authority places is always higher than the mean, which implies that a small minority of authorities have almost completely divested themselves of in-house provision, while the majority demonstrate a more balanced mix. Nationally, the private sector dominated residential care for elderly people in 1990, holding almost 60 per cent of the market. However, in only fifty-four of the 109 authorities was private sector provision larger than statutory and voluntary sector provision combined. In other words, the private sector's dominance of market share is not nationwide.

The proportion of independent sector places supported by local authority funds is small, comprising less than 10 per cent of the total number of supported places (Table A.2). It is instructive to note that local authority purchasing does

Table A.1 Residential care places for elderly people, England, 1993: market shares

	Residential care places for elderly people – market share					
	All LAs		25 LA sample		8 LA sample	
	Mean	Median	Mean	Median	Mean	Median
Sector	(%)	(%)	(%)	(%)	(%)	(%)
Local authority	27.5	34.8	27.6	35.1	28.1	39.7
Voluntary	13.6	12.5	13.7	11.3	9.9	8.6
Private	58.9	51.7	58.7	50.3	62.0	51.8

Source: Department of Health RA and AF PSS statistics.

not in any way reflect the prevailing market share of places in 1993. Indeed, local authorities buy far more voluntary sector places than private sector places. This contrasts strongly with the private sector's dominance in terms of market share.

Expenditure data for services funded by local authorities come from the annual Revenue Outturns submitted to the Department of the Environment. However, these RO3 statistics are not collected on the same basis as the activity data, and hence are not directly comparable with the data in Table A.2. Moreover, they relate to the period before local authorities assumed their current purchasing role. None the less, they provide an indication of local authority support of residents in the independent sector leading up to the April 1993 implementation date, and can be disaggregated into direct contractual payments and grants. Grants to voluntary organizations are substantially bigger than contractual payments to private and voluntary organizations (Table A.3), where both are taken as a proportion of the same total spend on *residential* care (although RO3 returns do not provide information on how grants are spent).

Table A.2 Local authority supported residential care by sector, England, 1993

	Percentage share of total local authority supported places in residential care for elderly people					
	All LAs		25 LA sample		8 LA sample	
	Mean	Median	Mean	Median	Mean	Median
Sector	(%)	(%)	(%)	(%)	(%)	(%)
Local authority	91.5	98.1	90.9	98.3	98.6	98.5
Voluntary	6.8	1.2	8.2	1.0	0.8	0.7
Private	1.8	0.2	0.8	0.2	0.5	0.2

Source: Department of Health RA and AF PSS statistics.

Table A.3 Local authority purchase of service, 1993

| Expenditure type | Payments to independent organizations as a percentage of total LA residential care expenditure | | | | | |
| | All LAs | | 25 LA sample | | 8 LA sample | |
	Mean (%)	Median (%)	Mean (%)	Median (%)	Mean (%)	Median (%)
Residential	4.1	0.3	1.6	0.2	0.9	0.5
Non-residential	2.0	0.2	2.9	0.2	4.9	0.3
Grants	23.8	19.8	20.0	18.4	20.3	25.0

Source: Department of Environment RO3 returns.

Spending on all forms of non-residential care by local authorities is broadly equivalent to spending on residential care. This is especially evident if we look at the median values. These are anyway more appropriate because analysis of the data shows that the higher mean values are accounted for by a very small number of authorities that spend considerable amounts on the independent sector.

Methods and samples: the 1994 provider study

Information on independent sector residential care for elderly people was gathered in 1994 by means of a postal questionnaire and face-to-face interviews in three shire counties, two London boroughs and three metropolitan districts. The subsample of authorities was selected so as to reflect national intersectoral patterns of residential care provision for elderly people and the patterns of over- or underprovision across authority types. Homes were selected within the authorities using sampling frames stratified by sector, size and ownership of providers. The aim was to obtain samples of ten homes per authority (with replacement), although this was not always possible.

Quantitative data on providers were first gathered by means of a short postal questionnaire, sent to the sampled providers in summer 1994. Fifty-eight usable questionnaires were returned (a response rate of 73 per cent). The questionnaire was addressed to 'the proprietor or manager' of the home, and sought data on the following:

- details of registration and provider association membership;
- current level of provision (numbers of permanent and respite places), plans for change in these levels, and home-based day care services for non-residents;
- funding sources of residents, and resident turnover between April 1993 and March 1994;
- home characteristics (rooms, facilities and additional services);
- residents' characteristics (age, ethnic mix and dependency); and
- details of pricing regimes, staffing levels and staff qualifications.

Face-to-face interviews took place in sixty-two homes, conducted by the authors of this book. These interviews generally lasted just over an hour. The target interviewees were the proprietors of owner-managed private homes, and the managers (or equivalents) of voluntary sector or 'corporate' private sector establishments, although occasionally officers-in-charge were interviewed. Interviews were semi-structured and gathered quantitative and qualitative information on providers. The topics covered were:

- details of home ownership, legal structure and status, and acquisition;
- admissions policy, marketing and advertising strategies;
- changes in patterns of demand since April 1993;
- pricing methods and strategies, and effects of main purchaser's policies;
- local authority regulation: contracts and specification;
- motivation and background of interviewee; and
- plans for diversification.

The 'unit of analysis' was the home itself, rather than any organization or federation of which it was a part, or of which it was a member.

The provider study: sample characteristics

Three-quarters of the homes covered by the survey were in the private 'for-profit' sector (forty-three of the fifty-eight for whom we had full postal questionnaire information). Legal structures were described by survey respondents as: husband and wife partnerships (twenty homes), other partnerships (five), private limited companies (ten), sole proprietors (seven), and public limited companies (two).

At a national level, the routine DH statistics do not break down patterns of ownership and legal structure beyond the crude private versus voluntary dichotomy. However, Laing & Buisson have been refining a database including this type of information since 1988, on the basis of which they suggest that 'most care homes are still run on traditional owner-manager lines, typified by the husband and wife team running a single care home' (Laing & Buisson 1995: 44). Our sample reflected this in the main, although this was not the outcome of deliberate stratification.

Of the fifty-eight homes in the sample, eight were voluntary and seven not-for-profit, including former local authority Part III homes now run as trusts. All providers who classified themselves as 'voluntary' were registered charities or part of larger registered charitable organizations, with the exception of those providers which were housing associations, some of which were exempted charities or were not charitable. In what follows, we treat all voluntary and not-for-profit bodies as 'voluntary sector' establishments, although we are of course aware that the latter have a somewhat ambiguous status as 'quasi-independent' or 'hybrid' agencies.

There were few large organizations (Table A.4). A quarter of these

Table A.4   Organizational size: all sectors

Number of other homes run by this organization	Homes in the registering local authority (N)	Homes in other local authorities (N)
0	47	45
1–2	8	8
3–10	6	4
More than 10	0	3

organizations ran homes in more than one local authority area. We compared national concentration of ownership with that apparent in our sample. According to the latest Laing & Buisson market survey (1995), just 3.6 per cent of residential homes and 5.6 per cent of places in the private sector were owned in 1994 by 'major providers': that is, companies or partnerships running three or more homes (Laing & Buisson 1995: 40, Table 4.6). Unlike the nursing home sector, where 'corporate penetration' has been rather more significant (one-fifth of these homes were run by 'major providers' in 1994), the residential care market remains highly diffuse. In this respect, it is unlike most other segments of the wider private economy, although the Laing & Buisson analyses suggest that corporate involvement is starting to expand from its very low base. If anything, our sample overrepresented the presence of large providers, as 11 per cent of *private* sector homes in our sample ran three or more homes.

In the case of *voluntary* providers, we selected our samples to include large national organizations, in cognisance of the very different extent of concentration in that sector. Laing & Buisson's national data indicate that voluntary 'major providers' in both residential and nursing care (their data do not separate these types of provision for the voluntary sector) accounted for 45 per cent of homes, and 51 per cent of places in 1994. In fact, around half of the homes in our sample were run by voluntary organizations controlling three or more establishments.

As well as different patterns of concentration, marked differences were evident in the longevity of homes, and the ways in which they had come to be run as residential homes. In the private sector, over half (53 per cent) of all homes had been purchased and then converted. Most began operating during the early and mid-1980s, presumably partly fuelled by the availability of social security funding (Day and Klein 1987; Bradshaw 1988). Nearly half (48 per cent) of the private sector homes began operating between 1984 and 1988. By contrast, just under one-third of the voluntary sector homes in the sample had been operating for more than twenty years, while just over one-third had begun operating since 1989. As many as half of the voluntary homes were purpose-built (compared with the 7 per cent of private sector homes that had been started from scratch).

The sample was dominated by medium-sized homes. The smallest had seven permanent places and the largest had sixty-two, but half the sample had between fourteen and twenty-seven places. Private sector homes tended to be smaller than voluntary homes (with means of twenty and thirty-one places, respectively). In addition to these permanent places, seven homes had one respite place each, and one home had four respite places. The voluntary sector was more likely to have dedicated respite places, having eight of the eleven places in our sample. Five homes (out of fifty) were planning to increase the number of permanent places, and two homes (out of fifty-one) were planning to increase the number of short-stay/respite places, but none was planning any size reductions. There were no differences in these respects between the sectors.

Staff-resident ratios varied widely across the sample, both within and between sectors, although the difficulties of computing these ratios (because of short-term fluctuations in resident numbers, temporary staff vacancies, potential double-counting of staff in some categories, and so on) should be noted. In the private sector there was an average ratio of 0.51 full-time staff (all staff categories) per resident and 0.75 part-time staff, compared to 0.60 and 0.50 in the voluntary sector. Compared to voluntary homes, private homes had higher ratios of care staff with social work qualifications to residents, but lower ratios of qualified nursing staff, ancillary staff and volunteers.

Relatively few homes provided either day care or the base for a home help service for non-residents. Private sector homes were less likely than voluntary homes to offer a home help service, but the proportions providing day care, were similar. On the whole, the sample homes were concentrating predominantly on their main business: residential care.

Occupancy rates averaged 90 per cent of places (excluding short-stay residents) during the year ending 31 March 1994, with no difference between the sectors. The average number of residents was 17.7 in the private sector, 28.4 in the voluntary and 20.4 overall. Again, these averages disguise wide variations: ranges of 5–50 in the private sector and 19–41 in the voluntary. Almost all residents were described as 'permanent'. More than half the residents were women aged 85 or over, and another 26 per cent were women aged 75–84.

We also used the postal questionnaire to collect information on client dependency: in terms of numbers of current residents with restricted mobility, incontinence, confused mental state, difficulty in performing basic tasks and toileting difficulties. (It should be noted that our ratings were simple and reliant on respondents' interpretations.) Private homes described themselves on average as being more likely to have clients in a confused mental state, and to have clients with more difficulties with respect to incontinence, toileting and basic living tasks, while the sectors were similar in the extent to which clients suffered from restricted mobility.

Twenty-two per cent of all residents in the fifty-seven homes for which we had these data were funded under contracts with local authorities (Table

A.5). There was no difference between the sectors in relation to residents funded by the local authorities in which homes were located (16 per cent of voluntary home residents, 18 per cent private), but more voluntary than private home residents were funded under contract by other authorities (8 per cent compared to 3 per cent). A third of the residents in voluntary homes and four out of ten in private homes were funded from private means, while the proportions funded from preserved rights (DSS) were 43 per cent and 36 per cent respectively. Approximately 2 per cent of the residents for whom we

Table A.5 Funding sources

	Residents by funding source, permanent and temporary					
	Voluntary sector		Private sector		All homes	
	Perm. (%)	Temp. (%)	Perm. (%)	Temp. (%)	Perm. (%)	Temp. (%)
Under contract with:						
− local authority in which home is located						
mean	15.5	0.9	17.7	0.3	17.2	0.4
maximum	62.1	0.9	55.6	13.3	62.1	13.3
− other local authority						
mean	7.9	0	3.4	0	4.5	0
maximum	80.1	0	33.3	0	80.6	0
− any local authority						
mean	23.4	0.9	21.1	0.3	21.7	0.4
maximum	86.1	8.7	66.7	13.3	86.1	13.3
− health authority in which home is located						
mean	0	0	0	0	0	0
maximum	0	0	0	0	0	0
− other health authority						
mean	0	0	0	0	0	0
maximum	0	0	0	0	0	0
Funded from private means						
mean	33.4	0	40.8	0.1	39.9	0.1
maximum	75.0	0	92.9	5.9	92.9	0.6
Funded from preserved rights (DSS)						
mean	43.0	0	35.8	0	37.5	0
maximum	81.0	0	100.0	0	100.0	0
Funded from income support, not preserved rights						
mean	0.2	0	2.3	0	1.8	0
maximum	3.3	0	30.0	0	30.0	0
Sample size	14	14	43	43	57	57

have data about funding source were funded from non-preserved rights income support.

Funding share from a single source was often very high: one voluntary home had 62 per cent of residents funded by its own local authority, and another had 80 per cent funded by other local authorities. One private home had all residents funded from preserved rights income support, and another had 93 per cent funded from private means. (Note that the percentages above, and in Table A.5, give the averages for homes, not the percentages of all individual residents; that is, they are not weighted for home size.)

Occupational background of providers

In addition to background characteristics from the postal questionnaire where the home was the 'unit of analysis', we also collected information on the backgrounds of interviewees. We used eight categories to describe interviewees' backgrounds, designed to reflect previous experience in terms of sector (public, private or voluntary) and field of work (health care, social care or non-care background). The categories are presented in Table A.6 along with the associated numbers of interviewees, broken down by sector. Within the largest category, those with NHS nursing backgrounds, we distinguished managers with no ownership stake in the organization from owner-managers. (We did not do this in all cases to avoid a proliferation of categories.) As indicated in the table, providers in our sample had varied career paths.

The single most common background among providers was nursing in the NHS: thirteen owner-managers or owners fitted this description, accounting for around one-third of all private sector establishments. In addition, three of the seven providers classified as 'partnerships' also involved one partner with an NHS background (see below). Including owners and managers, twenty of the fifty-three homes across *all* sectors (38 per cent) involved former NHS employees. As Table A.6 shows, social care and mixed care backgrounds were also to be found in the sample, and 11 per cent of respondents across all sectors had worked in Part III homes. One of the owner-managers with a joint health and social care background, who had worked first as a nurse and then as a social worker, had bought the home he had previously managed for the local authority when offered the chance to do so in 1989.

Just under one in five of the sample (17 per cent) was accounted for by providers *without* any kind of caring or social welfare background. The majority of these operated in the private sector. In fact, only one interviewee with this background worked in the voluntary sector. That interviewee was the manager of a regional Christian charity home who had previously been in the catering business.

In the private sector, the next most common category comprised partnerships combining caring and non-caring backgrounds. (As we have

Table A.6 Interviewee backgrounds

	Current sector (sector of home)			
	Private (N)	Voluntary (N)	Not-for-profit (N)	All sectors (N)
Former NHS nursing, currently owner/manager or owner	13	0	0	13
Former NHS nursing, currently manager (not owner)	2	3	2	7
Former LA residential home or other SSD	4	2	1	7
Individual with both health and social care background	2	1	0	3
Non-care background	8	1	0	9
Partnership: care and non-care background	5	0	0	5
Partnership: both care background	2	0	0	2
Voluntary organization background	2	4	1	7
Total	38	11	4	53

The two 'partnership' categories shown represent only those partnerships for which information on the background of all (usually two) partners was available, and which involved at least one partner with a caring profession background. Thus non-care partnerships have been classified as 'non-care background', and the other categories include partnerships, but with information available on only one of the partners.

stressed, a number of other interviewees where single person information only was available would have been added to this category if full information were available.) Examples included: a woman who had worked as a geriatric nurse in the NHS and her husband with a 'management and industry' background who 'decided to combine their two skills'; and a partnership comprising a former manager of a local authority home and a driving instructor.

Our table shows that 60 per cent of our voluntary and not-for-profit sector interviewees' backgrounds could most easily be summarized as public sector health or social care, but five of the interviewees had pursued a career wholly within the voluntary sector. All had moved between establishments or posts *within* their respective organizations to get to their current jobs.

References

Arrow, K.J. (1969) The organization of economic activity: issues pertinent to the choice of market versus nonmarket allocation, in J.E. Commitee (ed.) *The Analysis and Evaluation of Public Expenditures*, G.P.O., Washington D.C.

Arrow, K.J. (1974) *The Limits of Organization*, Norton, New York.

Association of Directors of Social Services (1994) *Towards Community Care: ADSS Review of the First Year*, Association of Directors of Social Services, London.

Audit Commission (1986) *Making a Reality of Community Care*, HMSO, London.

Audit Commission (1992a) *Community Care: Managing the Cascade of Change*, HMSO, London.

Audit Commission (1992b) *The Community Revolution: Personal Social Services and Community Care*, HMSO, London.

Audit Commission (1993) *Taking Care: Progress with Care ·in the Community*, Health and Personal Social Services Bulletin No. 1, Audit Commission, London.

Audit Commission (1994) *Taking Stock: Progress with Community Care*, Community Care Bulletin No 2, HMSO, London.

Bacon, R. and Eltis, W. (1976) *Britain's Economic Problem: Too Few Producers*, Macmillan, London.

Bebbington, A.C. and Davies, B.P. (1983) Equity and efficiency in the personal social services, *Journal of Social Policy*, 12, 309–30.

Beecham, J.K., Knapp, M.R.J. and Fenyo, A.J. (1991) Costs, needs and outcomes, Discussion Paper 730/2, Personal Social Services Research Unit, University of Kent at Canterbury.

Beresford, P. and Croft, S. (1984) Welfare pluralism: the new face of Fabianism, *Critical Social Policy*, 9, 19–39.

Beveridge, W. (1942) *Social Insurance and Allied Services*, Cmd. 6404, HMSO, London.

Beveridge, W. (1944) *Full Employment in a Free Society*, Allen and Unwin, London.

Bottomley, V. (1992) *Speech to Social Services Conference*, 2 October, Isle of Wight.

Bradshaw, J. (1988) Financing private care for the elderly, in S. Baldwin, G. Parker and R. Walker (eds) *Social Security and Community Care*, Avebury, Aldershot.

Brooke, R. (1989) *Managing the Enabling Authority*, Longman, Harlow.

Brown, C. (1992) Major demands review of care in the community, *The Independent*, 23 June, 7.

Buchanan, J.M. (1978) *The Economics of Politics*, IEA Readings No. 18, Institute of Economic Affairs, London.

Buchanan, J.M. (1986) *Liberty, Market and State*, Wheatsheaf, Hemel Hempstead.

Butler, R. (1994) Reinventing British government, *Public Administration*, 72, Summer, 263–70.

Challis, L., Fuller, S., Henwood, M., Klein, R., Plowden, W., Webb, A., Whittingham, P. and Wistow, G. (1988) *Joint Approaches to Social Policy*, Cambridge University Press, Cambridge.

Clarke, K. (1989) *Secretary of State's Statement to Parliament on the Future Arrangements for Community Care*, Press Release 89/298, Department of Health, London.

Clarke, M. and Stewart, J.D. (1988) *The Enabling Council*, Local Government Training Board, Luton.

Clarke, M. and Stewart, J.D. (1990) *General Management in Local Government: Getting the Balance Right*, Longman, Harlow.

Cyert, R. and March, J. (1963) *A Behavioral Theory of the Firm*, Prentice-Hall, Englewood Cliffs, New Jersey.

Davies, B.P. and Knapp, M.R.J. (1981) *Old People's Homes and the Production of Welfare*, Routledge and Kegan Paul, London.

Day, P. and Klein, R. (1987) Residential care for the elderly: a billion-pound experiment in policy-making, *Public Money*, March, 19–24.

Deakin, N. (1994) *The Politics of Welfare: Continuity and Change*, Harvester Wheatsheaf, Hemel Hempstead.

Deakin, N. and Wright, A. (eds) (1990) *Consuming Public Services*, Routledge, London.

Department of Health (1990a) *Community Care in the Next Decade and Beyond: Policy Guidance*, HMSO, London.

Department of Health (1990b) The Government's Plans for the Future of Community Care: The Government's Reply to the Third, Fifth, Sixth, Seventh and Eighth Reports from the Social Services Committee Session 1989–1990, Cmd. 1343, HMSO, London.

Department of Health (1990c) *Care in the Community*, CI(90)3, Social Services Inspectorate, Department of Health, London.

Department of Health (1992a) *Implementing Caring for People*, EL(92)13/CI(92)10, Department of Health, London.

Department of Health (1992b) *Implementing Caring for People*, EL(92)65/CI(92)30, Department of Health, London.

Department of Health (1992c) *National Assistance Act 1948 (Choice of Accommodation) Directions 1992*, LAC(92)27, Department of Health, London.

Department of Health (1992d) *Caring for People Who Live at Home*, LASSL(92)7, Department of Health, London.

Department of Health (1992e) *Priorities and Planning Guidance for the NHS, 1993/94*, EL(92)47, Department of Health, London.

Department of Health (1993a) *Monitoring and Development: First Impressions, April to September 1993*, Department of Health, London.

Department of Health (1993b) *Community Care Plans (Consultation) Direction 1993*, 25 January 1993, Department of Health, London.

Department of Health (1993c) *Implementing Caring for People*, EL(93)18/CI(93)12, Department of Health, London.

Department of Health (1994a) *Implementing Caring for People: Impressions of the First Year*, Department of Health, London.

Department of Health (1994b) *Putting People First*, Third Annual Report of the Chief Inspector, Social Services Inspectorate, 1993/94, HMSO, London.

DiMaggio, P.J. and Anheier, H.K. (1990) The sociology of nonprofit organizations and sectors, *Annual Review of Sociology*, 16, 137–59.

DiMaggio, P.J. and Powell, W.W. (1983) The iron cage revisited: institutional iso-morphism and collective rationality in organizational fields, *American Sociological Review*, 822, 147–60.

Donnelly, M., McGilloway, S., Mays, N., Perry, S., Knapp, M.R.J., Kavanagh, S., Beecham, J.K., Fenyo, A.J. and Astin, J. (1994) *Opening New Doors: An Evaluation of Community Care for People Discharged from Psychiatric and Mental Handicap Hospitals*, HMSO, London.

Downey, R. (1994) Community care choice limits, *Community Care*, 3 November, 1.

Downs, A. (1967) *Inside Bureaucracy*, Little, Brown, Boston, Massachusetts.

Dunleavy, P. and O'Leary, B. (1987) *Theories of the State: The Politics of Liberal Democracy*, Macmillan, Basingstoke.

Ellis, K. (1993) *Squaring the Circle: User and Carer Participation in Needs Assessment*, Joseph Rowntree Foundation, York.

Ennals, K. and O'Brien, J. (1990) *The Enabling Role of Local Authorities*, Public Finance Foundation, London.

Ferris, J.M. and Graddy, E. (1988) Production choices for local government services, *Journal of Urban Affairs*, 10, 273–89.

Flynn, N. (1990) *Public Sector Management*, Harvester Wheatsheaf, London.

Forder, J.E. (1995a) Transaction cost theory and health and social care, Discussion Paper 1158, Personal Social Services Research Unit, University of Kent at Canterbury.

Forder, J.E. (1995b) Optimal governance structures in social care, Discussion Paper 1170, Personal Social Services Research Unit, University of Kent at Canterbury.

Forder, J.E., Knapp, M.R.J. and Wistow, G. (1996) Competition in the English mixed economy, *Journal of Social Policy*, 25(2), forthcoming.

Friedman, M. (1976) The line we dare not cross, *Encounter*, November 1976.

Gamble, A. (1988) *The Free Economy and the Strong State: The Politics of Thatcherism*, Macmillan, London.

Granovetter, M. (1995) Economic action and social structure: the problem of embeddedness, *American Journal of Sociology*, 91, 3, 481–510.

Griffiths, R. (1988) *Community Care: Agenda for Action*, HMSO, London.

Gutch, R. (1992) *Contracting Lessons from the US*, NCVO, London.

Hardy, B., Wistow, G. and Leedham, I. (1994) *Analysis of a Sample of English Community Care Plans 1993/94*, Department of Health, London.

Harrison, S. and Pollitt, C. (1994) *Controlling Health Professionals*, Open University Press, Buckingham.

Harrison, S., Hunter, D.J., Pollitt, C.J. and Marnoch, G. (1990) *The Dynamics of British Health Policy*, Unwin Hyman, London.

Henwood, M. (1995) *Making a Difference: Implementation of the Community Care Reforms*

Two Years On, King's Fund Centre, London and the Nuffield Institute for Health, Leeds.

Henwood, M. and Wistow, G. (1994) *Monitoring Community Care: A Review*, Report to the Joseph Rowntree Foundation, Nuffield Institute for Health, University of Leeds.

Henwood, M. and Wistow, G. (1995) The tasks in hand, *The Health Service Journal*, 13 April, 24–5.

Hodgson, G. (1988) *Economics and Institutions: A Manifesto for a Modern Institutional Economics*, Polity Press, Cambridge.

Hodgson, G. (1994) The return of institutional economics, in N.J. Smelser and R. Swedberg (eds) *The Handbook of Economic Sociology*, Princeton University Press, Princeton, New Jersey.

Hood, C. (1991) A public management for all seasons?, *Public Administration*, Spring, 1, 3–19.

House of Commons Health Committee (1993a) *Community Care: The Way Forward*, HMSO, London.

House of Commons Health Committee (1993b) *Community Care: Funding from April 1993*, Third Report, Session 1992–93, HC309, HMSO, London.

House of Commons Social Services Committee (1990) *Community Care: Funding for Local Authorities, Third Report, Session 1989–1990*, HC277, HMSO, London.

Hughes, J.A., Martin, P.J. and Sharrock, W.W. (1995) *Understanding Classical Sociology: Marx, Weber, Durkheim*, Sage Publications, London.

Ibbs, Sir R. (1988) *Improving Management in Government: The Next Steps*, HMSO, London.

James, E. (1987) The nonprofit sector in competitive perspective, in W.W. Powell (ed) *The Nonprofit Sector: A Research Handbook*, Yale University Press, New Haven, Connecticut.

James, E. and Rose-Ackerman, S. (1986) *The Nonprofit Enterprise in Market Economies*, Volume 9 of *Fundamentals of Pure and Applied Economics*, Harwood Academic Publishers, London.

Jeavons, T. (1992) When the management is the message: relating values to management practice in nonprofit organisations, *Nonprofit Management and Leadership*, 2, 4, 403–18.

Judge, K.F. (1984) Caring for profit private residential homes for the elderly: the establishment of family enterprises, Discussion Paper 311, Personal Social Services Research Unit, University of Kent at Canterbury.

Judge, K.F. and Knapp, M.R.J. (1985) Efficiency in the production of welfare: the public and private sectors compared, in R. Klein and M. O'Higgins (eds) *The Future of Welfare*, Basil Blackwell, Oxford.

Kendall, J. and Knapp, M.R.J. (1994) A loose and baggy monster: boundaries, definitions and typologies, in J. Davis Smith, C. Rochester and R. Hedley (eds) *An Introduction to the Voluntary Sector*, Routledge, London.

Kendall, J. and Knapp, M.R.J. (1995) *Voluntary Means, Social Ends*, Personal Social Services Research Unit, University of Kent at Canterbury.

Kendall, J. and Knapp, M.R.J. (1996) *The Voluntary Sector in the UK*, Manchester University Press, Manchester.

Knapp, M.R.J. (1984) *The Economics of Social Care*, Macmillan, London.

Knapp, M.R.J. (1986) The relative cost-effectiveness of public, voluntary and private providers of residential child care, in A.J. Culyer and B. Jönsson (eds) *Public and Private Health Services*, Blackwell, Oxford.

Knapp, M.R.J. (1995) Are voluntary agencies really more effective?, in D. Billis and M. Harris (eds) *Voluntary Agencies: Organisation and Management in Theory and Practice*, Macmillan, London.

Knapp, M.R.J. and Forder, J.E. (1996) *Shaping Social Care Markets*, Personal Social Services Research Unit, University of Kent at Canterbury.

Knapp, M.R.J. and Wistow, G. (1993) *Welfare Pluralism and Community Care Development: The Role of Local Government and the Non-Statutory Sectors in Social Welfare Services in England*, Organization for Economic Cooperation and Development, Paris.

Knapp, M.R.J., Wistow, G., Forder, J. and Hardy, B. (1994) Markets for social care: opportunities, barriers and implications, in W. Bartlett, C. Propper, D. Wilson and J. Le Grand (eds) *Quasi-Markets in the Welfare State*, School for Advanced Urban Studies, Bristol.

KPMG Management Consultants (1992) *Implementing Community Care: Improving Independent Sector Involvement in Community Care Planning*, Department of Health, London.

KPMG Management Consultants and Department of Health (1993) *Diversification and the Independent Residential Care Sector*, HMSO, London.

Kramer, R.M. (1994) Voluntary agencies and the contract culture: 'dream or nightmare?', *Social Science Review*, March, 33–60.

Laffont, J.-J. and Tirole, J. (1993) *A Theory of Incentives in Procurement and Regulation*, MIT Press, Cambridge, Massachusetts.

Laing & Buisson (1994) *Care of Elderly People: Market Survey 1994*, Laing & Buisson Publications, London.

Laing & Buisson (1995) *Care of Elderly People: Market Survey 1995*, Laing & Buisson Publications, London.

Lawrence, R. (1983) Voluntary action: a stalking horse for the right?, *Critical Social Policy*, 3, 14–30.

Le Grand, J. and Bartlett, W. (1993) *Quasi-Markets and Social Policy*, Macmillan, Basingstoke.

Leach, S., Stewart, J. and Walsh, K. (1994) *The Changing Organisation and Management of Local Government*, Macmillan, London.

Leedham, I. (1993) *Contracting for Community Care: A Survey of Local Authorities in the North-West*, Social Services Inspectorate, Department of Health and Association of Directors of Social Services, London.

Leibenstein, H. (1980) *Beyond Economic Man*, Harvard University Press, Cambridge, Massachusetts.

Lewis, J. (1993) Developing the mixed economy of care: emerging issues for voluntary organisations, *Journal of Social Policy*, 22, 2, 173–92.

London Research Centre (1994) *From Social Security to Community Care 2: The Impact of the Transfer of Funding on Local Authorities*, The Local Government Management Board, Luton.

Mawhinney, B. (1992) Speech to IHSM/ADSS Conference, 10 July, Department of Health, London.

Mawhinney, B. (1993) *Purchasing for Health: A Framework for Action*, NHS Management Executive, Leeds.

Metcalfe, L. and Richards, S. (1990) *Improving Public Management*, 2nd edition, Sage, London.

Milgrom, P. and Roberts, J. (1990) Bargaining costs, influence costs, and the organization of economic activity, in J. Alt and K. Shepsle (eds) *Perspectives on Positive Political Economy*, Cambridge University Press, Cambridge.

Mirvis, P. (1992) The quality of employment in the non-profit sector: an update of employee attitudes in non-profits versus business and government, *Nonprofit Management and Leadership*, 3, 1, 23–42.

Niskanen, W.A. (1971) *Bureaucracy and Representative Government*, Aldine-Atherton, Chicago, Illinois.

Niskanen, W.A. (1978) Competition among government bureaux, in J.M. Buchanan (ed.) *The Economics of Politics*, IEA Readings Number 18, Institute of Economic Affairs, London.

Onyx, J. (1993) Career paths in the third sector: implications for human resource management, Queensland University of Technology Working Paper No. 30, Sydney.

Osborne, D. and Gaebler, T. (1992) *Reinventing Government*, Addison-Wesley, Reading, Massachusetts.

Paton, R. (1991) The emerging social economy: value-based organisations in the wider society, in J. Batsleer, C. Cornforth and R. Paton (eds) *Issues in Voluntary and Nonprofit Management*, Addison-Wesley, Wokingham.

Perkin, H. (1989) *The Rise of Professional Society*, Routledge, London.

Rasmusen, E. (1992) *Games and Information: An Introduction to Game Theory*, Blackwell, Oxford.

Rees, R. (1989) Uncertainty, information and insurance, in J. Hey (ed.) *Current Issues in Microeconomics*, Macmillan, Basingstoke.

Rhodes, R.A.W. (1995) *The New Governance: Governing Without Government. The State of Britain*, Joint ESRC/RSA Seminar Series, Economic and Social Research Council, Swindon.

Richardson, J. (1995) *Purchase of Service Contracting: Some Evidence on UK Implementation*, Inter-Agency Services Team of the National Council for Voluntary Organisations, London.

Ridley, N. (1988) *The Local Right: Enabling not Providing*, Policy Study No. 92, Centre for Policy Studies, London.

Robinson, J. and Wistow, G. (1994) *Community Care, Year 2. Developments on the Health and Social Care Boundary*, King's Fund Centre, London and Nuffield Institute for Health, Leeds.

Russell, L., Scott, D. and Wilding, P. (1995) *Mixed Fortunes: The Funding of the Voluntary Sector*, Department of Social Policy and Social Work, Manchester University, Manchester.

Sako, M. (1992) *Prices, Quality and Trust: Inter-firm Relations in Britain and Japan*, Cambridge University Press, Cambridge.

Salamon, L.M. (1987) Partners in public service: the scope and theory of government–nonprofit relations, in W.W. Powell (ed.) *The Nonprofit Sector: A Research Handbook*, Yale University Press, New Haven, Connecticut.

Scase, R. and Goffee, R. (1982) The Entrepreneurial Middle Class, Croom Helm, London.

Secretaries of State (1989) *Caring for People: Community Care in the Next Decade and Beyond*, Cmd. 849, HMSO, London.

Self, P. (1993) *Government by the Market?*, Macmillan, London.

Simon, H. (1957) *Models of Man: Social and Rational*, Wiley, New York.

Simon, H. (1961) *Administrative Behaviour*, Macmillan, New York.

Smeltzer, N.J. and Swedberg, R. (1994) *The Handbook of Economic Sociology*, Princeton University Press, Princeton, New Jersey.

Smith, J. (1994) *A Wider Strategy for Research and Development Relating to Personal Social Services*, report to the Director of Research and Development by an independent review group (Chair Mr John Smith), HMSO, London.

Stevenson, O. and Parsloe, P. (1993) *Community Care and Empowerment*, Joseph Rowntree Foundation, York.

Stewart, J. and Walsh, K. (1992) Change in the management of public services, *Public Administration*, 70, Winter, 499–518.

Tilly, C. and Tilly, C. (1994) Capitalist work and labor markets, in N.J. Smelser and R. Swedberg (eds) *The Handbook of Economic Sociology*, Princeton University Press, Princeton, New Jersey.

Walsh, K. (1995) *Public Services and Market Mechanisms*, Macmillan, Basingstoke.

Willetts, D. (1993) Why Tories ought to care, *The Independent*, 1 October, 25.

Williamson, O.E. (1975) *Markets and Hierarchies: Analysis and Antitrust Organization*, Free Press, New York.

Williamson, O.E. (1985) *The Economic Institutions of Capitalism*, New York, Free Press.

Wilson Committee (1979) *The Financing of Small Firms*, Interim Report of the Committee to Review the Functioning of Financial Institutions, Cmd. 7503, HMSO, London.

Wistow, G. (1990) *Community Care Planning: A Review of Past Experience and Future Imperatives*, Caring for People Implementation Document, CCI3, Department of Health, London.

Wistow, G. (1995a) Aspirations and realities: community care at the crossroads, *Health and Social Care in the Community*, 3, 4, 227–40.

Wistow, G. (1995b) Ambiguity and mistrust: a case study of community care and central local relations, Paper presented to British Council 'Know-How' Programme Seminar on Central Local Relations, Dobogoko, Hungary, March. Available at Nuffield Institute for Health, Leeds.

Wistow, G. (1995c) Coming apart at the seams, *Health Service Journal*, 2 March, 24–5.

Wistow, G. and Barnes, M. (1993) User involvement in community care: origins, purposes and applications, *Public Administration*, 71, 3, Autumn, 279–99.

Wistow, G. and Hardy, B. (1994) Community care planning: learning from experience, in C. McCreadie (ed.) *Planning and Updating Community Care Plans: The Needs of Older People and their Carers*, Age Concern Institute of Gerontology, King's College, London.

Wistow, G. and Hardy, B. (1996) Competition, collaboration and markets, *Journal of Interprofessional Care*, 10, 1, forthcoming.

Wistow, G., Leedham, I. and Hardy, B. (1993) *A Preliminary Analysis of a Sample of English Community Care Plans*, Department of Health, London.

Wistow, G., Knapp, M.R.J., Hardy, B. and Allen, C. (1994) *Social Care in a Mixed Economy*, Open University Press, Buckingham.

Young, R. and Wistow, G. (1995) *Experiences of Independent Sector Home Care Providers: Analysis of the January 1995 UKHCA Survey*, UKHCA.

Name index

Subject index